WOODALL'S FAVORITE RECIPES FROM AMERICA'S CAMPGROUNDS

Edited by ANN EMERSON

ISBN - 671-688-58-8

Other publications available from WOODALL'S:

WOODALL'S CAMPGROUND DIRECTORY
WOODALL'S TENT CAMPING GUIDE
WOODALL'S RV BUYER'S GUIDE
WOODALL'S CAMPSITE COOKBOOK
WOODALL'S RV OWNER'S HANDBOOKS VOLS. 1 - 3
WOODALL'S RV HOW-TO GUIDE
WOODALL'S TRAVEL AMERICA NEWS

Cover Design: Brad Hook & Associates

Cover Photo: Autumn Color by Glenn Jahnke

FOREWARD

Camping and cooking seem to go together. Everything tastes better when cooked in an outdoor atmosphere.

Why is it that sliced potatoes with the skins still on them, smothered in butter and onions tastes so good when cooked in foil over an open fire? Why does the smell of chicken and ribs cooking outdoors make my mouth water?

'Cause everything cooked outdoors tastes good. Now I, like you, don't go RVing or camping to cook. But somehow, cooking is part of the outdoor experience and I like to make it as pleasurable and special as the rest of our trip.

So we've put together a cookbook containing favorite recipes from campgrounds and RV parks across North America. Each one contains a narrative about the park and why the recipe is a favorite. We hope they'll be favorites of yours. Maybe you'll find a recipe from a park where you've enjoyed camping.

A recipe we received from a campground in Michigan sums it up —

FRIENDSHIP RECIPE
KOA-Monroe County — Petersburg, MI

Our campground offers a country, forest setting with easy access to the expressway. We provide over 30 activities for the active camper. Our well-stocked store meets our campers' needs. KOA-Monroe County loves campers! As owners, we have watched children grow up and bring their children back to stay at our campground. This recipe IS KOA-Monroe County!

INGREDIENTS
One or more camping families and friends
A forest setting
Lots of sunshine
Many activities
A campfire for roasting marsh-mallows and hot dogs
A camping unit (any size or shape)

DIRECTIONS
Mix all of the ingredients together with laughter, love and consideration. Add to this a pinch of compassion. Leave the above mixture in a campground for a weekend or more and the results are excellent!

We hope you will use the recipes in this book to add to your outdoor experiences. Try them at home or on the road.

Wishing you good camping and good cooking!

Linda L. Profaizer
President, Woodall's

P.S. Special thanks to the many campground and RV park owners across the country who took the time to send their favorite recipes to us for inclusion in this book. It couldn't have been done without you.

Contents

WOODALL'S FAVORITE RECIPES FROM AMERICA'S CAMPGROUNDS

Outdoor Cooking Made Easy

By J. Wayne and Sherry K. Fears

Cooking over the open flame of campfire or campstove can be the highlight of any overnight venture into the outdoors. With some basic know-how and simple gear, campers can prepare meals with the ease and convenience of cooking in the home kitchen.

For the newcomer to open fire cooking, getting a suitable and safe fire going may be a somewhat difficult chore. However, this need not be: The first step in building a fire is to select a safe place for the fire, assuming there is not an established fireplace. Pick a site that is at least 15 feet from tents, RVs, green trees, dry grass, or anything else that could catch fire or be damaged from the heat or sparks. Also be sure to check overhead, as an overlooked tree branch may hang directly over the fire area. Be careful of building a fire over roots or peat moss. Fire can burn and smolder within roots and pop up as wildfire around the base of the tree, and peat moss can burn underground for days, starting a major fire long after you have left the campsite. If there are pine needles, leaves, or other materials at your fire site, clear them away, exposing the bare earth for 10 to 15 feet. Put the cleared material in a pile nearby for use in restoring your site to its original condition when breaking camp.

Many campgrounds have permanent fire rings or open fire grills for campers to use. If not, you will want to construct your own. The best type fire ring for cooking is the keyhole ring, which is simply a rock outline in a keyhole shape. Since the best cooking fire is a small one consisting mostly of hot coals, a fire is kept going in the round end of the keyhole to provide a supply of hot coals for the narrow part where most cooking is done. As more coals are needed for cooking, use a stick or shovel to move hot coals from the fire.

A word of caution about using rocks: use only dry rocks, as porous ones gathered from stream beds or wet ground may contain enough water to build up steam and explode when heated in a fire.

Once you have selected a safe site for your fire and constructed a rock ring if there wasn't one, you must gather an adequate supply of firewood. Knowing which wood burns best is the mark of an experienced fire builder. The best woods for cooking are hardwoods, such as ash, beech, birch, maple, and oak, which burn less vigorously and with a shorter flame. The coals of such woods last longer and do not give food a resinous flavor as softwoods, such as pine, spruce, and fir, do. Oak gives the shortest and most uniform flames and produces steady, glowing coals.

Before you begin your wood-gathering, find out the regulations of the campground regarding firewood gathering. Use dead wood only; never cut anything green. Your first choice should be dead sticks in the immediate area, then use larger dead trees that may be standing.

If you are caught in a rainstorm, look for standing dead wood, as it is often much drier than wood lying on the ground. However, splitting dense hardwood logs found in the ground may reveal dry firewood at the center, even after several days of rain.

To get the fire going, collect a supply of easily ignited tinder, such as deserted bird nests, birch tree bark, dry cedar bark, dry evergreen twigs, sagebrush bark, dead lower twigs on evergreen trees, and perhaps best of all, the rich, resinous dead stumps and roots of the southern pine called "fat lighter," "lighter knot," or "lighter wood." Many campers use short, thick candles and commercial fire starters as tinder.

Never use gasoline, kerosene, alcohol, or other such combustible materials as fire starters. More than one backcountry traveler has gone to his reward early trying to start a quick fire with gasoline.

Once you have a good supply of tinder, place it in the fire ring. Next, get a generous supply of small sticks and twigs. Place these small sticks over the tinder and slowly add slightly larger sticks until you have a fire that can catch the larger wood. Remember not to rush the fire. If you place the heavier wood on too soon, you will smother the fire.

Safety with a campfire cannot be overemphasized. Every year many camps are burned to the ground and forest fires are started by campfires left unattended. Never leave a fire or even hot coals unattended. It is also a good precaution to keep a bucket of water and shovel handy in the event a campfire does get out of control.

When you are ready to break camp and move on, do the following: (1) pick up all trash of any kind to pack out with you; (2) put your fire out several hours before you leave, if possible, by dousing the fire until it is soaked, then smothering with soil, if available; (3) scatter the rocks, firewood, dead charcoals, etc; (4) replace the ground cover as it was when you arrived, leaving the site as though no one had been there.

If you have been using a permanent fire ring or open fire grill, make sure the fire is out and leave the area as clean as you found it, or follow any special procedures required by the campground.

Of course, today we don't have to depend upon the campfire or fire grill for cooking as we once did, so the camper who doesn't want to bother with firewood or doesn't desire the "atmosphere" of the campfire can choose from a wide selection of camp stoves which burn bottled or liquid gas, such as the famous Coleman stoves. Many of us who camp often like to use both a stove and open fire, frequently at the same time when cooking for a large group or preparing several hot dishes at the same time.

The same safety precautions should be used with a stove as with a campfire. Also, the operator of a camp stove should be very familiar with the stove's proper use. The stove

should always be placed on a level, solid base. Midway through preparation of a meal is no time to have a stove with pots on it come tumbling down without warning.

There are many types of cook kits available for whatever heat source you choose. One of the most complete units that serves all cooking purposes is the Camper's Kitchen. This unit has a complete cook kit including cooking and eating utensils, plates, cups, dishwashing pans, food storage containers, aluminum pots and pans, even measuring spoons and can opener. All of these are stored in a metal box which forms an excellent working cabinet when opened. A second box made by the same company is available for food storage.

There are two schools of thought on the best way to care for aluminum cookware used over open fires. Some people prefer to coat the shiny cookware's outer surface with a paste of soap and water. The soot from the fire gets on this coating and washes off easily, leaving shiny cookware. If you try this, be careful not to get the soap inside the cookware. Other people prefer not to pre-treat the aluminum but to let the cookware blacken over the fire to collect heat faster, and thereby cook faster. Both ways work well.

If the weight of your gear is not a consideration, old-fashioned cast iron cookware is still an excellent choice for camp cooking. Ironware dates back for centuries, and the only significant change is that it is now available in many additional shapes and sizes. Cast iron is extremely durable, has excellent heat retention, and distributes heat well so you don't have hot spots. There is even nutritional value in using cast iron because the iron imparts dietary iron into the food. Cleanup is easy by simply wiping clean.

The most versatile piece of cookware available is the ironware Dutch oven, which has a flat, flanged lid upon which hot coals can be placed for even baking, a bail for hanging over a fire, a flat bottom, and three legs to keep the bottom from sitting directly on hot coals when placed in the fire. Since many modern flat-bottomed pots are called Dutch ovens, make sure you are getting the one described, as it is made specifically for open-fire cooking. This pot can be used for deep fat frying, shallow frying, roasting, baking, boiling, broiling, or stewing. When the Dutch oven lid is turned upside down and placed on a small bed of hot coals, it makes an excellent frying pan. You can also turn the pot upside down, place coals on the bottom of the pot, and set the lid upside down on the pot legs to make an excellent camp griddle. If you are using more than one Dutch oven, you can "stack cook." After you have the first Dutch oven heating properly, set the second on top of the first and add hot coals to its lid. The multitude of uses for the Dutch oven is limited only by the imagination.

Another versatile "utensil" is ordinary aluminum foil. You can cook almost anything in it, including vegetables, meats, and even fruits such as apples. Perhaps best of all, foil cooking can save on the number of pots you have to take with you and reduces clean-up time for pots and pans to zero.

When you make an envelope of the foil and seal properly, each foil bundle becomes a pressure cooker. The steam that is confined in the bundle retains flavor and prevents scorching. Fish can be especially good when cooked in foil, particularly when butter and vegetables are added for a one-pot meal.

It is very important that only the coals of the fire be used when cooking with aluminum foil. You can either place the foil bundles on the coals or rake away enough coals to expose the ground, place the foil package on the ground, and cover with the hot coals. Cooking times will vary, depending upon how hot your coals are. Experiment for the best method for your needs.

Baking is often left out of camp cooking, but it can be conquered with fun and ease with a reflector oven. Tasty breads, pies, cakes, biscuits, puddings, roasted meat and fish, casseroles, and any other food that can be cooked in the home oven can be cooked in this simple oven.

The reflector oven is made from polished aluminum or sheet metal so that dry heat from a nearby fire is reflected from the walls of the oven around the food. The best fire for reflector oven cooking is one that has some hot flames. It is important to care for the reflector oven properly, keeping the surfaces shiny with soft wool pads and non-abrasive soaps.

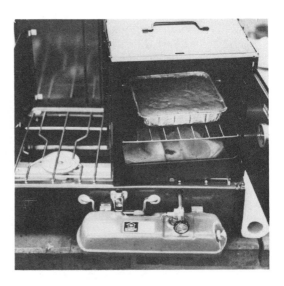

Badlands Goulash

6 medium potatoes, peeled and diced
1 lb. Polish sausages
2 Tbsp. bacon fat or oil
2 onions, slices
1 can (1 lb. 12 oz.) tomatoes
salt and pepper

In stewing pot or Dutch oven, simmer potatoes until tender, using as little water as possible. Slice sausages into bite-sized pieces; fry in bacon fat (or oil) with onions until latter are light brown. Add tomatoes (including juice) andd simmer. When potoates are tender, drain if necessary, then stir into meat-to-mato mixture. Season with salt and pepper to taste. Makes 6 servings.

Breakfast Apples

Large baking apples
Orange marmalade
Chopped walnuts
Lemon juice

Core apples and peel skin from upper part. Place on square of aluminum foil. Fill centers with orange marmalade, top with chopped walnuts, and sprinkle with lemon juice to keep cut surface from discoloring. Wrap in foil, twisting at top to close. Place in coals and cook about 45 min. Test for doneness by piercing with fork through foil.

Campfire Tuna

1 pkg. dehydrated spaghetti sauce mix
1 can (1 lb. 12 oz.) tomatoes
1 pkg. (8 oz.) egg noodles
½ c. water
1 tsp. seasoned salt
1 can (13 oz.) tuna
½ c. grated American cheese

Using a small stewing pot or Dutch oven, combine spaghetti sauce mix, tomatoes, water, and seasoned salt; blend thoroughly. Bring to a boil, reduce heat, cover, and simmer over very low heat for 20 min. Meanwhile, cook noodles according to package directions until just tender. Drain. Stir in spaghetti sauce mixture, tuna, and cheese. Makes 6 to 8 servings.

Banana Dessert

Take a banana (leaving peel on), split it down the middle, and fill the split with caramel candy. Wrap the banana with aluminum foil and toss into a bed of hot coals. Remove in about 10 minutes when the candy has melted into the hot banana.

Campfire Meat Loaf

½ c. dry bread crumbs
1 c. milk
1½ lbs. ground beef
2 beaten eggs
Catsup or sauce
¼ c. grated onion
1 tsp. salt
½ tsp. sage
Dash of pepper

Soak bread crumbs in milk; add meat, eggs, seasonings, and onion; mix well. Form into individual loaves or place into greased muffin pans. Cover with catsup or sauce of your choice.

Bake in moderate reflector oven at 350° for 45 min. to 1 hr. Makes 8 servings.

Note: All pans must be greased.

Almost any dish you can cook in the home kitchen can be prepared outdoors, and there is no end to the number of ways campers can prepare these meals. Learning exciting new cooking techniques and recipes can add to the entire family's adventure of being in the great outdoors. □

BREAKFAST IN CAMP

By Gertrude Olinghouse

Except for the up-before-daybreak fisherman, campers tend to take their time beginning the day. Breakfast is usually a family affair, often the only time during daylight hours a family or camping group gets together. This later start makes the first meal of the day resemble brunch in that heartier foods and larger servings are in demand. By the time breakfast reaches the table, even the fisherman may have returned, demanding that his freshly caught finnies be cooked. Fish for breakfast is acceptable only if the angler has cleaned his catch, so that cooking it requires but a few minutes.

Breakfast Fish

½ c. flour or bread crumbs
¼ tsp. salt
⅛ tsp. pepper
4 to 6 small fish
fat for frying

Put flour or crumbs in a paper bag, add the salt and pepper. Drop in the fish and shake well. In the meantime have the fat heating in a skillet. When it is hot, lay in the fish and cook for 10 min., turning once. An old-fashioned cast iron frying pan creates crispness.

Right here seems a good place to mention pans and other things. Old hands at camping have long since gathered together cooking gear that fits their needs comfortably; new hands are probably using cast-off kitchen pots and pans. If this describes your situation, do begin replacing these with utensils better suited to camping and keep them just for that.

Among the necessities of equipment for cooking breakfast are a coffee pot ranking first with a large heavy frying pan running a close second. Two or three nesting frying pans or skillets should be a part of the camp kitchen gear. Three well-seasoned, cast iron skillets are worth every ounce of their weight at camp. Cast iron does require care, as does aluminum or steel. If you decide on one of these, make it cast aluminum or the heaviest steel possible. You'll have less scorched food and your pans will not warp out of shape as lighter ones may.

A griddle and Dutch oven can be included but are not strictly necessary. Add a heavy saucepan or two, mixing bowls and spoons, pancake turner and/or spatula and a long handled sharp-tined fork. A wire whip or rotary beater is handy.

For the table, heavyweight plastic plates are suggested rather than paper or metal. Metal cups have burned many an unwary lip, and metal plates, while they can be heated, cool too rapidly. Warm the plastic in hot water.

Breakfast is not complete without biscuits. Muffins are easily baked in the oven of an RV range, but can readily be baked in a skillet having its own cover, or at least a well fitting cover of some sort. If you use a mix, reduce the amount of liquid called for, so the resulting dough is near the consistency of drop biscuits. Preheat the skillet, and add a little fat to prevent sticking. Keep the heat moderate, especially if the mix contains sugar. Spoon the dough by heaping tablespoonfuls into the skillet. When all the dough has been used, cover the skillet and leave about 10 min., peeking after the first 5 to lift the edge of a muffin (now more like a scone) to check the browning. The heat may need to be raised or lowered. When the tops of the muffins lose their shine and the bottoms are nicely browned, carefully turn each one with a spatula or pancake turner. Adjust the cover and continue cooking until this side browns, about 8 min. Serve at once from the pan. Put out lots of butter, jam or honey, crisp bacon and eggs, coffee, and milk for the kids. Breakfast is ready in less than half an hour. The hardest part is getting the kids out of the creek and the teenagers out of the sleeping bags.

You can make your muffins from any recipe, just remember to reduce the amount of liquid if they are to be baked over heat instead of in the oven. Biscuits and cornbread batter take to skillet baking with no changes in the basic recipe. Pour the batter into a heated and greased skillet, and bake until the top appears dull; carefully turn and bake the other side, about 10 min. per side.

All sorts of goodies can be added to plain muffin mixes: chopped raisins, blueberries, chopped apples, dates and nuts.

Muffins (Basic Recipe)

2 c. sifted flour
3 tsp. baking powder
½ tsp. salt
2 Tbsp. sugar
1 egg, well beaten
4 Tbsp. melted fat or salad oil
Milk to make soft dough (about ⅔ c.)

Sift together (or stir) all dry ingredients. Combine remaining ingredients, and add all at once to flour mixture, stirring, not beating, quickly and vigorously until just mixed. Bake in skillet as directed. Use 1 cup milk if muffins are to be baked in muffin cups in the oven.

And then there's pancakes in their endless interesting, tasty varieties. These, of whatever kind, should be served hot off the griddle (or fry pan). One way to manage this is to let each person cook his or her own, even the kids who are old enough to do it safely. They'll love it and will make fanciful shapes and sizes until the last drop of batter disappears.

These buckwheat griddlecakes can be mixed ahead and somewhat resemble sourdough pancakes.

Buckwheat Griddlecakes

½ pkg. (1 and ½ teaspoons) active dry yeast
1½ c. plus 1 Tbsp. lukewarm water
¼ tsp. salt
2½ c. buckwheat flour
1 c. milk, scalded, cooled to lukewarm
½ tsp. baking soda

Before you go to bed, dissolve the yeast in one and one-half cups of water. Combine the flour, salt, yeast and milk in a glass, stainless steel or good plastic bowl. Beat well, cover and set in warm place.

The next morning, dissolve the soda in the tablespoon of water and add it to the batter. Test the batter by pouring a little on your hot griddle. If the batter is too thin, add a little buckwheat flour; if it's too thick, thin with warm water or milk. Makes 2 to 3 dozen griddlecakes, depending on size. Serve with maple syrup or other syrup, honey or jam. Have butter handy, too.

Omelets top any list of things for breakfast, but why not make it easy for yourself and cook scrambled eggs instead? Almost anything that can be carefully folded into an omelet can be less carefully incorporated into scrambled eggs.

Basic Omelet (French)

1½ Tbsp. fat or salad oil
6 eggs
⅓ c. milk
salt and pepper to taste

Heat a skillet, add the fat, tipping skillet to grease sides and bottom. Beat the eggs, using a hand-turned beater, wire whisk or large fork. Add the salt and pepper; a dash of red pepper or Tabasco is all right, too. Beat in the milk. Pour into the skillet and allow to set a moment. Add whatever "stuffing" wanted and begin to

stir and lift the mixture gently with a spoon; don't overdo this as too much stirring makes the eggs look curdled. The idea is to move the mixture just enough to prevent scorching. When the eggs have set, but have not entirely lost their shine, your scrambled eggs are ready to serve. Scrambled eggs are not browned.

Breakfast in a Skillet

8 slices Canadian bacon
3 Tbsp. bacon fat
1 Tbsp. chopped onion
2 c. cooked potatoes, cubed
4 or 5 eggs, beaten
1/8 tsp. pepper

Brown the bacon on both sides, remove from skillet. Leave about 3 tablespoons of fat in skillet. Add the onions, stir until limp. Add the potatoes and brown. When potatoes are nearly as brown as wanted, add the eggs, pepper and salt. Stir carefully until eggs are done and very lightly browned. Toasted, well-buttered English muffins go well with this dish.

Note: Frankfurters cut in thin rounds or thin-sliced ham may be used in place of the Canadian bacon. Corned beef or luncheon meat could be substituted in a pinch.

Suppose you have a small slice of ham and one rasher of bacon, but not enough of either for more than one serving? Chop the ham, fry the bacon crispy and crumble it. Add both to the egg mixture after pouring it into the skillet. Sauted mushrooms, leftover vegetables that seem suitable, grated cheese, and chopped cooked meat will add interest to either an omelet or scrambled eggs.

Hashed brown potatoes go with scrambled eggs like Punch goes with Judy. Leftover boiled potatoes, or potatoes boiled in their jackets for this purpose are diced and browned in butter or bacon fat. This is where a second heavy skillet comes in handy, because the

potatoes must be browning while the eggs are cooking. Season the potatoes as you like: salt, pepper, red pepper, your favorite herb, a shake of garlic powder or garlic salt.

If your morning, even midmorning appetite does not respond to the more robust foods mentioned, or your health is less than perfect, or you aren't as young as you once were, perhaps soft boiled eggs, fruit and toast are more appropriate. However, some effort should be made to make camp breakfast a little different from the one at home every day. Suggestions are canned applesauce sprinkled with cinnamon, a dollop of whipped topping added, or other canned fruit with a different spice. You do, of course, carry as many herbs and spices as are practical. Toast can be readily made on a hot griddle or in a skillet. And hot water makes soft-boiled eggs. Coddle them. Bring a pan of water to a full boil—about 1 qt. for two eggs—and carefully lower the eggs into the water; cover the pan and remove from heat. Allow to stand for 8 min. Remove the eggs from their shells and season as you wish. A cup of hot tea is a change instead of coffee.

Apple Toast

6 tart apples, cored, peeled and sliced
6 Tbsp. butter
1/3 c. powdered sugar
2 Tbsp. water
3 slices bread
2 Tbsp. granulated sugar
1/4 tsp. cinnamon

Place apple slices in a saucepan with 2 tablespoons of the butter, powdered sugar and water. Cook quickly, tossing lightly, over medium high heat until just tender.

Melt the remaining butter in a skillet and fry the bread slices in it until golden on both sides. Place each slice of bread on a plate, top with apple mixture and sprinkle with granulated sugar. Little pig or smoked sausages are delicious with Apple Toast, as are ham and bacon.

More good things for camp breakfasts include old-fashioned, rolled oat porridge with raisins added; long grain rice, cooked the night before and reheated in a double boiler, or freshly cooked in the morning, raisins can be added to rice as well. Serve either one in bowls with sugar and milk within reach. Even the small fry will eat porridge at camp.

Since it's difficult to keep coffee hot and tasting fresh for more than a short time, why not keep water hot and have instant coffee, tea bags, sugar and coffee whitener handy? Each camper can then make his or her own at any time and how they like it.

Keep your cooking fire small, if used at all. Charcoal's hard to beat, if you give it time to heat. If two burners are your choice, keep the fuel tank filled, and the cook will rejoice. ☐

TAKE A WOK ON THE ROAD

By Ann Manes

How would you like to sit down to a campground dinner of Chinese cuisine? You can discover the fun of a new world of quick and easy food when you take a wok on the road.

During ten years of trailering, a Chinese wok has been a standard cooking utensil. A wok is a bowl-shaped frying pan that can be used to stir-fry, boil, steam and pan-fry. You can also toss salads and noodles in the wok. Its versatility is amazing. And its greatest feature for campers is that a wok is perfect for fast cooking over charcoal, a campfire, a camp stove or in an RV. Usually a complete main dish can be cooked and served right in the wok. How fancy you decide to make your wok cooking is up to your palate and pocketbook. I've enjoyed boiled lobster on the Gaspe Peninsula in Quebec, Canada . . . . delicate steamed salmon in Seattle . . . . stir-fried Mazatlan shrimp in Mexico. One of my more simple favorites is ham and eggs wok style.

With the current popularity of Chinese cooking, woks are easily available in a variety of price ranges. There are stainless, black and carbon steel woks, as well as aluminum. All woks are sold with a supporting ring to stabilize them, and wok covers can be bought separately or come with the more expensive and complete wok sets. Do buy the long handled shovel and spoon designed for woks, because

they're especially convenient when cooking outside over the coals or campfire. The 14-inch wok size is the most popular and fits well in any mini kettle barbecue.

Using your wok over charcoal is probably the most fun way of cooking with it, because you can put the grill or cooker right on the picnic table and prepare dinner in front of your eager eaters. Especially in the stir-fry method, the cooking time is so short that ingredients become dinner in minutes. Then you simply whisk the wok from charcoal to table and you have an edible centerpiece.

When cooking over charcoal, prepare the coals in the usual manner, and when they're grey, place the wok ring in the middle of them. The ring has slanted sides, so the circle can be flipped over and made larger or smaller to help control the heat. You may have to rearrange a few coals, because you must be sure that none of them actually touch the wok when it's placed on the ring. A little experimentation will teach you how many coals to use for your barbecue and the dish you're preparing.

Stir-fry cooking is just what it says . . . . you stir and fry. This is the quickest and most popular type of wok cooking. Any number of ingredients can be used in any combination that appeals to you, and with the addition of a simple sauce and seasoning you create an interesting main dish. Because stir-frying is so fast, it's important to assemble the ingredients first, more time will be needed to cut up the food than to cook it. Always pre-heat the wok, because stir-fry food is best when cooked quickly in a hot pan over high heat. Only a minimum of oil is needed. Vegetables should remain crisp, so the dish shouldn't be allowed to overcook. When the food is cooked, remove it immediately from the fire . . . . the heat of the wok will keep the food warm while you put last minute accompaniments on the table. Serving a main dish meal directly from the wok is casual and fun and makes for less cleanup. Put the wok on a paper towel if you're bringing it in your RV to serve, so you won't get soot on your table. Speaking of soot, don't scour the outside of the wok since you'll use it so much over the coals. Wash it inside, wipe the outside with a paper towel and store it in a large plastic bag.

Boiling in a wok is a handy way to make noodles, and eliminates the need to carry another large pot. If your taste leans toward lobster, a 14-inch wok accommodates them.

Steaming is an excellent method to prepare fish and fresh vegetables. It's easy to do in a wok by boiling a little water in the bottom, placing a round cake rack in the wok, setting an oven-proof plate on top of the rack with the food in it, and putting on the wok cover. You can steam and serve the food on the same plate, too.

Pan-frying in a wok is sometimes better than doing it in a conventional frying pan. The bowl shape is a great advantage in frying fish, for example. Because the sides of the pan are not as hot as the middle, you can fry whole fish more evenly. Just put the thickest part of the fish at the bottom and run the tail up the side of the pan. Bacon is expertly drained in a wok by frying it on the sides; the grease drips down into the center. Chicken is extra crispy when panfried in a wok.

Don't forget that a wok makes a fine soup kettle . . . . and chili pot . . . . and stewing pan. And when you tire of frying fish, bacon and eggs, and chicken in your wok, buy one of the many Chinese cookbooks and expand your wok cookery.

Here are six easy wok dishes while camping.

Teriyaki Steak or Meatballs

1 lb. flank or sirloin steak, or ground beef
2 Tbsp. teriyaki sauce
2 Tbsp. oil
½ tsp. garlic salt
1 c. sliced onion
2 c. green pepper, sliced lengthwise
2 c. tomatoes, cherry tomatoes or chunks
2 Tbsp. flour
1 c. chicken bouillon
1 Tbsp. teriyaki sauce

Slice steak into strips 1½" long by ⅛" thick, or roll ground beef into small meatballs. Marinate in teriyaki for an hour or more. Mix flour, bouillon and teriyaki sauce and set aside. Heat wok for 30 seconds, add 1 Tbsp. oil and swirl. Add steak or meatballs and stir-fry 2 min. or until meat is pink inside. Remove. Add 1 Tbsp. oil and garlic salt and swirl. Add onion and green pepper and stir-fry 2 min. Add bouillon mixture, cover and cook 3 min. Add steak or meatballs and tomatoes, stir-fry 1 min. and serve over rice. Serves 4.

Ham 'n Eggs Wok Style

6 eggs
1 c. diced ham
½ c. fresh or canned bean sprouts, optional
½ c. fresh or canned mushrooms
¼ tsp. onion salt
1 Tbsp. oil

Beat eggs lightly in bowl and add remaining ingredients. Heat wok for 30 seconds, add oil and swirl it around. Pour in about ¼ c. of the egg mixture, letting it cook for about 1 min. or until lightly browned. Turn and cook for another minute. Remove, keep warm, and repeat to use up the mixture. Serve with soy sauce or catsup. Serves 4.

Steamed Whole Fish

Make slits 1" apart the entire length of the fish, cutting down to the backbone. Slit both sides of fish. Open slits and sprinkle with desired seasonings; salt, garlic, onion, paprika, or Chinese seasonings. Also season cavity of fish. Place fish on oven-proof plate and marinate an hour or more before steaming. Set plate on round cake rack over boiling water in wok. Put on wok cover. Fish is done when flesh flakes.

Chicken with Zucchini

1 lb. diced chicken breast
¼ tsp. garlic powder
2 Tbsp. soy sauce
1 to 2 Tbsp. oil
2 oz. canned sliced mushrooms
¼ c. water chestnuts, optional
½ c. celery
1 generous c. diced zucchini
Prepare vegetables above.
1 tsp. flour
½ c. water
Mix flour and water.

Heat wok and add oil. Stir-fry chicken and garlic powder until chicken turns white. Add soy sauce and stir-fry another minute. Add vegetables and cook covered about 5 min. Stir flour and water, then add to wok, simmering and stirring for at least 1 min. until mixture thickens. Serves 4.

Sweet and Sour Pork

1 lb. pork tenderloin
2 Tbsp. teriyaki sauce
cut pork into 1-inch cubes and marinate in teriyaki 1 hr.
1 c. canned pineapple slices, cut in cubes
1 c. sliced carrots
1 c. sliced green pepper
1 lg. tomato, cut in wedges
¼ c. diced sweet pickles
1 sliced onion

Prepare vegetables above and set aside.
½ c. vinegar
2 Tbsp. honey or syrup
1 c. brown sugar
1 tsp. teriyaki sauce
1 c. pineapple juice and water (use juice from pineapple slices)
Blend sauce ingredients above.
3 Tbsp. flour
⅔ c. water
Blend flour and water until smooth and slowly add to sauce.
1 Tbsp. oil

Heat wok for 30 seconds; add oil and swirl. Add pork and stir-fry 4 to 5 min. Remove meat. Stir sauce and add to wok, cooking until sauce thickens and becomes glossy. Add vegetables and meat and cook covered for 12 to 15 min. Serves 4.

Beef with Broccoli
1 lb. sirloin steak
1 Tbsp. flour
1 Tbsp. soy sauce
Slice steak into strips 1½″ long by ⅛″ thick and toss in mixture of soy and flour.
2 c. sliced broccoli
2 oz. can sliced mushrooms
½ c. chicken bouillon
1 Tbsp. soy sauce

Prepare vegetables and set aside. Mix soy sauce and bouillon.
1 or 2 Tbsp. oil
½ tsp. garlic salt
Heat wok for ½ minute, add oil and garlic salt and beef and stir-fry two minutes or until pink inside. Remove meat. Add vegetables and bouillon mixture, and cook covered for about 5 min. Add meat, stir-fry 1 min. and serve with rice. A sprinkle of toasted almonds adds nice texture. Serves 4.

Remember that the recipes here are chosen for their simple preparation, and because the ingredients are easy to find in any market. Remember, too, that you can substitute other meats, vegetables and leftovers as you choose. Once you begin camp cooking in Chinese, you'll undoubtedly want to expand your culinary experiments. This will involve familiarizing yourself with Chinese seasonings, sauces and vegetables. These are becoming easier to find in gourmet sections of your supermarket. Or visit a Chinese grocery if you're fortunate enough to have one in your town. Very small quantities of these Chinese ingredients are used at one time, so tiny containers of them are easily tucked in with other foodstuffs in your RV.

Once you whet your appetite for Chinese cuisine, experiment with ingredients and soon you'll have your own favorite wok dishes. □

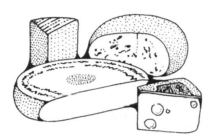

APPETIZERS

DUSTY'S SALSA DIP
Sun Vista RV Resort – Yuma, AZ

Dusty's Salsa Dip is popular at our park's Happy Hours and is a spicy complement to barbequed beef dinners on the patio. Sun Vista is located in the Southwest Arizona desert just minutes away from Mexico. The Yuma area is of great historical significance in the settling of the West. Historic sites such as the old Territorial Prison, also known as the "Hell Hole", draw thousands of visitors each year.

INGREDIENTS
- **1 28 oz. can crushed tomatoes**
- **1 bunch green onions, chopped**
- **1 green bell pepper, chopped**
- **2 chili peppers, chopped**
- **6 yellow banana peppers, chopped**
- **6 cerrano peppers, chopped ***
- **1 sm. bunch of cilantro**
- **2 Tbsp. vinegar**
- **2 Tbsp. vegetable oil**
- **2 Tbsp. hot taco sauce**
- **1 sm. can tomato sauce**
- **garlic salt & pepper to taste**
- *** may substitute jalapeno peppers**

DIRECTIONS
Mix all ingredients and chill. Mixture will keep for up to two weeks in refrigerator. Serve with corn or nacho chips.

TANGY TOMATO DIP
KOA Snug Harbor – Williamsport, MD

This recipe is low in fat and cholesterol and is easy to prepare. Not only is it good for you, it tastes great as well.

Snug Harbor offers grassy, creekfront sites, modern restroom and laundry facilities, game room, creek fishing and a variety of group activities such as Sunday pancake breakfasts, church services and bingo. We're located in the Civil War area and the scenic Mason Dixon line area. You can enjoy our peaceful atmosphere or take advantage of the many attractions in the Washington D.C. or Baltimore area.

INGREDIENTS
- **¾ c. low-fat cottage cheese**
- **2 Tbsp. horseradish**
- **2 dashes Tabasco sauce**
- **1 Tbsp parsley**
- **2 Tbsp. chopped onion**
- **¾ c. cocktail sauce**

DIRECTIONS
Mix all ingredients together. Serve with fresh vegetables.

AVOCADO DIP
Rancho Corrido Campground – Pauma Valley, CA

Avocados are plentiful in our area and this recipe has proven popular at some of our potlucks. It's not a spicy dip so it is enjoyed by all. We are at an elevation of 700 ft in a valley with avocado and citrus groves surrounding our area. Our park is 31 acres of grass with 170 sites and a view of Palomar Mountain.

INGREDIENTS
- 8 oz. cream cheese
- 1 c. sour cream
- 2 avocados, mashed
- 2 sm. cans chopped green chilies
- 1 garlic clove, mashed
- salt & pepper to taste

DIRECTIONS
Whip cream cheese. Add remainder of ingredients in order listed. Refrigerate for 1-2 hrs. for flavors to blend. Onions and more garlic can be added for variety and more zest to the dip.

KAMPERSVILLE PINEAPPLE KIELBASA
Lake Dunmore Kampersville – Middlebury, VT

Every family has many favorite recipes which have been carried down through the years. Our family has picked one of our favorite recipes to pass it on to all you folks. We hope you enjoy this recipe as much as we have. This particular hors d'oeuvre is wonderful for any holiday or occasion.

INGREDIENTS
- 1 kielbasa, precooked
- 2 cans pineapple, sliced
- 1 24 oz. jar duck sauce

DIRECTIONS
Cut up the pineapple into 1-inch chunks, and drain the remaining juice. In a large saucepan combine the duck sauce and pineapple. Simmer over low heat. While warming the sauce, grill kielbasa until it is warmed through. Cut the kielbasa into ½-inch chunks and add to the sauce mixture. For serving, place a large spoon into the saucepan and place small bowls around the pan. Self-serving always works best for this recipe.

SOUTHWESTERN MEXICANA DIP
KOA-Albuquerque Central – Albuquerque, NM

Our park is in the heart of the Southwest and Mexican flavor can be found anywhere, in clothing, architecture and in food as well.

Albuquerque Central KOA is located at the base of the spectacular Sandia Mountains. The campground offers shuttle service to historic Old Town, Albuquerque, a quaint part of the city which promises a taste of the unique blend of Spanish, Mexican and Indian. The shuttle takes campers to the Sandia Tram, the world's longest tram as well. While at the campground, enjoy miniature golf, swimming pool, hot tub and full amenities.

INGREDIENTS
- 1 can cheddar cheese soup
- 1 lb. velveeta cheese
- 1 can chopped green chilies
- 1 jar taco sauce

DIRECTIONS
Melt cheese in pot over campfire. Add chilies and taco sauce. Once sauce is warmed, add cheese soup (do not add water). Mix thoroughly and warm slightly to taste. Can be served directly from pot, using your favorite chips as dippers.

MEATBALLS IN BAR-B-QUE SAUCE
Del-Raton Mobile Headquarters – Delray Beach, FL

Each year we host a New Year's Party at our park. We serve this tasty appetizer and it's always a big hit.

Del-Raton offers a quiet, clean and comfortable atmosphere. We're close to shopping, fishing, golfing and the beach. Located in the heart of tropical weather, there's always a gentle breeze to keep you comfortable.

INGREDIENTS
- 1½ lbs. ground beef
- 1 egg
- ½ c. bread crumbs
- 1 pkg. dry onion soup mix
- 1 c. barbeque sauce (your favorite)

DIRECTIONS
In large bowl, mix first four ingredients together. Form mixture into meatballs and saute lightly in frying pan. Drain and place in casserole dish. Cover with barbeque sauce and bake at 350° for 30 min.

SUGAR COATED NUTS
Travelers Campground U.S.A. — Cecil, GA

This easy-to-prepare treat is great for your holiday get-togethers.

Travelers Campground U.S.A. is located off I-75 at exit 8. Our campground has level open sites with full and partial hookups. We have a variety of amenities with reasonable rates. Come visit us and you'll see how convenient and comfortable our campground is.

INGREDIENTS
- 1 egg white
- 1 Tbsp. water
- 1½ qts. pecan halves
- 1 c. sugar
- 1 tsp. cinnamon
- ¼ tsp. salt

DIRECTIONS
Mix sugar, cinnamon and salt together. Beat egg white and water until soft peak forms. Add nuts to egg white mixture and mix well. Add sugar mixture. Place on ungreased cookie sheet. Bake at 250° for 1 hour, stirring every 15 min.

JAKIE BOB FINGERS
Green Acres Family Camping Resort—Williamston, NC

Our park is a full service campground — country-style — with lots of activities for all ages.

In our haunted house at Halloween, Jakie Bob loses his arm. Then in the kitchen, Jakie Bob fingers are served to all guests.

INGREDIENTS
- **10 lbs. wieners (Carolina Packers preferred)**
- **3 (18 oz.) bottles hot barbecue sauce**
- **1 box toothpicks**

DIRECTIONS
Cut wieners into quarters. Simmer in hot sauce 30 to 45 min. Add a small amount of water if needed. Yields 400 nubs.

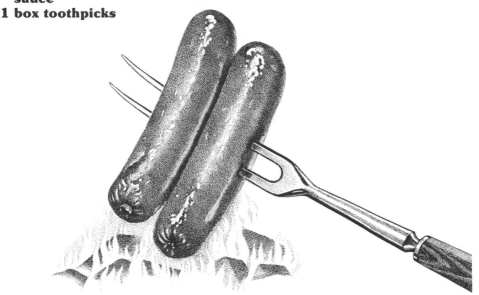

PARTY FINGER GRINDERS
White Pines Campsites – Winsted, CT

We are a family campground located in the heart of the Connecticut Berkshires. White Pines Campsites offers miles of woodlands and fragrant fresh air, historic landmarks and the serene majesty of the Litchfield Hills. White Pines is snuggled between Winsted and Barkhamsted in the northwestern corner of the state. Spacious wooded or open sites with all the necessary facilities located on the grounds are available here. This recipe is a favorite of many of our campers and was in fact provided by one of our campers.

INGREDIENTS
- **½ lb. Genoa salami**
- **½ lb. ham**
- **½ lb. Provolone cheese**
- **2 pkg. crescent rolls**
- **6 eggs**
- **½ c. Parmesan grated cheese**
- **1 jar of roasted peppers**

DIRECTIONS
Place crescent rolls on bottom of lightly greased 9″ x 13″ aluminum pan. Layer with half of salami, provolone cheese and ham. Beat eggs and Parmesan cheese together and pour over meats and cheese in pan. Layer again with remainder of meats and cheese and cover with the roasted peppers. Add the second package of crescent rolls on top and bake 45-50 minutes in a 325° oven. Cool and cut into squares and serve warm or cool. Makes 40 servings.

CAVIAR PIE
RiverBend Park and Campground – Forestville, CA

This is an exceptional hors d'oeuvre that complements the many varieties of wines available from our area.

Located 11 miles off the freeway at Santa Rosa, RiverBend provides the ideal location for exploring the varied produce and vineyards of the area. Our location, in the heart of the Russian River Valley, is the perfect spot from which you can explore the best the area has to offer including Caviar Pie which is available in our store in season.

INGREDIENTS
1 lg. jar lumpfish black caviar
6 hard boiled eggs, finely diced
1 sweet onion, finely diced
   (drain on paper towel 1 hr.)
6 oz. cream cheese
2/3 c. mayonnaise

DIRECTIONS
Soften cream cheese and combine with mayo. Prepare 10″ spring form pan with wax paper bottom and buttered sides. Layer ingredients in following order: eggs, onion, cream cheese, and mayo mixture. Chill for 3 hrs. Remove from form and spread caviar on top like you would cake icing. Serve with crackers.

EGGPLANT FRITTERS
Capri Court Campground – Houma, LA

Southern Louisiana has long been famous for its cajun food & hospitality. The ingredient for this unique cuisine is grown in the lush family gardens.

At Capri Court Campground, in the heart of Bayou-Cajun country, 50 miles southwest of New Orleans, you can enjoy the food & culture of the area while camping in the shade of huge, moss-draped cypress trees.

While seafood dishes are usually associated with the bayous, this recipe offers a traditional food served at family gatherings and restaurants "down home".

INGREDIENTS
2 lg. eggplants
3 Tbsp milk
1/2 tsp. vanilla extract
1/4 tsp. pumpkin pie spice
2 Tbsp. granulated sugar
2 Tbsp. brown sugar
flour (self-rising)
cooking oil
powdered sugar

DIRECTIONS
Peel and cut up eggplant. Boil eggplant in water until tender. Drain, mash, and mix eggplant with remaining ingredients except flour, powdered sugar, and oil. Add enough flour to mixture to make a pancake batter consistency. Drop by spoonfuls into thin layer of cooking oil. Brown fritters on both sides. Sprinkle with powdered sugar and serve warm.

CINDY'S CHEESE BALL
Yogi Bear Jellystone Camp-Resort – Caledonia, WI

Located near Lake Michigan, and only twenty minutes from downtown Milwaukee this Jellystone features a full complement of facilities for resort recreation and relaxation. Planned activities appeal to all family tastes. The resort is ideally located to take advantage of the metropolitan cultures of Milwaukee and Chicago. And everyone from all walks of life enjoys this appetizer at our annual New Year's Eve Party in July.

INGREDIENTS
- 4-5 oz. blue cheese or roquefort cheese
- 2 lg. pkgs. cream cheese
- 1 sm. jar very sharp processed cheddar cheese
- 1 c. ground pecans
- 1 palmful parsley flakes
- 1 sm. grated onion
- 2 tsp. Worchestershire sauce
- 1 tsp. salt

DIRECTIONS

Grind nuts and parsley together. Let all ingredients come to room temperature. Mix all ingredients together at high speed. Add half of the parsley and nuts, place in the refrigerator overnight so it can mellow. When ready to mold, mix balance of parsley and nuts and cover molded ball. Makes 2 lb. ball or 5 small balls. Wrap in plastic wrap, can be frozen for 1 yr. or will keep in refrigerator several weeks.

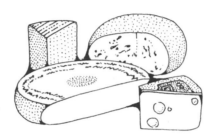

CHEESE FONDUE
Ship Ashore Resort – Smith River, CA

We have been serving cheese fondue in our restaurant for 15 years and people love it.

Ship Ashore Resort is in the heart of the redwood forest on the beautiful northern California coast, just 3 miles south of the Oregon border. In addition to a variety of amenities, we also offer great salmon and steelhead fishing.

INGREDIENTS
- 1-2 lb. pkg. Velveeta Cheese
- 1-4 oz. can chili strips, diced
- ½ c. diced tomatoes (can)
- 1 tsp. garlic, granulated
- 1 tsp. onion, granulated
- 1 tsp. Worcestershire Sauce
- 1 Tbsp. oil
- 1 Tbsp. prepared mustard
- ⅛ tsp. Accent
- 1-11 oz. can cheddar cheese soup

DIRECTIONS

Heat in double boiler until cheese is melted. Do not overheat. Do not dilute with water. Serve with breadsticks, varieties of rye, celery sticks, or fresh cauliflower.

CLAM BALLS
Rod's Beach Resort – Copalis Beach, WA

Located on the Pacific coast, our family oriented resort is ideal for clam digging. Clams dug on the beaches of the blue Pacific are the main ingredient of this "Gourmet's Delicacy". The area is also great for beachcombing or just getting away from it all.

INGREDIENTS
1 egg
1 c. minced clams, raw or canned
¼ c. bread crumbs
2 Tbsp. pancake flour
dash of minced onion
dash of parsley
salt to taste

DIRECTIONS
Mix all ingredients into stiff batter and spoon into deep fat fryer until golden brown — 2-3 min.

CRAB DIP
Bridgeview Family Campground – Emerald Isle, NC

We have a boat ramp and a dock right on the Intercoastal Waterway where you can set your crab cages and have fresh crab meat. We are located on the Intercoastal Waterway (Bogue Sound) with shady rustic sites, ceramic-tiled bathhouse, and swimming pool. We are surrounded by excellent fishing and shellfishing and are close to the ocean, theme parks, and restaurants.

INGREDIENTS
2-6 oz. pkg. cream cheese
1½ Tbsp. mayonnaise
1 Tbsp. cream
¼ tsp. salt
1 tsp. grated onions or chives (optional)
1 tsp. Worcestershire sauce
1 c. cooked crab meat, flaked
round loaf of dark rye bread (optional)

DIRECTIONS
Mix all ingredients except crab meat and bread. Beat with a spoon until smooth. Fold crab meat into mixture. Slice off the top of the loaf of bread and remove the soft inner part, leaving about 1 inch thickness at sides and bottom. Use the removed bread later as chunks for dipping. Fill the hollow with the dip.

SAUSAGE BALLS
Chattanooga South KOA – Ringgold, GA

This recipe is a quick and easy snack. At Christmas we bake cookies, cakes and sausage balls for our campers. That is our way of thanking them for staying with us.

Our campground is wooded and nature has landscaped our campground with plenty of tall trees and hills. We're just off I-75 at exit 141 with easy off and easy on access. We're only minutes from Chattanooga and all the attractions of the area. We offer shaded, pull-thru sites, laundry and restroom facilities, a rec hall, swim pool, playground, Kamping Kabins and much more.

INGREDIENTS
1 lb. breakfast sausage, sliced
1 c. Bisquick
½ c. sharp cheddar cheese, diced
milk

DIRECTIONS
Mix all ingredients together. Add just enough milk to form mixture into dough-like consistency. Roll into small balls and bake at 350° for 15 min.

CHEESE BALLS
Nashville East/Lebanon KOA – Lebanon, TN

This recipe is easy to make and is a tasty appetizer for any party. We occasionally have parties here at the campground and serve this cheese ball.

Our campground offers a country feeling with grassy, shaded and level spaces. We have pull-thru sites, laundry, grocery items and barbeque grills. There's always plenty to do here. Right here at the park you can swim, play tennis or shuffleboard, or take advantage of our rec hall. You can also tour the attractions of Nashville, or visit Opryland which is only 30 min. away.

INGREDIENTS
2 8-oz. pkgs. cream cheese
1 jar Old English cheese
2 Tbsp. mayonnaise
2 Tbsp. lemon juice
1 Tbsp. grated onion
2 Tbsp. Parmesan cheese
crushed pecans

DIRECTIONS
Combine all ingredients and form ball. Roll ball in crushed pecans. Cover and refrigerate for at least 2 hrs.

SWEDISH PORCUPINE MEATBALLS
Budget RV Park – Donna, TX

This recipe is a favorite of mine because it is delicious, quick and easy to prepare. There are never any leftovers! It's ideal for picnics and potlucks.

We are located 2 mi. east of Alamo, 2 mi. west of Donna, and 10 mi. north of Mexico — right in the center of the beautiful Rio Grande Valley. Ours is a small park with a rec hall, showers, laundry room and paved streets. Since we are small, close relationships are formed and everyone goes home having met many new friends. Our people are the greatest and are always ready to help out whenever needed. They have become our family and we love them all. So ya'll come on down and be part of our big happy family.

INGREDIENTS
1½ lb. ground beef
1 can or jar applesauce
1 c. pre-cooked rice
½ c. onion
1½ tsp. salt
¼ tsp. pepper
1 c. catsup
1 c. water

DIRECTIONS
Mix all ingredients except catsup and water. Shape into balls. Place 1 layer deep in a 13" x 9" pan. Mix catsup and water. Pour over meatballs. Bake at 350° for 1 hr.

MEATY FONDUE
Lickdale Campground – Jonestown, PA

Lebanon County is known for its delicious bologna. Each year our county tourist bureau holds a Bologna Fest where you can buy bologna made in different ways.

Our family oriented campground is located along the Swatara Creek. We are centrally located to Hershey, Lancaster and Reading in a semi-wooded area.

INGREDIENTS
1¾ c. milk
2 8-oz. pkg. cream cheese, cubed
2 tsp. dry mustard
¼ c. chopped onion
1 8-oz. pkg. regular Lebanon bologna, diced
French Bread (cut into bite size pieces)

DIRECTIONS
Heat milk in crockpot on high. Add cream cheese. Stir until cream cheese is melted. Add dry mustard, onion and bologna. Stir thoroughly. Set on low for serving.
Note: This recipe may be prepared on top of the stove and served in a fondue pot. Serve with french bread or you may wish to try cherry tomatoes and raw cauliflower.

ARTICHOKE SCRAMBLE
Marina Dunes RV Park – Marina, CA

Marina Dunes RV Park is on the beautiful Monterey Peninsula. Our neighbor, just 5 miles to the north, is Castroville, the Artichoke Capital of the World, where artichokes are available year round. This recipe is just one of our favorites.

Marina Dunes is a serene, landscaped, full service park nestled in the sand dunes, a comfortable stroll to the beach, 8 miles to historic Monterey and 14 miles to quaint Carmel and the world famous Pebble Beach golf courses.

INGREDIENTS
3 lb. sm. fresh artichokes (1½″-2″ dia.)
1 lb. ground beef
1 sm. onion, chopped
2 Tbsp. minced parsley
2 cloves minced garlic
⅓ c. white wine
2 Tbsp. grated parmesan cheese
salt & pepper to taste

DIRECTIONS
Remove outer leaves of artichokes, cut off tough ends, cut in quarters and wash. Soak in water and lemon juice until ready to use. Saute beef until pink is gone. Add onion, parsley, garlic, salt and pepper, and saute about 5 min. Add drained artichokes and wine. Stir, cover and cook over med. heat until artichokes are tender (about 15 min.) Sprinkle with parmesan cheese before serving. Serve with sliced tomatoes, crusty French bread and a good California cabernet sauvignon. Serves 4.

SOUPS, STEWS & CHILIES

"BLACK POT" STEW
The Heritage – Whispering Pines, NC

This is a no-way-to-fail recipe that can serve any size group. It turns into an outdoor function and everyone enjoys taking their turn with the stirring stick! As a matter of fact, Robert Foxworth, star of TV's Falcon Crest, visited us during a political function. We served Black Pot Stew and it was a big success.

The Heritage is a private 200-acre country estate nestled in the heart of the "Golf Capital off the World." In 1978 the Sadler family began a camping and recreation program on the wooded slope overlooking the 14-acre springfed lake. With natural growths of pines, dogwoods and oaks, camping guests enjoy large pull-thru sites (full hookups/50 amps), full facilities, laundry and a large meeting room. Guests may enjoy swimming, fishing, canoeing, pedal boats, the sandy beach, nature trails, shuffleboard, croquet, basketball, horseshoes or volleyball in a private setting; and yet you're still only minutes from famous golf courses, fine shopping and elegant restaurants.

INGREDIENTS
  any kind of meat including
    pork, beef, poultry or game
  any kind of vegetable including
    potatoes
    carrots
    celery
    corn
    green beans
    peas
    onions
    peppers
    tomatoes
  salt & pepper to taste

DIRECTIONS

In large pot, add water, meat, salt and pepper. Simmer over open fire until meat falls away from bones. Remove bones and add vegetables. Season to taste. Stir and continue to simmer until vegetables are tender.

NEW ENGLAND FISH CHOWDER
Great Bay Camping Village – Newfields, NH

Our pot luck dinners are fast becoming a favorite activity at Great Bay Camping during May, September and October. This is one dish we prepare to warm up our campers on these cool evenings.

New Hampshire is not only known for being a shopper's paradise (no sales tax), and for its beautiful foliage and ski slopes, but also for its beautiful "Great Bay". Bluefish, striped bass and salmon — just a few of the species of fish waiting to be hooked. You may depart from our docking facilities at Great Bay Camping Village located on the Sqwamscott River. We are just a 5 min. boat ride away from an afternoon of GREAT fishing.

INGREDIENTS
- ¼ lb. salt pork, diced
- 2 sm. onions, diced
- 2 c. hot water
- 3 med/lg potatoes, peeled & diced
- 3 stalks celery, chopped
- 1 bay leaf
- 1 tsp. salt
- ¼ tsp. pepper
- 2 lb. fish fillets, cut into 1-inch cubes
- 4 c. hot milk
- 2 Tbsp. butter
- parsley

DIRECTIONS

In a large pot, saute salt pork for 1 min. Add onions and cook until golden. Add water, potatoes, celery, bay leaf, salt, and pepper. Cover and cook 10 min. then add the cubed fish. Simmer 10 min. or until fish flakes with a fork. Add the hot milk and stir, checking seasoning. Serve garnished with bits of butter and chopped parsley. Makes 4 to 6 servings.

HAM & BEAN SOUP
Hay Creek Valley Campground – Red Wing, MN

Campers love this recipe. They often buy a pot or two to take home with them.

Hay Creek Valley Campground is located on 30 acres bordered by a state-stocked trout stream. We're adjacent to Memorial Hardwood Forest where hiking, skiing and miles of trails await you. We offer water and electric hookups, dump station, modern bathhouses, heated pool, camp store, volleyball and horseshoes. We're just six miles from the Mississippi River and historic Red Wing. Come stay with us and enjoy our rural setting.

INGREDIENTS
- hambone
- 7 lbs. ham, cut in pieces
- 6 lbs. navy pea beans
- 4 lg. onions, chopped
- 6-8 carrots, chopped
- salt & pepper to taste
- water

DIRECTIONS

For best flavor, start with a leftover baked ham and the drippings. Soak beans in drippings and 2 gallons of water overnight. On low heat, simmer beans, onions, ham and hambone for 3 to 4 hrs. or until beans start to soften. Add carrots, salt and pepper and two more gal. of water. Simmer until carrots are cooked and beans are soft. Remove about 4 cups of beans, mash and return to soup to thicken. Freezes nicely.

QUICK BRUNSWICK STEW
Mountain View Campground – Cleveland, GA

We are located 11 miles northwest of Cleveland in the Chatahoochee National Forest on a trout stream. Quick Brunswick Stew is a great favorite at our restaurant which features barbeque and mountain trout. Our campers enjoy the barbeque dinners which we cater throughout the season in our pavilion. We also offer gold and gem grubbin, fishing in the trout pond, country music, and hiking. We hope you enjoy this Brunswick Stew. It's great with mashed potatoes, noodles or biscuits for sopping up the juices. Add a green salad and the meal is complete. Y'all come and visit us soon!

INGREDIENTS
- ¼ c. flour
- ½ tsp. salt
- ½ tsp. pepper
- 1 frying chicken
- 3 Tbsp. butter
- 1 onion, thinly sliced
- 1-14 oz. can tomatoes
- ½ c. chicken stock
- 2 tsp. Worcestershire sauce
- 1 tsp. dried thyme
- 1 c. green baby lima beans
- 1 c. okra
- 1 c. corn kernels
- ½ tsp. Tabasco sauce
- 1 Tbsp. sherry

DIRECTIONS
Heat butter in large skillet. Dip chicken in flour, salt and pepper. Brown over medium heat for 10 min. Remove chicken. Pour off all but 3 Tbsp. of drippings from skillet. Add onions and crushed tomatoes. Simmer for 5 min. Return chicken and any accumulated juices to pot. Bring to boil, cover, lower heat and simmer for 20 min. Uncover and add lima beans, okra and thyme to skillet. Simmer for 12 min. Add corn and simmer 5 min. or until lima beans and okra are tender. Stir in Worcestershire, Tabasco and sherry.

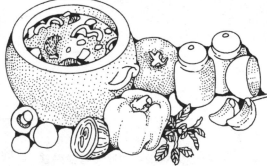

HAMBURGER STEW
Enon Beach Campground – Springfield, OH

Enon Beach Campground is on a small lake in a suburban setting, near the Air Force Museum. We host numerous guests visiting the museum. In addition, many nearby city dwellers come for a weekend getaway at our beach. One of our favorite meals is this delicious stew, a mild version of the chili family, which we call Hamburger Stew. When served with a salad, it makes a complete meal. For dessert we recommend watermelon or soft ice cream from our snack bar.

INGREDIENTS
- 10 lbs. hamburger
- 5 lg. onions
- no. 10 can of tomatoes
- no. 10 can of red kidney beans
- no. 10 can of tomato sauce
- 1 celery bunch
- water
- salt, pepper & chili powder to taste

DIRECTIONS
Brown hamburger and chopped onions in a large (at least five gallon) kettle. Ladle off and discard excess grease. Add the canned ingredients and water to make four gallons. Simmer for at least 15 min. Add chopped celery and season to taste. Serves 30.

YUMA CHILI (1986 Cook-off Popular Vote)
Villa Alameda R.V. Park – Yuma, AZ

Our recipe received the "PEOPLES CHOICE AWARD" in 1986 and 1988 in the annual chili cook-off sponsored by the Yuma Fine Arts Association. We are the friendliest R.V. Park in Yuma, Arizona!

INGREDIENTS
**2-3 lb. dried New Mexico Red
   medium-hot chile pods
garlic cloves
6 lb. lean pork cut into
   ½-inch cubes
2 c. flour
1 lb. lard
4 tsp. garlic salt
1 gal. water**

DIRECTIONS
Make a chile puree by placing chiles in a saucepan and covering with hot water. Bring to a boil and simmer for ten minutes or until the pulp is tender. Blend a few at a time in an electric blender at high speed using the simmer water as liquid. Add about 2 garlic cloves per blender. The amount of liquid used will determine the consistency of the sauce. If a blender is not available, the chiles can be cooked until soft and put through a colander to remove the peel. This is also suggested for those with digestive trouble.

Heat lard in 4 gallon pan. Place flour in plastic bag. Put pork cubes in flour and shake well to coat pork. Brown pork well in hot lard, stirring to keep from burning. Add 8 cups of the chile puree and stir well. Simmer over low to medium heat for at least 1½ hours. Freezes well.

HOMEMADE CHILI
Americamps Lake Gaston – Bracey, VA

Americamps is nestled on the Virginia side of Lake Gaston where anglers will find excellent fishing year round. We have wooded sites, a convenience store, marina, swimming pool, mini golf and much more. Actually, our complete camping facility has something for everyone.

INGREDIENTS
**2 lbs. hamburger
1 lg. onion
1 green pepper
1 pkg. chili seasoning
2 garlic cloves or
   1 tsp. garlic powder
1 lg. can tomato sauce
1 can crushed tomatoes
2 cans kidney beans or
   pinto beans
salt & pepper to taste
hot sauce to taste**

DIRECTIONS
Brown hamburger. Add chopped onions, green pepper and garlic. Cook for about 5 min. Sprinkle entire pkg. of chili seasoning over mixture. Stir. Add tomato sauce plus 1 can of water. Then add tomatoes and beans. (Add more water if too thick.) Add salt, pepper and hot sauce to taste. Let simmer — the longer it simmers, the better the flavor.

KENTUCKY BURGOO
Kentucky Horse Park – Lexington, KY

Our park contains 260 water and electric sites with many activities for our campers' enjoyment. As you might expect, we also provide a horse museum, hall of champion films, horseback riding and horse drawn tours.

INGREDIENTS
- 5 lb. veal bones
- 2 Tbsp. shortening
- ¼ c. flour
- 1 gal. water
- ¼ lb. shortening
- 2 lb. diced beef
- 2 lb. diced pork
- 2 lb. diced veal
- 1 qt. dried onions
- 6 carrots
- 1 celery stalk
- 1 bunch green onions
- 1 garlic clove
- 1 can okra
- 1 can corn
- 1 can peas
- 18 oz. tomato sauce
- 1 can string beans
- 1 can lima beans
- 1 Tbsp. salt
- 1 tsp. black pepper
- 1 tsp. ground allspice
- 3 drops Tabasco sauce
- 1 Tbsp. Worcestershire sauce
- 2½ lb. chicken

DIRECTIONS
Place veal bones and 2 Tbsp. shortening in a roasting pan; brown with flour. Remove veal bones and place them in a large kettle with 1 gal. of water. Cook for 5-6 hrs. Make sure water covers veal. Strain and place bones in separate container. Let cool. Note: It is better to make beef stock the day before you plan on serving this dish.

Next, in a steel jacketed kettle, place shortening, diced beef, diced pork, diced veal, dried onions, carrots, celery, green onions and garlic clove. Brown all ingredients.

In a large roasting pan, take soup stock (made previously) and add with water to make 4 gal. Add meat and vegetables and cook for 10 to 12 hrs. Keep at a hot simmer; do not let boil.

Two hrs. before burgoo is to be served, add the remainder of vegetables to roasting pan. Then add salt, black pepper, allspice, Tabasco sauce, and Worcestershire sauce. Simmer but don't boil.

Separately, boil chicken until well done. Strain soup stock and stir into Burgoo. Dice chicken and add to roasting pan.

Should yield about 5 gal. It is important to stir this recipe constantly.

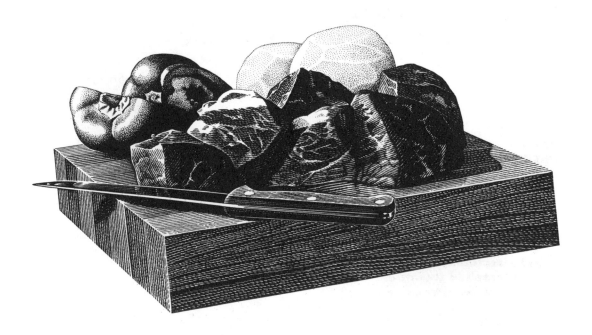

TWO SPRINGS CHILI
Two-Springs RV Resort – N. Palm Springs, CA

I've enjoyed cooking for many years. I knew the first time I tried this chili recipe that it was a winner. I took second place in a Houston cook-off.

Two Springs RV Resort is one of the few RV parks that offer permanent living conditions. We also have many trailers for lease. Some of our features are laundry rooms, showers, large heated pool and spa, tennis and volleyball courts.

INGREDIENTS
- 3 lbs. boneless chuck roast, cubed
- 2 lg. cans peeled tomatoes, chopped
- 14 oz. can diced green chilies
- 1 med. onion, diced
- 2 fresh jalepenos, finely diced
- 2-3 oz. Mexican chili powder
- 1/8 tsp. oregano
- 1/4 tsp. ground cumin
- 1/2 tsp. garlic salt
- 1/2 tsp. pepper
- 2 15-oz. cans chili or kidney beans, optional

DIRECTIONS
Combine meat, onion, garlic salt, and pepper. Simmer 45 min. Drain and return to stove. Add tomatoes, green chilis, chili powder, jalepenos, oregano and cumin. Simmer for 1 hr., stirring occasionally. Add beans if desired and simmer for 30 min. For thick chili, add 4 Tbsp. cornstarch mixed with water. Stir in slowly.

CLARK'S CHILI
Blackstone RV Park – Bullhead City, AZ

We had a big party and Mr. Paul Clark conjured up this big pot of mild chili. We all loved it and I continue to cook it for groups and always get rave reviews about it. I like to serve it with cornbread and butter.

We are a new 133 site RV park located south of Bullhead City in a quiet, desert setting with beautiful views of all the surrounding mountains. Blackstone RV Park is an adults only park with a peaceful atmosphere. Come visit us and let us know how you like this recipe.

INGREDIENTS
- 1 lb. ground hamburger
- 1 med. onion, chopped
- 1 bell pepper, chopped
- 1 c. celery, chopped
- 1 12-15 oz. can tomatoes
- 1 2-3 oz. can tomato sauce
- 1 can red kidney beans
- salt, pepper & chili powder to taste

DIRECTIONS
Fry hamburger and drain. Saute onion, bell pepper and celery until tender. Then add hamburger, tomatoes, tomato sauce, kidney beans and seasonings. Simmer 20 min. You'll love it!

DAN'S CATFISH STEW SPECIAL
Rocks Pond Campground — Eutawville, SC

Rocks Pond is located on the Rocks Plantation, the oldest continuous working plantation in South Carolina. Bordered on three sides by Lake Marian, Rocks Pond offers a variety of activities for you to enjoy. Whether you enjoy the water, land, or simply peace and tranquility, Rocks Pond is the place to be. But most of all we offer Southern hospitality to ensure that you and your family enjoy your stay with us. Rocks holds a National Catfish Stew Cookoff once a year. This recipe was one of our winners last year.

INGREDIENTS
- 3 lbs. bacon or seasoning meat, cut in small pieces
- 2 lg. onions, diced
- 3 lg. bell peppers, diced
- 1 102-oz. can tomatoes
- 1 115-oz. can catsup
- 1 8-oz. bottle Texas Pete Sauce
- 10 lbs. potatoes, peeled, diced, boiled and drained
- 10 lbs. catfish, cooked and cut into small pieces

DIRECTIONS
Prepare ingredients, then cook bacon down in large pot. Add onions and bell peppers and saute. Add tomatoes, catsup, and Texas Pete. Cook on low until heated. Then add catfish and potatoes. Simmer for 1½ - 2 hours. Salt and pepper to taste.

FROGMORE STEW
Point South KOA – Yemassee, SC

Frogmore stew is a favorite South Carolina low country recipe dating back to plantation days.
Point South KOA, at Exit 33 on I-95, is nestled in a beautiful oak and pine forest in South Carolina's historic low country near Beaufort, Hilton Head, Charleston and Savannah, GA.

INGREDIENTS
- 1 lb. shrimp
- ½ lb. smoked link sausages cut in 2-in. chunks
- 4 ears of corn
- chopped celery
- chopped onion
- salt to taste
- seafood seasoning

DIRECTIONS
Bring 2-3 gal. water to a boil. Add ¼ cup salt per gal. of water. Add seafood seasoning, chopped celery and onion as desired. Add sausage and boil 7 min. Add corn and boil for 7 min. Add shrimp and cook for 4 min. Add water to cover as needed. Drain and serve in large bowl. Serves 2.

MEXICAN SOUP
Pleasant Valley Campground – Wells River, VT

We serve this recipe at our potluck dinners. Our campground overlooks a lake with a beautiful view. It is mostly wooded with pine trees. We also have some grassy sites.

INGREDIENTS
- 1 lb. ground beef
- 1 lg. onion, chopped
- 1 lg. pepper, chopped
- 1 pkg. chili mix
- 5 c. water
- 1 tsp. garlic salt
- 1 32 oz. can whole tomatoes
- 8 oz. whole kernel corn
- 1 c. elbow macaroni

DIRECTIONS
Cook ground beef and drain. Stir in chili mix, water, garlic salt, and tomatoes (broken up with a fork) including liquid. In a separate pan, saute onion and pepper. Stir into beef mixture. Bring to a boil, stirring constantly. Stir in macaroni and corn with liquid. Cover and cook an additional 10 minutes.

PA. DUTCH CORN-CHICKEN SOUP
Ridge Run Campground – Elizabethtown, PA

Ridge Run Campground is located in Lancaster County, surrounded by Pennsylvania cornfields and chicken farms. We are 15 miles west of the heart of the Amish country and only 15 miles to Hershey Park. We are located off Rt. 283-Rheems-Elizabethtown exit. Our campground has over 100 shady sites in a park-like setting. We are an easy ride to all of the area attractions.

INGREDIENTS
- 1½ c. cooked whole-kernel corn
- 1 10½ oz. can condensed chicken-rice soup
- 2 chicken bouillon cubes
- water
- salt & pepper
- dumpling batter (optional)

DIRECTIONS
Combine corn, soup, and bouillon cubes in large saucepan. Add 3 soup cans of water. Bring to boil. Season to taste with salt and pepper. Dribble dumpling batter from spoon into gently boiling soup. Simmer for 5 min., or until dumplings are cooked. Makes 1½ quarts or 4 to 6 servings.

AUTUMN SOUP
Cowlitz Motel and RV Park – Toledo, WA

This recipe is a favorite since it's simple to prepare and it's very tasty. Although we call it Autumn Soup, it's good any time of year — just use veggies that are in season.

We are located 60 mi. north of Portland, OR, at the I-5 Cowlitz River Bridge. We are situated on the banks of the Cowlitz River, one of the best fishing rivers in western Washington. We have 50 spaces with full hookups and many pull-thru sites. We offer free hot showers and clean restrooms. Also available are 17 clean, comfortable motel rooms.

INGREDIENTS
  1 lb. ground beef
  1 c. chopped onion
  3 c. beef broth or water
  2 tsp. salt (less if using broth)
  ¼ tsp. pepper
  1 c. carrots, cut
  1 c. celery, diced
  1 c. potatoes, diced
  other vegetables, optional
  1 tsp. brown bouquet sauce
  ½ tsp. basil
  1 bay leaf
  1 28-oz. can stewed or whole
    tomatoes

DIRECTIONS
  Cook and stir meat until brown. Drain off fat. Cook and stir onions with meat until tender. Combine everything together in a crockpot or simmer on stove until veggies are tender.

PUMPKIN SOUP
Papoose Pond Resort & CG – No. Waterford, ME

We offer a special weekend package in the spring and fall which includes accommodations, five meals, free rental boats, activities and nightly entertainment. Pumpkin soup has become a favorite to start off the Friday night roast beef buffet. We serve the soup in a hollowed-out pumpkin.

Papoose Pond Resort is situated on a lake in southwestern Maine. It is within an hour's drive of the picturesque Maine coast or the White Mountain National Forest. You can choose luxury campsites with their own private bath, beachfront or wooded sites, rental trailers or cabins. In season supervised activities are offered all day, everyday, as well as nightly entertainment.

INGREDIENTS
  1 lg. onion, diced
  2½ c. chicken stock
  2½ c. half & half
  1 no. 2½ can (1 lb. 3 oz.)
    pumpkin
  salt, pepper & curry to taste

DIRECTIONS
  Saute onion in small amount of stock until transparent. Add remaining stock and the rest of the ingredients. Heat slowly stirring occasionally.

5-WAY CINCINNATI CHILI
Cave Lake Park – Hillsboro, OH

Having five children and working long hours in our park, I have used this recipe often. Once made, it can be a dinner or a supper and can be served 5 different ways.

Our park consists of 115 acres with a 40 acre lake for swimming, fishing and boating. In the spring and fall we have a potluck and the whole campground is invited. 5-Way Chili is included along with other favorites. We are located 20 miles SE of Hillsboro and 20 miles west of Latham.

INGREDIENTS
2 lbs. hamburger, raw
2 chopped onions
1 qt. water
2 8-oz. cans tomato sauce
½ tsp. allspice
¼ tsp. garlic powder
4 Tbsp. chili powder
1 tsp. cumin
2 Tbsp. vinegar
½ tsp. red pepper
¼ tsp. cloves
1 bay leaf
½ oz. unsweetened chocolate
2 tsp. Worcestershire Sauce
2 tsp. cinnamon
1½ tsp. salt
4 drops Tabasco sauce

DIRECTIONS
Combine hamburger, onions and water and simmer for 30 min. Add remaining ingredients and simmer uncovered 2 to 3 hrs. until thickened. Remove grease from top. Serve in any of the following ways:
1. In a bowl with crackers.
2. On top of your favorite hot dog.
3. Over cooked spaghetti, topped with shredded cheese.
4. In a bowl with hot beans and cheese.
5. In a bowl with beans, onions and cheese.

BEAN POT BEAN SOUP
Bean Pot Campground – Crossville, TN

This is a good hardy soup that goes well with any type of meal, especially a potluck. We often serve it at small group gatherings.

Our park is located half-way between the Smoky Mountains and Music City, U.S.A. (Nashville). We're situated in a quiet, serene, wooded area and are within a "stone's throw" of four of the finest golf courses in the U.S. We are open year 'round for RVers demanding tops in accommodations.

INGREDIENTS
1 iron pot hanging from a tripod over hot coals
4 lbs. white or navy beans
8 qts. water
4 lbs. smoked ham hocks
2 tsp. black pepper
2 c. celery, finely chopped
4 med. onions, finely chopped
4 med. carrots, finely chopped
4 bay leaves

DIRECTIONS
Pick over and wash beans carefully being sure to remove any stones and dirt. Soak beans overnight in enough water to cover. Drain, reserving liquid. Pour soaking liquid into pot adding additional water to total 8 qts. Scrub hocks under running water. Add hocks, soaked beans and all other ingredients to pot. Bring to a low boil and simmer (a bubble or two now and then). Cook for several hours or until the soup has reached desired doneness. Remove hocks. Cut off meat and return to pot. Discard skin, fat and bones. Adjust seasonings to taste. Makes approx. 10 qts.

TRAIL STEW
Wheel-In Campground – Shelocta, PA

This recipe is easy, delicious, and nutritious. Make this main dish ahead of time, leaving more time to enjoy the many things to do in our park or to just relax and do whatever you want to do. Wheel-In Campground is in a scenic rural valley, through which flows a popular trout stream, Plumcreek. We are located midway between Indiana and Kittaning, Pennsylvania near the junction of US 422 and SR 210.

INGREDIENTS
- **2 lbs. ground beef**
- **1 pkg. dry onion soup mix**
- **4 med. potatoes**
- **4 carrots**
- **½ pkg. frozen green beans**
- **½ pkg. frozen corn**
- **salt & pepper to taste**

DIRECTIONS

Brown the meat lightly in a heavy kettle or large skillet. Add raw vegetables, covering with water and cooking with the cover on. Frozen or canned vegetables can be added later. Add more water as necessary. Cook until all the hikers have been rounded up. Serve in bowls with crusty homemade or Italian bread.

Note: The ingredients may be determined according to your family's taste and the contents of your cupboard. If you're traveling, canned vegetables can be used.

BUFFALO CHILI
Flat Branch Campground & RV Park – Gulfport, MS

Buffalo meat is low in cholesterol and high in protein. The excitement of the hunt adds extra spice to this recipe.

We're an overnight park located just ½ mile north of I-10 on Hwy. 49. Since we're near the Mississippi golden coast beaches, we offer fun in the sun year round!

INGREDIENTS
- **5 strips bacon**
- **1½ lb. ground buffalo meat**
- **1 lg. can tomatoes**
- **1 Tbsp. chili powder**
- **1 lg. onion, chopped**
- **1 can kidney beans**
- **salt to taste**
- **½ tsp. pepper**

DIRECTIONS

Fry bacon and chop in pieces. Fry onions and ground buffalo over medium heat. Add tomatoes, beans, bacon and seasonings. Simmer for 45 min. to 1 hr.

CLAM CHOWDER
Florida Pines Mobile Home Court – Venice, FL

It is very hard to find a good clam chowder anywhere. This recipe is a family favorite and one that your family is sure to enjoy.

Florida Pines Mobile Home Court is located four miles south of Venice. We offer full hookup sites, RV storage and laundry facilities. Enjoy our planned activities, rec hall and shuffleboard courts; or visit one of the many beaches nearby.

INGREDIENTS
19½ oz. minced clams
1 c. finely diced celery
1 c. finely diced onion
2 c. finely diced raw potatoes
2 Tbsp. cooking sherry,
  optional
¾ c. butter or margarine
¾ c. flour
1 qt. milk or half & half
½ tsp. sugar
salt & pepper to taste

DIRECTIONS
Drain juice from clams and pour over prepared vegetables. Add sherry and simmer over medium heat until potatoes are tender. Make white sauce from remaining ingredients. Add to vegetables and clam mixture and simmer.

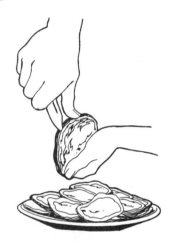

BILL'S CLAM CHOWDER FOR A CROWD
Shady Pines Campground – Savoy, MA

Being clear across the state from the ocean, good chowder is hard to find. This recipe was refined over the last five years catering to campers and clambakes.

We are a destination park located in a rural area, situated on grassy flatlands on top of a mountain.

INGREDIENTS
2 – 51 oz. cans clams
2 – 51 oz. cans clam juice
1½ qts. onions, diced
2 qts. carrots
1½ qts. celery
1 – 6 lb. can diced potatoes
5 med. cans cream corn
2 Tbsp. parsley
1 tsp. black pepper
1 Tbsp. salt
½ lb. butter
½ gal. milk
1 pt. heavy cream

DIRECTIONS
Add all ingredients except milk and cream to an 18-quart cooker and simmer slowly for 3-4 hours. When vegetables are tender, add milk and cream.

Chowder may be thickened by mixing 2 cups of milk with 1 cup cornstarch. Bacon bits may be added for a finishing touch.

MARILYN'S BEEF CABBAGE SOUP
Little River Village Campground – Townsend, TN

For great Southern Mountain cooking, no Sunday table is complete without a platter of country ribs, cole slaw, ramps, beans and cornbread or biscuits with homemade strawberry jam. Little River Campground, located at the Cades Cove entrance to the Great Smoky Mountain National Park has a pavilion and BBQ pit that is a hot bed of activity for catered dinners throughout our long season. We hope you and your family enjoy this down home recipe!

INGREDIENTS
- 1 lg. onion
- 1 lg. green pepper
- 2 stalks celery
- 2 cloves garlic
- 1 sm. cabbage
- 1½ lb. ground chuck
- 6 beef bouillon cubes
- 1½ c. hot water
- 1-46 oz. can tomato juice
- 1-12 oz. can V-8 juice
- 2-14½ oz. cans tomatoes, chopped
- 2 cans kidney beans
- 1 tsp. dried basil
- 1 tsp. marjoram
- pepper to taste

DIRECTIONS

Chop and saute first four vegetables in small amount of oil or margarine. Brown ground beef, drain fat. Combine with sauteed vegetables. Add tomato juice, V-8 juice, tomatoes, bouillon dissolved in hot water, finely chopped cabbage, herbs and spices. Bring to a boil, then turn down to simmer for about 1 hr. until cabbage is tender. Add kidney beans (juice and all) and simmer another 15 min. or until beans are hot. This is a good hearty meal served with country biscuits and butter or hot crusty rolls.

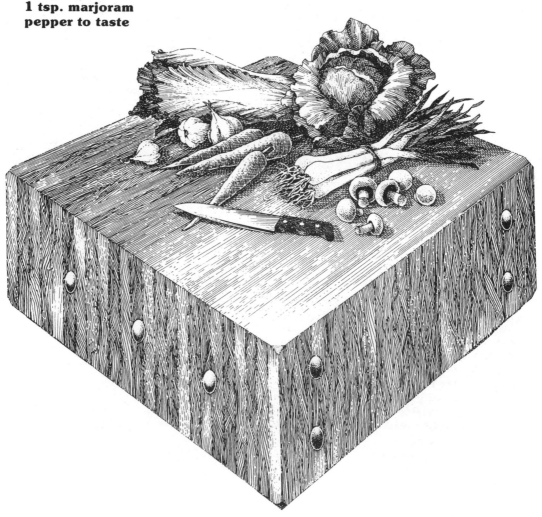

ITALIAN WEDDING SOUP
Kozy Kampground – Celina, OH

Kozy Kampground is located on Grand Lake St. Marys, near Celina, Ohio. We have many campers that come to this former reservoir for boating, fishing, swimming, skiing and relaxation. Kozy offers mini-golf, pools, boating, dances, parties and lots of fun. As the main season draws to an end each year the idea of a soup supper has grown to a full scale holiday. Campers bring all kinds of soups and breads to start the evening. Then they disappear and strange shapes and sizes emerge in costumes to claim prizes. An evening of music and dancing follows. It's a Happy Halloween to all, as the ghosts disappear until another year.

INGREDIENTS
   4 lb. boned chicken, cut in
      pieces
   5 qt. cold water
   2 stalks of celery, diced
   1 med. onion, diced
   1 bay leaf
   salt & pepper to taste
   ¼ lb. fresh spinach or kale
   1 lb. ground veal
   1 egg
   ¼ c. bread crumbs
   3 Tbsp. milk
   2 Tbsp. butter

DIRECTIONS
   Combine chicken, water, all vegetables (except spinach), and seasonings. Bring to a boil slowly. Cook over low heat until meat is tender. While chicken is cooking, combine veal, egg, bread crumbs, and milk. Salt and pepper to taste. Roll in 1″ balls and brown in melted butter until golden. Add to soup with fresh torn strips of spinach leaves and simmer for 30 minutes. Some folks like to add a cup of cooked rice to the final pot, others prefer some very fine noodles. Sprinkle each bowl lightly with grated Italian cheese.

"DUMP CHILI"
Indian Point RV Park – Eddyville, KY

This recipe is a favorite at Indian Point RV Park. Not only do you get a great bowl of chili, you also get to enjoy the good company of other campers.
We are located on beautiful Lake Barkley in the heartland of Western Kentucky — where camping, boating and fishing go hand in hand.

INGREDIENTS
   a batch of your favorite chili
   lots of family campers
   good camping stories for
      telling around a campfire
   a beautiful sunset

DIRECTIONS
   Each family prepares its favorite chili. Gather all families around a campfire. Dump each batch of chili in the big community pot. Bring to a boil over the campfire, taking turns stirring. When the aroma fills the campground, it's time for everyone to enjoy the greatest chili ever made!

CATFISH STEW
Mansard Island Campground — Springville, TN

This is my husband's mother's recipe. It is just one of many good southern recipes we share with our campers.

Mansard Island Campground is a world away from the stresses of life! When getting away is your goal — Mansard Island is your destination. It's quiet, it's sports, it's excellent fishing, it's laid back, it's affordable. Located 20 miles from Paris, Tenn., we're only minutes away from Paris Landing State Park and only a short drive to the Land Between the Lakes. Come on over and get away from it all!

INGREDIENTS
- **4 oz. salt pork**
- **1 med. onion**
- **2 cans stewed tomatoes**
- **1 sm. can tomato paste**
- **2 cans tomato soup**
- **1 bottle catsup**
- **1 Tbsp. Worcestershire sauce**
- **½ tsp. sugar**
- **salt to taste**
- **6-7 boneless filleted catfish**

DIRECTIONS

Cut and dice salt pork and onions very fine. Cook together until light brown. Cut stewed tomatoes very fine. Add tomatoes, tomato paste, tomato soup, catsup, Worcestershire sauce, sugar and salt. Bring to a boil and continue to boil lightly for 15 min. Drop in fish and cook until they fall apart. Serves 6-7.

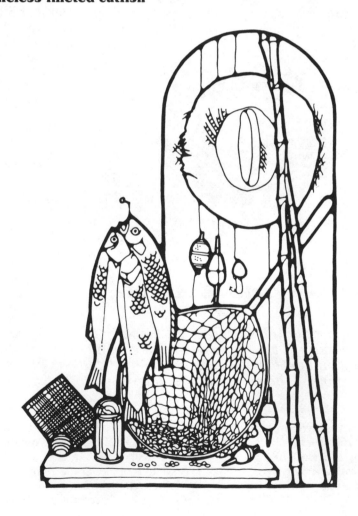

HAMBURGER CAMP STEW
Holiday Trav-L-Park – North Platte, NE

This is an old recipe of my own. I serve it to my family because it is so easy to prepare and is very nutritious.

Our park is located just off Interstate 80 and Highway 83 at exit #177. North Platte is in the center of Nebraska and is known for its western hospitality. While this one-dish casserole dinner is cooking in your RV oven, your whole family will be enjoying our heated pool, shaped like the state of Nebraska, or taking swings on our mini-golf course. There is also a water slide and go cart track so everyone can "play" up an appetite.

INGREDIENTS
- 1 lb. lean hamburger, raw
- 3 peeled, quartered potatoes
- 3 peeled, quartered carrots
- 3 stalks quartered celery
- 1 onion, sliced
- 1 can beef bouillon
- salt & pepper to taste

DIRECTIONS
Mix all ingredients together and place in a large casserole dish. Cover and bake at 325° for 2 hrs.

NO-MEASURE CAMPER'S BEEF STEW
Sundermeier Mobile Home & RV Park-St. Charles, MO

This recipe is ideal for camping or RVing. You can prepare over your campfire or in the kitchen of your RV. It's easy to make, it tastes great, and it's very nutritious. I receive many compliments whenever I serve this stew.

Sundermeier offers tree shaded sites with full hookups, restroom and laundry facilities, dusk-to-dawn lighting and paved streets. We're conveniently located to swimming, downtown St. Louis, historic St. Charles and the Shrine of Rose Philippine Duchesne all nearby. Come enjoy a restful, quiet stay with us.

INGREDIENTS
- 2 lb. beef for stew, cut in 1" pieces
- 1-16 oz. can whole tomatoes, broken up
- 1 envelope Italian salad dressing mix
- 2 lg. carrots, cut in ½" pieces
- 3 sm. onions
- 3 potatoes, quartered

DIRECTIONS
Combine beef pieces, tomatoes and salad dressing mix in Dutch oven. Cover tightly. Simmer one hour over medium coals or on camp stove. Add carrots. Continue cooking covered for 30 min. Add onions and potatoes. Continue cooking covered for 30 min. or until beef and vegetables are tender. Serves 6.

HOBO STEW
Bake Oven Campground — Ashfield, PA

Every year we have a Hobo Weekend. Everyone dresses as a hobo — some of the outfits are really clever. We serve this stew in our pavilion and we all have a lot of fun.

We're located at the west entrance of the Pocono Mountains at the foot of Bake Oven Knob - Blue Mountain range. We have large, flat grassy sites with full and partial hookups. Lizard Creek runs through our campground and offers great trout fishing. Visit nearby attractions in Beltville Lake, Ashland and Allentown.

INGREDIENTS
20 lbs. potatoes, quartered
10 lbs. carrots, sliced
5 lbs. onions, sliced
3 lg. celery stalks
1 lg. head of cabbage
10 lbs. ripe red tomatoes, quartered
20 lbs. chuck roast, cooked and cubed
4 lg. cans beef broth
6-8 gal. water
seasoning to taste

DIRECTIONS
Fill large pot with water, add meat and broth. Simmer. Add vegetables. Simmer until done.

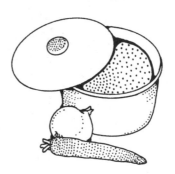

BAKED STEW
Peacock Landing RV Park – Everett, WA

This recipe is one of my favorites because it's so easy to make, yet it feeds a large crew.

Peacock Landing offers spotless restrooms, laundry facilities, cable TV, and level, paved, full hookup sites. We're close to shopping and Boeing's plant. We have a small stocked trout fishing lake which is also visited by Canadian geese and ducks. The geese will even eat right out of your hand. For your enjoyment we also offer lakeside jogging trails, jacuzzi, basketball, volleyball, horseshoes and more. Come join us — we'd love to have you.

INGREDIENTS
2-3 lbs. stew meat or short ribs
1 onion, whole
1 potato, whole
1 celery stalk, sliced
carrots, sliced
2 Tbsp. instant tapioca
salt & pepper to taste
2 Tbsp. brown sugar
1 can tomato soup
½ can water

DIRECTIONS
In large casserole dish, add meat, onion, potato, celery and carrots. Sprinkle with tapioca, then brown sugar, salt and pepper to taste. Pour soup and water over top. Cover. Bake at 250° for 5 to 6 hrs.

COUNTRY COWBOY CHILI
A Wheel Inn – Gila Bend, AZ

Since we have no rec room, everyone gathers around an open campfire to socialize. This recipe is ideal for these gatherings.

Our RV park offers pull-thru spaces, clean restrooms, cable TV, laundry and planned group activities. We're conveniently located on your way to Phoenix, San Diego, Los Angeles, Yuma, Tucson and Mexico. We're also close to Painted Rock and Organ Pipe National Park.

INGREDIENTS
- **10 lbs. ground beef**
- **6 onions**
- **1 pkg. carrots**
- **chili powder**
- **6 cloves garlic**
- **salt & pepper to taste**
- **10 lbs. kidney beans**
- **3 cans tomato juice**

DIRECTIONS
In large skillet, brown ground beef. Add onions and seasonings. Add cooked beans and remaining ingredients. Cook over open campfire until beans are soft. Serves 30 to 40 people. Serve with grated cheese and chopped onion.

ANTELOPE STEW
Western Hills Campground – Rawlins, WY

Pronghorn antelope are abundant in our area. Our campers often see the antelope along the interstate and around our campground. Actually, our county provides more trophy antelope than any other county. From our campground you can also see prairie and rolling hills. We offer a quiet and peaceful environment and one can see for miles.

INGREDIENTS
- **antelope, cut in 1″ chunks**
- **3 or 4 potatoes**
- **several carrots**
- **1 onion**
- **1 can cream of tomato soup**
- **1 can cream of celery soup**
- **1 can cream of mushroom soup**
- **salt & pepper to taste**
- **1 bay leaf**

DIRECTIONS
Stew antelope until tender. Cut up potatoes and carrots in small pieces. Add chopped onion and stewed meat. Salt and pepper to taste. Add soups, diluted with ⅓ can of water. Add bay leaf. Cook in crockpot or slow oven at 250° for 5 hrs.

SALADS

SHRIMP STUFFED ARTICHOKE SALAD
KOA-Santa Cruz — Watsonville, CA

The Monterey Bay area is blessed with coastal waters and lush, green farms with an abundance and variety of favorite fruits and vegetables.

KOA-Santa Cruz is situated on Monterey Bay amidst rolling hills, fresh produce farms and abundant cedar, pine and eucalyptus trees. This area and KOA-Santa Cruz provide a countryside respite from populated, hot, urban areas. The campground provides all amenities to deliver a true, resort-type camping vacation "get-away".

INGREDIENTS
- 4 lg. artichokes
- 1 garlic clove
- 1 bay leaf
- 4 lettuce leaves
- 1 Tbsp. olive oil
- ½ lb. bay shrimps
- 1 c. sliced ripe olives
- 1 c. fresh mushrooms (thinly sliced)
- ½ c. minced celery
- 2 Tbsp. chopped green onions
- 1 Tbsp. lemon juice

Dressing (optional)
- ½ c. mayonnaise
- 2 Tbsp. tarragon vinegar
- 1 Tbsp. chopped parsley
- ¼ tsp. whole dill seed
- ¼ tsp. salt
- ¼ tsp. onion powder
- dash white pepper

DIRECTIONS

Cook artichokes in water with bay leaf, olive oil and garlic until done. Remove center section, choke, drain and refrigerate. Combine shrimp, olives, celery, mushrooms, onions. Toss lightly with lemon juice. Mix dressing until smooth and creamy. Pour over salad, toss and refrigerate for at least one hour. When ready to serve, place artichoke on lettuce leaf and fill with shrimp salad. Serves 4.

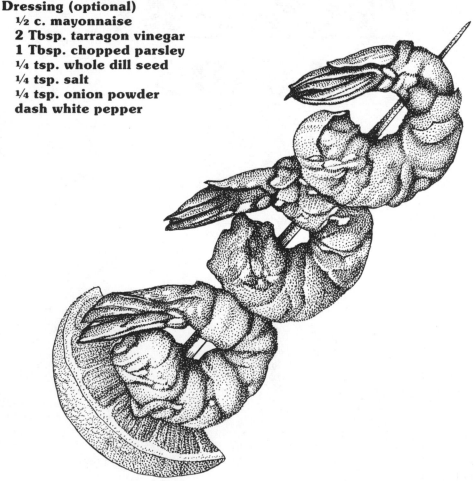

CONFETTI SALAD
RV Park of the Big Spring — Big Spring, TX

This is a very easy but tasty and colorful salad. After preparing, you'll know why it's called confetti salad.

The park is built in great semi-circles in a scenic area of west Texas. We're a new park and we offer paved streets, full service pull-thrus in a quiet area. Cable TV and telephone are available. We're located next to the city's Commanche Trail Park offering great golf, tennis, trails and a lake.

INGREDIENTS
- **1 12-oz. can white shoepeg corn**
- **6 cherry tomatoes, sliced in half**
- **4 green onions, chopped**
- **2 Tbsp. mayonnaise**
- **salt and pepper to taste**

DIRECTIONS
Mix all ingredients and chill in refrigerator.

COMMUNITY SALAD & SWEET/SOUR DRESSING
Mammoth Mountain RV Park — Mammoth Lakes, CA

These recipes are used with our square dance club weekend festivals. We are beginning barbecues and potlucks this summer at Mammoth Mountain RV Park.

Our park is the only RV Park in Mammoth Lakes. We're located on the eastern side of the Sierra Nevada Mountains. We are open all year for winter skiing and summer hiking and fishing in a majestic and scenic mountain area.

INGREDIENTS
Salad:
- **any salad ingredient such as**
  - **lettuce**
  - **tomatoes**
  - **seafood**
  - **etc.**
Dressing:
- **¼ c. salad oil**
- **¼ c. vinegar**
- **¼ c. catsup**
- **¼ c. sugar**

DIRECTIONS
Salad: Each couple brings 1 cup of their favorite salad ingredient to the Community Salad Bowl. There's always plenty as the salad grows with the size of the crowd. Serve with sweet/sour French dressing or other dressings of your choice on the side.

Dressing: Mix all ingredients together until sugar is dissolved. Serve with Community Salad.

DRY JELL-O SALAD
Rio Penasco RV Camp — Mayhill, NM

I like this recipe simply because it is quick and easy and will keep for 2 weeks.

We have 22 full hookup sites, shower and laundry facilities and a large pavilion. We are at an altitude of about 6,750 feet, so the summers are pretty mild. Daily, weekly and monthly rates are available. We also have a river running through the camp, so trout fishing is also available.

INGREDIENTS
- 1-3 oz. pkg. orange Jell-O
- 1 ctn. cottage cheese
- 8 oz. Cool Whip
- 1-11 oz. can mandarin oranges, cut in half & drained

DIRECTIONS

Mix dry Jell-O with cottage cheese until dissolved. Add oranges and fold in Cool Whip. Pour into salad mold, cover and refrigerate.

MANDARIN ORANGE SALAD
Sierra Springs Trailer Resort — Portola, CA

Every 4th of July management and campers have a potluck barbecue. This recipe is good either as dessert or salad. It is cool and refreshing on a warm afternoon. The barbeque has been a tradition for 10 years; started by seasonal regular campers who missed each other during winter months.

We are located on beautiful Hwy 70 in a wonderful group of pine trees. We receive an afternoon breeze and are a quiet park up on a knoll surrounded by a national forest. Excellent hiking can be taken advantage of and we are nearby the river, lakes, golf courses, etc. There is a railroad museum in Portola, and the State Park museum nearby. We have several Arts and Crafts Fairs during the season and are only 1 hr. from Reno.

INGREDIENTS
- 3 c. boiling water
- 1 sm. box orange Jell-O
- 2 sm. boxes Americano Jell-O Tapioca Pudding
- 2 sm. cans Mandarin oranges
- 1 8-oz. container Cool Whip

DIRECTIONS

Mix water, Jell-O, and pudding in bowl until well blended. Place in refrigerator until slightly thickened. Stir every 10 min. Then mix in Cool Whip. Add Mandarin oranges. Pour into mold. Recipe may be doubled for large groups.

SAUERKRAUT SALAD
Pelican Point RV Park — Half Moon Bay, CA

Having made this for one of our potlucks here, I am always asked to make it again.

Our park is located 30 miles south of San Francisco, and is near the ocean. We have perfect summer weather, and many things to do no matter what season. Trees and grass can be found at all our sites. We're a quiet park with all the amenities needed to make your stay with us a pleasant one.

INGREDIENTS
- 1 lg. can sauerkraut
- 1 lg. green pepper
- 1 lg. onion
- 1 4-oz. jar pimento
- ½ c. sugar
- ½ c. wine vinegar

DIRECTIONS

Rinse kraut and drain. Cut pepper and onion in thin strips. Add pimento, sugar and wine vinegar. Put in tight container and keep in refrigerator. This is great for traveling, and will keep for six weeks in the fridge.

HOT GERMAN POTATO SALAD
Sunrise Lake Family Campground – Nicholson, PA

In Nicholson, a lot of bridge and railroad people come to look at the fine bridge that was built for the Lackawanna Railroad in 1912. People are just amazed at the size and height of it — and the beautiful arches. They cannot believe it is still used today.

INGREDIENTS
- 5 lbs. white potatoes
- 1 med. onion
- 1 lb. bacon
- 6 sticks celery
- ½ tsp. salt
- ¼ tsp. pepper
- 1 tsp. parsley flakes
- 3-4 Tbsp. white vinegar
  (depends on your taste)
- 1 c. hot water

DIRECTIONS

Boil potatoes and peel. Cut them to medium size bites. Dice the celery and onion in a large bowl with potatoes, add the salt, pepper, and parsley flakes. Dice and fry the bacon until crispy brown. Pour the bacon bits and drippings over the mixture. Add hot water and vinegar and mix well. Put in a crock pot and leave it on low heat. Should be eaten warm. Let it stand for about 1 hr. for juices and flavor to set in.

SPAM & CHINESE NOODLE SALAD
Ione Motel & RV Park – Ione, WA

This salad is easy, tasty and always gets compliments.

Our park has beautiful green grass. We're located ½ block from the town of Ione on the Pend Oreille River, where you can enjoy boating, water skiing, and fishing. We offer laundry and restroom facilities. The Canadian border is only 26 miles from us. We hope you come and enjoy our beautiful country setting.

INGREDIENTS

1 lg. can spam, diced
1 c. celery, diced
2 Tbsp. chopped onion
1 sm. can chopped dark olives
1 c. mayonnaise
2 tsp. dark vinegar
1-5 oz. can Chinese noodles

DIRECTIONS

Mix spam and celery together. Add onion, olives, mayonnaise and vinegar. Mix well. Add noodles and mix again. Chill. Stir salad before serving.

Note: If you like crunchy noodles, add them ½ hr. before serving. If you like soft noodles, add them 2 hrs. before serving. If salad seems dry, add more mayonnaise.

GERMAN POTATO SALAD
Plymouth Rock Camping Resort – Elkhart Lake, WI

German Potato Salad and Sheboygan Bratwurst are very popular in our park and in this area. People come from miles around for a Sheboygan Brat and Potato Salad.

Plymouth Rock is a family oriented park with a strong emphasis on recreation and entertainment. We are located in Sheboygan County which has the beautiful Kettle Moraine, Lake Michigan fishing, Road America race track and many quaint shopping areas from riverfront shopping to country crafts barn. Bratwurst Days and the County Fair are also summer favorites of many of our campers.

INGREDIENTS

1½ lb. potatoes
1 med. onion
½ c. vinegar
½ c. sugar
1 sprig parsley
1 c. water
2 Tbsp. flour
3 tsp. salt
4 slices bacon

DIRECTIONS

Boil and slice potatoes. Add onion (cut fine) and salt. Fry sliced bacon and add bits to potatoes. Stir flour, sugar, vinegar and water into bacon grease, stirring over low heat until thick. Add to potato mixture. Serves 6.

HOT TACO PASTA SALAD
Vagabond Campground – Rapid River, MI

This recipe is quick and easy to prepare during the busy camping season. This salad is enjoyed by family and friends and is very satisfying.

Our campground is located among stately Norway Pines on the Stonington Peninsula which has an original lighthouse at its Point overlooking the three waters of Big and Little Bays de Noc and Lake Michigan in Michigan's Upper Peninsula.

INGREDIENTS

2 c. white or vegetable spiral
  noodles
1 lb. ground sirloin or ground
  venison
1 tsp. salt
1 pkg. taco seasoning
½ c. water
1 c. grated Cheddar or
  Monterey Jack cheese
1 chopped onion

DIRECTIONS

Cook noodles in boiling water. Brown meat with onion. Add package of seasoning with water and salt. Simmer for 10 min. Add cheese and cooked pasta. Remove from heat, cover and let sit for 5 min. to allow the cheese to melt. Serve on shredded lettuce and top with tomatoes and taco sauce.

TACO SALAD
Santa Barbara RV Park – Santa Barbara, CA

Santa Barbara is a famous Spanish settled community, dating from the 1500's. It's red-tiled roofs and Spanish architecture remind us of the gentle hospitality offered by its citizens. In keeping with this, our park is a small, family owned park, nestled in the city. We are just blocks from the beach and sight-seeing activities.

INGREDIENTS
1 lb. hamburger
pinch of onion
pinch of garlic
pinch of chili powder
salt & pepper to taste
1-16 oz. can chili beans
1 head lettuce
2 tomatoes
1 sm. can sliced black olives
3 green onions
8 oz. shredded cheddar cheese
1 bottle Green Goddess
  dressing
1 lg. pkg. taco flavored tortilla
  chips

DIRECTIONS
Fry hamburger with onion, garlic, chili powder, salt and pepper. Add 1 can chili beans with liquid. Set aside to cool. Make tossed salad with head of lettuce, tomatoes, black olives and onions. When meat mixture is cool, toss with salad. Add shredded cheddar cheese and toss with Green Goddess dressing. At last minute, add package of coarsely crushed taco flavored tortilla chips. Serves four as a main dish.

TACO SALAD
Port of the Islands RV Park – Naples, FL

I bring this to our bi-weekly cookouts and it is well received. Our park is located in southwest Florida. We are 22 miles from Naples, 85 miles from Miami and 65 miles from Ft. Myers. There are a lot of attractions in this area — the biggest of course, being the weather.

INGREDIENTS
1 head lettuce
tomatoes
green pepper
chopped onion
shredded cheddar cheese
kidney beans
1 pkg. taco seasoning mix
1 lb. ground chuck
Western dressing
1 c. water
tortilla chips

DIRECTIONS
Cut lettuce, tomatoes, green pepper, and onion into small pieces. Put in large bowl. Brown the ground chuck and add pkg. of taco seasoning mix and water (Follow directions on pkg.). Let cool and add to above vegetables. Add shredded cheddar cheese, kidney beans (drained). Pour over desired amount of Western Dressing and add small bag of Tortilla chips (break into pieces).

COUNTRY SPINACH SALAD
Flatrock Campsite — Mexico, NY

Flatrock Campsite is located on the eastern end of Lake Ontario, three miles north of Mexico and a mile south of Texas in New York State. The campground consists of 124 sites ranging from rustic to full hookups. Its location is excellent for both the transient and vacationing camper, as well as the camper coming to the area for the excellent lake and stream fishing. The Little Salmon River flows through the campground providing bass fishing in the spring and salmon fishing in the fall. A state boat launch and several private marinas are located within two miles of the campground. Shuffleboard, horseshoes, swimming pool and playground are provided at no charge. Cro-golf and a new challenging miniature golf course (Golf of Mexico) are provided on the premises for a small fee. For the traveler without an RV unit, park model RVs completely furnished and with housekeeping services are available for daily or weekly rental.

INGREDIENTS
Salad:
    1 bag of spinach
    1 c. fresh mushrooms, sliced
    3 eggs, boiled and chopped
    6 slices of bacon, cooked crisp
      and crumbled
    1 sm. red onion, sliced thin
    ½ c. cheese, diced
    shredded carrots, for color
    croutons
Dressing:
    1 med. onion
    ⅔ c. sugar
    1 tsp. salt
    ½ tsp. pepper
    1 Tbsp. prepared mustard
    1 Tbsp. celery salt or celery
      seed
    ⅓ c. vinegar
    1 c. shortening or corn oil

DIRECTIONS
    Prepare salad. Mix all dressing ingredients in a blender. Pour over salad, there will be dressing left over as too much makes it soggy. Gently toss salad and serve.

GUACAMOLE SALAD
Lakeview Mobile Home Park — Weslaco, TX

We grow avocado trees that have reached nearly 30 ft. Their fruit is used to make this salad. Our park contains shaded and open sites along with many recreational activities for our campers to enjoy.

INGREDIENTS
    6 soft ripe avocados
    1 tomato
    1 med. onion
    1 lg. lime
    garlic salt
    pepper
    Tabasco sauce

DIRECTIONS
    Cut avocados in half. Remove seeds and scoop fruit out of peel. Mash in a bowl. Add diced tomato, onion and the juice of one lime. Add garlic salt, pepper and Tabasco sauce to taste. Mix well, refrigerate and serve with crackers or chips.

MACARONI AND CORN RELISH SALAD
Spartanburg Cunningham KOA – Spartanburg, SC

I like to make a different dish than what is expected — something out of the ordinary. And this recipe, while different, is always a crowd pleaser. Our campground is set in the foothills of the Great Smoky Mountains. The weather is so mild, we can operate every day. We treat every camper as the most welcome person traveling through the Carolinas. We like to be your tourist guide offering information brochures whether you are going to the mountains, the beaches, or visiting nearby areas. We are here for you!

INGREDIENTS
1 lb. elbow macaroni, cooked
12 oz. jar corn relish
4 oz. pimiento, drained & chopped
1 tsp. parsley flakes
2 tsp. grated onion
1 c. mayonnaise
½ c. sour cream

DIRECTIONS
Mix all ingredients together and store 24 hours in large container. This recipe serves 15-20 people and will keep well for a week.

CREAMY JELL-O SALAD
Wildwood Campground – Kalona, IA

Not only is this an attractive dish, it's also very creamy and delicious. Our family and friends love it!

We're located on 110 acres of beautiful timberland in the heart of Amish Country. Near a golf course, tennis, antique shops and Amish stores, there is always something to do here. Fishing is available in our private pond and a variety of wildlife is found here. You can also enjoy two bluegrass festivals during the year.

INGREDIENTS
2 c. water
1 box peach Jell-O
1 box vanilla pudding mix (the kind you cook)
½ oz. cream cheese
1 c. Cool Whip

DIRECTIONS
Stir pudding mix and Jell-O together in saucepan. Add water and bring to a boil. Boil gently for 1 min. Cool thoroughly. Cream whipped topping and cream cheese together. Beat Jell-O mixture with beaters then add half of Jell-O mixture to cheese mixture. Swirl together slightly and put in glass serving dish. Any flavor Jell-O can be used, and a small amount of fruit may be added.

CRAB MEAT SALAD
West Gate Campgrounds – Perry, FL

Our campground has 60 spaces located in the city of Perry. Although we do not entertain personally, groups that travel together love to share the hospitality room we have at the campground to get together and enjoy a good meal. Crabmeat salad is a popular dish.

INGREDIENTS
1 can condensed tomato soup
8 oz. cream cheese
1 envelope unflavored gelatin
½ c. cold water
¼ c. chopped onions
¼ c. chopped green peppers
1 c. celery
1 tsp. salt
1 tsp. pepper
1 c. mayonnaise
2 c. flaked crabmeat*

* crabmeat may be substituted
   with chicken or tuna

DIRECTIONS
In a large pan, heat condensed tomato soup over low heat. Stir in cream cheese. Mix gelatin and water until dissolved and add to pan. Mix well. Remove pan from fire and stir in remainder of ingredients. Chill until firm.

LOBSTER SALAD A LA PENINSULA'S
The Landing Campground – Sylvan Beach, NY

This recipe came from the Yucatan Peninsula and was Americanized, or I should say "Landing Ownerized". The Landings is a 15 acre peninsula and the owner is often saved by this recipe when company is coming and there is no time to cook on schedule. It leaves time for the guests and there are no last minute pots and pans.

INGREDIENTS
2 sm. cold boiled potatoes,
   diced
1 lg. onion, finely chopped
3 lg. hard boiled eggs, diced
1 lg. tomato, diced
½ lb. shredded lobster tail
   (broiled or boiled)
1 can peas, drained
mayonnaise to taste
1 tsp. lime juice (optional)

DIRECTIONS
Mix all ingredients in a 2-3 qt. bowl. Chill for at least 2 hours. Serve as main course with corn tortillas or fresh tortilla chips. Great with avocado salad on the side. Serves 4.

RAPIDS RIGATONI SALAD
Silver Rapids Lodge – Ely, MN

Silver Rapids is known for our deluxe salad bar. Guests from throughout the United States have delighted in the variety of items we have to offer, all homemade, of course.

Silver Rapids Lodge is so named as early prospectors found silver here. We are located on a picturesque point adjoining White Iron Lake to Farm Lake. There is a rapids where it narrows. We are located in the Superior National Forest with many pines, birch, maple and many natural rock outcroppings and islands creating a very scenic tour. One can paddle into the boundary waters wilderness park without portaging. This area is rich in wildlife, most in their natural habitat. It's truly a unique vacation area.

INGREDIENTS
- 1 med. box cooked vegetable rigatoni
- 1 tub cherry tomatoes, whole
- 1 can black pitted olives
- 1 can green pitted olives
- 1 med. onion, chopped
- 1 med. stalk celery, chopped
- ½ lb. sliced pepperoni
- ¼ tsp. pepper
- ¼ tsp. garlic salt
- 2 tsp. Italian seasoning
- 1 tsp. oregano
- 8 oz. Italian dressing

DIRECTIONS

Combine dressing and seasonings into a marinade sauce. Add other ingredients to marinade, toss well. Refrigerate overnight before serving.

PASTA SEAFOOD SALAD
Aqua Barn Ranch Campground – Renton, WA

This recipe is so easy and it goes with all the great seafood we have here in the Northwest. If you enjoy seafood, you'll love this dish. It's always been a big success in our family.

We are located about 20 miles from Seattle and about 3 miles off the freeway. While we're out in the country, we're still convenient to the area's cities and attractions. We have an indoor, heated swimming pool and horseback riding for the children, but we're just a short way from shopping centers and the waterfront.

INGREDIENTS
- 1 pkg. 8 oz. Chinese noodles
- 1 c. sliced celery
- ½ c. sliced green onions
- 6 oz. shrimp or crab, canned or fresh
- 1 can sliced water chestnuts
- 2 c. mayonnaise
- 1 pkg. Uncle Dan's dressing

DIRECTIONS

Cook noodles according to directions. Mix all ingredients together and refrigerate overnight.

RIGATONI CUCUMBER SALAD
KOA of Topeka – Grantville, KS

This recipe was given to me by a camper after I supplied the parsley for her salad at our campground. This recipe has become a favorite of our extended stay campers. We exchange food and everyone loves this long keeping salad.

We are an overnight campground in a rural setting five miles from Topeka City limits. We have the best of all worlds — quiet nature setting with 15 minutes to entertainment, restaurants, and shopping. Our park contains an area "Extended Stay" for those who are working in the area and live in their RVs. They all enjoy this salad, and cucumbers come from my small garden during summer.

INGREDIENTS

8 oz. pkg. cooked rigatoni pasta
2 cucumbers (peeled or unpeeled, sliced thin)
2 onions sliced thin

Dressing
1¼ c. cider vinegar
1½ c. salad oil
1 c. sugar
2 tsp. garlic salt
2 tsp. coarse ground black pepper
2 tsp. parsley flakes

DIRECTIONS

Drain pasta and let cool. Combine vinegar, oil, sugar, garlic salt, pepper and parsley. Mix well. Chill at least 8 hrs. before serving. Keeps fresh a week or longer.

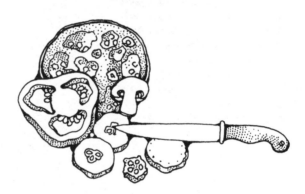

MARINATED VEGGIE SALAD
Junction West RV Park – Grand Junction, CO

This salad can be made well in advance, at your leisure, and is a sure hit at the covered dish dinners that abound in campgrounds.

We're a quiet, country campground located in the high desert valley of western Colorado. Enjoy the scenic views of the nearby Colorado National Monument and the Grand Mesa. We offer a variety of amenities and activities including level sites, RV and boat storage, modern laundry and restroom facilities, rec room, playground and hiking trails.

INGREDIENTS
1 lg. sweet onion
1 med. celery bunch
1 lg. green pepper
1 can sweet peas
1 can french cut green beans
1 lg. jar diced pimentos
Dressing:
1½ c. sugar
1 c. vinegar
½ c. salad oil
paprika

DIRECTIONS

Dice onion, celery and green pepper. Place in large mixing bowl with the undrained peas, beans and pimento. Sprinkle with salt. Let stand overnight or longer.

Dressing: Mix all ingredients together. Refrigerate to thicken. Shake dressing well and pour on salad. Drain and toss before serving.

WILTED LETTUCE
Indian Waters Hideway — Indio, CA

This recipe is my family's favorite because it came from our Grandmother in Wales.

We are located in Indio, known as the date capital. We are just minutes from Palm Springs, and have a winter temperature on the average of 74°. We swim all winter in our heated pool. We offer free cable TV and all the amenities. Our big date festival, which is always great fun, is celebrated in February. Come and see us.

INGREDIENTS
3-4 bunches of red leaf lettuce, chopped
2 bunches of green onions, sliced
6 strips of bacon diced
1 pt. sour cream

DIRECTIONS
Fry bacon bits until crispy. Pour in sour cream and bring to the boiling point. Pour over lettuce and green onion. Toss and serve.

HOT SHRIMP SALAD
Cooksey's Camping Resort — St. Augustine, FL

We are situated between the Atlantic Ocean and the Intracoastal waterway on a canal. Our resort is on a very large tract of land with beautiful trees and large sites. You can fish and crab on our property. Seafood is very much a part of our area.

At Cooksey's we have a covered dish supper every Tuesday night. We have put out two cook-books free to our campers. We collected recipes from them, had a cover contest and a name contest. The recipes are great.

INGREDIENTS
1 lb. shrimp, boiled & cleaned (small or chopped large ones)
2 cans cream of shrimp soup
4 tsp. lemon juice
1 sm. jar pimientos, chopped
4 hard boiled eggs, chopped
2 c. chopped celery
2 c. cooked rice
2 c. mayonnaise
2 tsp. Accent
potato chips

DIRECTIONS
Mix all ingredients except chips and pour into 9"x 13" baking dish. Sprinkle crushed potato chips on top and bake at 350° for 30 min. Serves 12 or more.

Delicious. Can be made early and placed in refrigerator until ready to bake. Add chips just before baking.

The same recipe can substituted with chicken and cream of chicken soup for hot chicken salad. Excellent way to use left-over turkey.

AMERICAN MEXICAN SALAD
Dogwood Valley Campground – Mt. Gilead, OH

Dogwood Valley Campground is a beautiful spot in the heart of Ohio. We have rolling hills, a six-acre lake, and lots of friendly folks who like to get-together to visit and share meals.

This salad is one of our best loved foods and is often prepared for our gatherings. I started making this meal for my family and friends. When the campers saw how easy it was to prepare, they all started fixing it. It can satisfy a lot of hungry people. It is so easy and so good!

INGREDIENTS
    1 lb. hamburger*
    1 med. onion
    1 pkg. taco seasoning
    1 can kidney beans
    1 can mushrooms
    1 head lettuce
    1 tomato
    1 can black olives
    1 c. shredded cheese
    1 bag Doritos (smashed)
    1 bottle 1000 Island dressing

* can substitute sausage or
    ground turkey for
    hamburger

DIRECTIONS
Brown ground meat, onions, and taco seasoning. Heat kidney beans and mushrooms in a saucepan. Prepare & combine remaining ingredients in a large salad bowl as you would for a regular salad. Drain all heated ingredients and add to salad bowl. Mix well. Serve and eat. Yields 6-12 servings.

Sour cream and/or salsa are well-liked additives to serve on the side.

CHARLIE'S SALAD
N.W. Houston Jellystone Park — Hempstead, TX

When my family camps, we all enjoy this easy and complete meal. I even suggest this to our campers when they are in our camp store wondering what to fix that's easy and satisfies everyone's tastes.

We have 70 acres with all types of campsites. All sites are shaded with hundreds of pine trees plus live oak, pecan and other trees. We have a stocked lake for fishing, a swimming pool, mini-golf, petting zoo, tennis court, planned activities with Yogi's help, and bluegrass festivals during the spring and fall. Exceptionally clean, quiet and friendly.

INGREDIENTS
    1 can chili with beans
    10 oz. grated cheddar cheese
    lettuce
    tomato
    onion
    1 bag corn chips
    salsa
    taco sauce

DIRECTIONS
Prepare tossed salad of lettuce, tomato and onion. Set aside. In saucepan, add chili and cheese. Bring to a boil. Pour chili and cheese mixture over salad. Add corn chips to salad. Toss well. Cover tightly 3 - 5 min. Serve with taco sauce or salsa.

BROCCOLI/CAULIFLOWER SALAD
Coastal Riverside Campground – Beaufort, NC

Coastal Riverside Campground is a quiet secluded area on the banks of a wide creek at the mouth of a river. We have 55 campsites on 22 acres. We offer a pool, pier, boat ramp, laundry room and bathhouse with hot showers. In addition to all this, we're close to historic Beaufort, Fort Macon, Atlantic Beach, Cape Lookout, New Bern and the Cedar Island to Ocracoke Ferry and the outer banks.

INGREDIENTS
- 1 head broccoli
- 1 head cauliflower
- 1 c. sharp cheddar cheese, shredded
- ½ c. chopped onion
- 1 3½ oz. bottle bacon bits
- 1 c. mayonnaise
- ½ c. sugar
- 3 Tbsp. vinegar

DIRECTIONS
Chop broccoli and cauliflower flowerets in small pieces. Add chopped onion and shredded cheese. Toss together. Mix mayonnaise, sugar & vinegar together and pour on broccoli/cauliflower mixture. Mix well and stir in bacon bits. Works well to make a day ahead. Diet mayonnaise and sugar substitute may be used to lower calories or for diabetics.

SPINACH SALAD
Palm Harbor Travel Trailer Park — Rockport, TX

This is a delicious, low-cal potluck favorite.
Our park is located 4 mi. south of Rockport on Redfish Bay. We offer 100 full hookups, rec hall, laundry facilities, lighted seawall, cabanas, fishing guides and salt water fishing. Come visit us and take advantage of all that we offer.

INGREDIENTS
- 1 sm. box lemon Jell-O with NutraSweet
- 1 c. hot water
- 1 c. lowfat small curd cottage cheese
- 1-10 oz. pkg. chopped frozen spinach, thawed and drained
- 1 c. mayonnaise
- 1 c. chopped onion
- 1 c. chopped celery

DIRECTIONS
Dissolve Jell-O in hot water. Add mayonnaise and blend well. Add remaining ingredients and blend together. Pour mixture into 9 x 9 inch dish and chill until set. Makes 9-12 servings.

PEAR SALAD
Sea Perch RV Park & Campground – Yachats, OR

This recipe is loved by everyone here and complements any meal.

We are a full service RV park, located in central Oregon. An open view of the ocean is seen from all sites. We have easy access to the beach, a gift shop, grocery items, full hookups and tent sites.

INGREDIENTS
- 1-3 oz. pkg. lime Jell-O
- No. 2½ can pears
- 1 c. pear juice, heated
- 1-8 oz. pkg. cream cheese
- ½ pt. whipping cream, whipped

DIRECTIONS
Mash cream cheese with fork. Mash pears and mix in hot Jell-O. Add hot pear juice to Jell-O mixture. Mix in cream cheese. Let stand until gelatin-like consistency. Fold in whipping cream. Cover and refrigerate.

RASPBERRY-CRANBERRY SALAD
Golden Pond R.V. Resort – Indio, CA

We have a salad luncheon once a month and this salad is a favorite of everyone.

Our park is for adults only. We have TV and phone hookups available at all spaces, large pool, jacuzzi and billiard and card rooms. Also available to our guests are a number of activities including bus trips to Vegas and Laughlin.

INGREDIENTS
- 2 pkg. cherry Jell-O
- 1 c. whole cranberry sauce
- 1 med. can crushed pineapple
- 1 pt. sour cream
- 2 pkg. frozen raspberries
- 1 pkg. raspberry Jell-O
- 3 c. hot water

DIRECTIONS
Combine cherry Jell-O, hot water, cranberry sauce, crushed pineapple and juices in a lg. bowl. Mix and let set. Pour in a 9" x 13" baking dish. Spread with sour cream. In a separate bowl, mix raspberry Jell-O, 1½ c. hot water, and frozen raspberries. Stir until thickened. Pour over the sour cream. Cut into squares. Makes 12 servings.

CINNAMON APPLE SWIRL SALAD
Woodburn I-5 RV Park — Woodburn, OR

This recipe is different, delicious and can be served as a salad or a dessert.

Woodburn is a medium-sized town, well known for its multi-cultural background and its farm produce — especially berries. Situated between Portland and Salem, it is a restful place to stay while visiting the larger cities. Our park is new and offers many luxury features, such as 150 paved sites, 60 ft. pull-thrus, cable TV, swimming pool and recreation room with kitchen and fireplace. We're located right off I-5 at the Woodburn exit. In summer, the local drag strip provides entertainment along with the many scheduled events such as the Hopps Festival, OctoberFest, Farmfest and numerous other events.

INGREDIENTS
- **2 3-oz. pkg. cherry gelatin**
- **2 c. boiling water**
- **dash of salt**
- **½-¾ c. red cinnamon candies**
- **2 c. applesauce**
- **1 Tbsp. lemon juice**
- **½ c. finely chopped celery**
- **½ c. chopped nuts**
- **6 oz. cream cheese, softened**
- **¼ c. milk**
- **2 Tbsp. mayonnaise**

DIRECTIONS

Dissolve gelatin and candies in boiling water. Stir in applesauce, lemon juice and salt. Chill until partially set. Fold in nuts and celery. Pour into 8 x 8 x 2-inch pan and refrigerate. Blend cream cheese, milk and mayonnaise; spoon on top of partially set salad. Swirl through salad to marble. Chill until firm. Cut into squares. Serves 9.

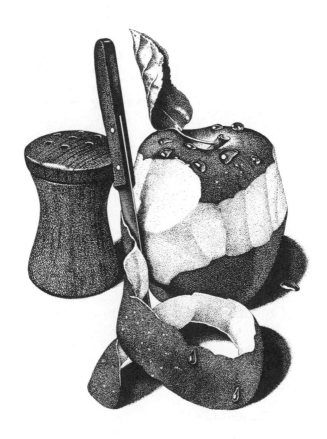

AVOCADO CHICKEN SALAD
Casa de Fruta RV Park – Hollister, CA

This salad is perfect for the RV lifestyle since the dish requires little cooking. Many ingredients used in this salad are also featured at our retail business.

We're a 300 site RV park with full hookups and cable TV available at most sites. We are located on scenic Hwy. 152 (Pacheco Pass Hwy.) and offer meeting rooms, modern restrooms, laundry facilities, lawn area, many fine specialty shops and a 24-hour restaurant.

INGREDIENTS
- **1½ c. diced cooked chicken**
- **1 c. thinly sliced celery**
- **1 Tbsp. lemon juice**
- **½ tsp. grated lemon rind**
- **2 green onions, finely chopped**
- **½ tsp. salt**
- **⅛ tsp. paprika**
- **¼ c. Chenin Blanc or other white table wine**
- **1 med. ripe avocado**
- **½ c. coarsely chopped salted cashew nuts**
- **⅓ c. mayonnaise**
- **crisp lettuce**

DIRECTIONS

Combine chicken, celery, lemon juice and rind, onion, salt, paprika and wine. Let stand in refrigerator for several hours to blend flavors. When ready to serve, cut avocado in half; remove pit and skin. Cut into small chunks or balls. Add with nuts and mayonnaise to chicken mixture. Toss lightly to blend ingredients. Serve in crisp lettuce cups. Serves 3-4.

BROCCOLI SALAD
Autumn Acres – Brownsville, TX

The combination of raisins and onions in this recipe may sound strange, but it was an instant hit at our monthly ladies' salad luncheons at the park.

Located in South Texas, we are close to South Padre Island, Boca Chica Beach, and Mexico. Our park is family owned and operated. Our ladies' salad luncheon is just one of many enjoyable activities at our park. Here you are known by name, not by a number. Your satisfaction is our main goal. We also have a heated pool and a whirlpool for your enjoyment.

INGREDIENTS
- **2 bunches broccoli**
- **2 med. red onions, sliced**
- **2 c. sunflower seeds**
- **1 c. raisins**
- **1 lb. bacon, fried and crumbled**

Dressing:
- **2 c. mayonnaise**
- **½ c. sugar**
- **4 tsp. vinegar**

DIRECTIONS

Break broccoli into small florets. Add onions, raisins, sunflower seeds, and bacon.

Dressing: Mix all ingredients together and pour over broccoli salad. Toss.

ENTREES

GRILLED TRI-TIP ROAST
Steckel Park Campground – Santa Paula, CA

This recipe is quick and easy! It's great with beans, potatoes, cole slaw and corn bread.

Our "getaway" campground is hidden in a beautiful wooded canyon, located 1-1½ hours north of Los Angeles. We're only minutes to the ocean. Year round camping, clubhouse, stone cabin with group and individual campsites are available. Come experience clean, fresh air, mild temperatures, cool mid-day breezes and long pleasant evenings where the sounds of nature and friendship abound.

INGREDIENTS
- **1 tri tip roast (3-5 lbs.)**
- **special tri tip seasoning**

DIRECTIONS

Marinate roast 2-3 hours. Place roast, fat side up over hot coals. Cook for 10 min. Turn roast and cook at 10 min. intervals until desired doneness.

MARINATED BEEF
Sunrise Beach — Mathis, TX

When we cook out, this is one of our favorite recipes. You can make an inexpensive cut of meat taste as good as any steak. Because you can marinate it overnight, it's great for outdoor cooking. We hope you enjoy it as much as we do.

Located three miles from Mathis on beautiful Lake Corpus Christi, Sunrise Beach is only 35 miles from the city of Corpus Christi. With 43 acres of mostly wooded, rolling terrain and a vast shoreline you feel akin to nature. Our 600-ft. fishing pier, boat launches, swimming and picnic areas allow you to choose your favorite leisure activity.

INGREDIENTS
- **4 lbs. round bone chuck**
- **soy sauce**
- **1 Tbsp. lemon juice**
- **1 Tbsp. Worchestershire sauce**
- **¼ c. brown sugar**
- **1½ c. water**

DIRECTIONS

Poke both sides of meat with fork prongs. Add tenderizer if desired. In pan, blend remaining ingredients. Place meat in 9″ x 13″ pan. Marinate at least 3 hours each side. Grill. Save juice to baste. Leftover meat can be warmed in juice and served over rice.

AUDREY'S COUNTRY FRIED STEAK
Perdido Bay KOA - Pensacola — Lillian, AL

The men in our family love it. It is prepared by a great cook, Audrey Auten.
We are located 15 miles west of Pensacola, Fla., out in the country. We're located right on beautiful Perdido Bay, where lots of seafood is just waiting to be caught. Half of our park is shaded by oak trees that are at least 200 years old. Here at our park there's something for everyone.

INGREDIENTS
- 1½ lb. ground chuck
- 4½ tsp. salt
- 1 tsp. pepper
- ¾ c. plus 3 Tbsp. flour
- 3 Tbsp. fat
- 2½ c. milk

DIRECTIONS

Combine meat, 1 tsp. salt, pepper and ¾ c. flour; mix well. Roll out to about ½ inch thick. Cut into 4 x 4 inch pieces. Place in hot fat in skillet. Cook until lightly browned. Remove from skillet. Add remaining flour; cook until browned. In separate pan, mix milk and remaining salt together and simmer until thick, gravy-like consistency. Pour gravy over steak. Serve hot.

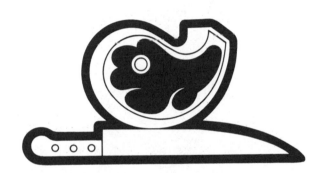

SASQUATCH SEOUL STEAK
Sasquatch Springs RV Resort-Harrison Hot Springs, BC

One of the problems of owning a camping resort is that of finding time to eat a regular evening meal. Real sit-down meals are something we enjoy in the off season! However, during the camping season we fend for ourselves. My technique is to adopt a well practiced "hungry dog" look and cruise around the campground following my nose to food on the grill. A casual inquiry such as "Are those pork ribs?" or "Did you make that delicious smelling BBQ sauce yourself?" will usually produce an invitation to sample the camper's meal. This recipe is not only easy to prepare — it's also easy to share!

INGREDIENTS
- 2 oz. sesame oil
- ¼ c. soy sauce
- 1 garlic clove, minced
- 4 ginger slices
- ½ c. chopped green onions
- 2 tsp. sugar or honey
- 2 lb. steak

DIRECTIONS

Combine sesame oil, soy sauce, garlic, ginger, green onions and sugar or honey. Slice steak into thin strips. Put steak and marinade in plastic bag and mix well. Squeeze air out of bag and seal with twist tie. After at least an hour, put the strips briefly on a very hot barbecue or frying pan and serve while sizzling.

BEEF RING
Valley Grande Mobile Home Park — McAllen, TX

Wintertime in the Rio Grande Valley means sunshine, activities and friendships, old and new. A big favorite at Valley Grande Mobile Home Park is Thursday evening potluck suppers. We enjoy the fellowship of sharing a lot of fun as well as the delicious variety of foods that are prepared. It is hard to choose one favorite from so many, but we decided on this tasty potluck recipe to share with you.

INGREDIENTS
- 1 lb. ground beef
- ½ c. cream
- salt & pepper to taste
- ⅔ c. oats
- 6 tsp. chopped onion
- 3 Tbsp. Worcestershire sauce
- 6 tsp. chopped onion
- ⅔ c. catsup
- 2 Tbsp. vinegar
- 3 Tbsp. sugar
- ½ c. water

DIRECTIONS

Blend beef, cream, salt, pepper, oats and onion together. Make a hole in the center. Bake 10 min. at 250°. Mix Worcestershire sauce, onion, catsup, vinegar, sugar and water together in a separate bowl. Pour mixture over ring and continue baking for 1 hr.

MARTY'S NORWEGIAN MEATBALLS
Camp Nebraska — Tampa, FL

This dish is very popular with our family. It's also a hit when served at potlucks.
Camp Nebraska has been catering to campers since 1921. We're located inside the city limits of Tampa so all the conveniences of the city are at your fingertips. Come enjoy the Florida sun.

INGREDIENTS
- 1 egg
- 1½ c. uncooked oatmeal
- 1 c. milk
- 1 med. onion, chopped fine
- 2 Tbsp. nutmeg
- 1 Tbsp. ginger
- 2 tsp. salt
- ½ tsp. pepper
- 2½ lb. ground meat *
- 1 pkg. dry onion soup mix
- 2½ c. water

* beef, pork, turkey or veal

DIRECTIONS

Mix spices, egg, milk and oatmeal; allow to stand until oats are moistened. Add meat and onion. Mix and form into golfball size meatballs. Brown. Drain off fat. Add soup mix and water. Simmer about 45 min. Thicken excess liquid with flour for gravy. Good when served with boiled potatoes and applesauce.

GRAB BAGS
Gold Mine RV Park — Greenwood, AR

This is a no mess, no clean up meal that's tasty and easy to prepare. It's perfect after a long, hard day of work or play.

Our park is located on Hwy. 71, just off I-10 with EZ-off and EZ-on access. We're a new park with modern facilities and full hookups. Our park was created with the traveler in mind.

INGREDIENTS
- 1 lb. ground beef
- 1 lg. onion, sliced
- 2 lg. potatoes, sliced
- 4 carrots, sliced

DIRECTIONS

Spread out a large sheet of aluminum foil. Press ground beef out in the center of foil. Place onions, potatoes and carrots on top of ground beef. Salt and pepper. Close foil tight. Bake at 400° for 15 min., then at 375° for 45 min.

VENISON STEAKS-JON WERTMAN STYLE
Almost Heaven Campground – Forksville, PA

We have many hunters in this area as well as fishermen. This recipe is very popular among the men. As a matter of fact, my son Jon is the cook around here for venison and trout and this recipe is his specialty.

Our campground is situated on 200 acres and we're surrounded by the Endless Mountains. Loyalsock Creek runs along our campground and since this creek is stocked by the state, fishing is excellent here. We have 200 sites and all modern conveniences.

INGREDIENTS
- 4 venison steaks
- 1 c. flour
- 1 pkg. dry onion soup mix
- ¼ tsp. salt
- ¼ tsp. pepper
- ¼ tsp. cumin
- ¼ c. oil
- ¼ c. margarine or butter

DIRECTIONS

Mix flour and dry soup mix together in a bowl. Add salt, pepper and cumin. Melt oil and butter in a skillet over medium heat. Dust venison steaks with flour mixture and fry in butter and oil mixture 3-5 min. on each side.

HOT BARBEQUED CHUCK ROAST
Granite Hill Campground & Waterpark-Gettysburg, PA

This recipe is a perfect camping family dinner because the whole family can participate in the cooking.

We are located 6 miles west of Gettysburg on a Civil War era farm. Our campground is very family oriented with lots of activities for everyone. We think cooking can be a fun family activity as well, with a meal prepared over the coals in a convenient grill basket. Come to Granite Hill Campground and Waterpark this summer and we'll show you how it's done!

INGREDIENTS
2 Tbsp. salad oil
½ c. finely chopped onion
¼ c. finely chopped green pepper
2 Tbsp. brown sugar
1½ c. catsup
dash hot sauce
2½ Tbsp. cider vinegar
½ tsp. garlic salt
½ tsp. salt
3 to 4 lb. chuck roast

DIRECTIONS
Heat salad oil in small skillet. Saute chopped onion and green pepper until tender. Stir in brown sugar, catsup, hot sauce, vinegar, garlic salt and salt. Bring to a boil and simmer for 10 min. Place roast in hinged basket or on grill over low heat for 10 min. Turn and cook another 10 min. Begin brushing sauce on roast and turn often. Use meat thermometer to cook to desired doneness. Serves 8.

BEEF 'N POTATO BAKE
Quail Run Campground – Zephyrhills, FL

This easy to prepare meal not only saves time in the kitchen, it also provides a hearty stick-to-your-ribs meal. Now you can take advantage of all that our campground has to offer — a clean, friendly and fun environment in close proximity to major attractions such as Busch Gardens, Disney World and Cypress Gardens.

INGREDIENTS
4 c. hash brown potatoes
3 Tbsp. vegetable oil
¼ tsp. ground black pepper
1 lb. ground beef
1 pkg. brown gravy mix
1 c. water
½ tsp. garlic salt
1 pkg. mixed vegetables
1 c. shredded cheddar cheese
1 can French fried onions

DIRECTIONS
Combine potatoes, oil and pepper in 1½ qt. baking dish. Firmly press mixture across bottom and sides. Bake uncovered at 400° for 15 min. Brown beef and drain. Stir in gravy mix, water, garlic salt and bring to a boil. Add mixed vegetables, reduce heat to medium, and cook 5 min. Stir in ½ c. cheese and ½ can French fried onions. Place in potato shell. Bake uncovered at 350° for 15 min. Sprinkle with remaining cheese and onions. Bake 5 min. or longer. Makes 4-6 servings.

SOUR CREAM STEAKS
Lavaland RV Park – Grants, NM

Lavaland RV Park offers convenient, easy on and off access to I-40. We offer reasonable rates, clean facilities and western hospitality to our guests. While staying with us, explore nearby lava beds, Acoma Sky City, mine museums and ice caves.

INGREDIENTS
1 lb. breakfast steak
8 oz. sour cream
1 bell pepper
1 tsp. oil
salt & pepper to taste

DIRECTIONS
Cut steak in strips and brown in oil together with bell pepper. Salt and pepper to taste and simmer for about 15 min. Mix in sour cream.

BAR-B-Q BEEF BRISKET
Suburban East RV & Mobile Home Park-Big Spring, TX

West Texas is noted for cattle, oil, cotton and Bar-B-Q's. Suburban East RV and Mobile Home Park offers a variety of facility amenities as well as a swimming pool and playground. At our annual picnic in the spring, someone always asks if I am going to serve that good Bar-B-Q. Here's my recipe!

INGREDIENTS
1 beef brisket, 8-10 lbs.
3-4 Tbsp. lemon pepper
3-4 Tbsp. garlic salt
3-4 Tbsp. seasoning salt
1 bottle barbeque sauce

DIRECTIONS
Smoke brisket over mesquite coals for 6-7 hrs. (DO NOT COOK.) Remove from smoker. Preheat oven to 250°. Cover meat with equal parts of lemon pepper, garlic salt and seasoning salt. Cover with barbecue sauce. Place meat in an oven baking bag. Place in oven and bake for 5 hours or until tender. This recipe can be frozen.

CORNISH PASTIES
Ekstrom's Stage Station – Clinton, MT

When you reach our park, you might think you've stumbled onto one of Montana's Ghost Towns. That's what we intended when we started reassembling century-old log cabins in the early 1970's. Ekstrom's Stage Station is more than just a campground and tourist attraction. You actually feel transported back in time!

INGREDIENTS
½-1 tsp. salt
3 c. flour
1¼ c. lard
¾ c. very cold water
5-6 med. potatoes
3 med. chopped onions
2 lb. loin tip beef
butter
salt & pepper

DIRECTIONS
Stir salt into flour. Cut in lard until lumps are pea-sized. Sprinkle water over flour mixture. Mix well and divide into 6 equal parts. Set aside.

Roll pastry slightly oblong. Peel and slice potatoes. Make a layer in center of pasty. Sprinkle with onions, top with meat, diced or cut into thin strips. Dot with butter and sprinkle with salt and pepper. Bring edges of pastry over filling to center. Crimp together well to seal. Bake at 375° for 1 hr. Makes 6 good-sized pasties.

HOG ROAST
Mountain Creek Campground – Gardners, PA

At Mountain Creek Campground we serve many meals to our campers. While all the meals are a hit, the hog roast is very popular with our guests. Our campground is located in a quiet, partially shaded mountain area. We have a trout stream, group activities and a rec hall. There is plenty to do here, or if you'd rather, there is nothing to do! Anyway you serve it, it's a great camping experience. We hope you enjoy this recipe and make a pig of yourself. And if you're lucky, you can give the squeal to a friend!

INGREDIENTS

200 lb. hog, dressed (hair removed, skin left on)
Stuffing:
  20 lb. bread cubes
  5 doz. eggs
  1 qt. whole milk
  2½ celery stalks, coarsely chopped
  12 med. onions, finely chopped
  2 lg. bunches parsley, finely chopped
  2 Tbsp. poultry seasoning
  2 tsp. salt
  2 tsp. pepper

DIRECTIONS

Remove head of pig. Slit the belly from shoulder to rear legs. Clean inside cavity thoroughly. Prepare filling and stuff hog. Using mason twine, sew opening shut. Using heavy duty foil, wrap hog to seal in the juices. Next, cover foil with chicken wire so hog retains its shape. Cook in hog cooker at 375°-400° for 12-15 hrs. Do not cook over open flame. Meat is finished when stuffing reaches 180°. Serves 200 people.

Stuffing: using a large tub, add bread cubes, celery, onions and parsley. In separate bowl beat eggs and add milk. Pour egg mixture over bread cube mixture. Work two mixtures into one another. Mix in poultry seasoning, salt and pepper. Place in hog cavity.

YOU'RE

INVITED

T
O

A

H
O
G

R
O
A
S
T

MOM'S BBQ COUNTRY PORK RIBS
Little River Village Campground – Townsend, TN

For great Southern Mountain cooking, no Sunday table is complete without a platter of country ribs, cole slaw, ramps, beans and cornbread or biscuits with homemade strawberry jam. Little River Campground, located at the Cades Cove entrance to the Great Smoky Mountain National Park has a pavilion and BBQ pit that is a hot bed of activity for catered dinners throughout our long season. We hope you and your family enjoy this down home recipe!

INGREDIENTS
- **country pork ribs cut with the bones**
- **your favorite BBQ sauce**

DIRECTIONS

Combine country ribs (bought pre-cut with the bones) in a large pot with enough water to cover. Bring to a boil and simmer 40-45 min. Place on a large foil covered baking sheet and baste with BBQ sauce on both sides. Bake at 375° for about ½ hr; turn once. Or, instead of an oven, finish on an open charcoal fire.

PORK SAUERKRAUT
Yogi Bear's Jellystone Park – Emporia, VA

Join us for Yogi antics, activities, "hey hey hey" rides, cool dips in the pool, and more. We are located 6 miles north of Emporia, home of the Virginia Pork Festival. Yogi's already licking his chops and dreaming of picnic baskets filled with the best pork smorgasbord anywhere. This recipe has long been a family favorite. Enjoy!

INGREDIENTS
- **pork loin or ribs**
- **1 apple**
- **sauerkraut**

DIRECTIONS

Simmer ingredients for 1-2 hrs. until meat is very tender.

BARBEQUED PORK CHOPS
Holiday Nashville Travel Park — Nashville, TN

This dish is easy and delicious. While the chops are baking, you can prepare the rest of your meal.

We have grassy, level and shady sites with full and partial hookups. All of our sites are also pull-thrus. We're located near Opryland and we also offer tours of Nashville and the surrounding area. We have clean restrooms, with plenty of hot water for showers. We offer a variety of activities to keep you busy such as swimming, mini golf, playground, indoor rec area and more. Come visit us soon and experience all the conveniences of home, and the excitement of a camping trip.

INGREDIENTS
- **8-10 lean pork chops**
- **¼ c. chopped onions**
- **½ c. chopped celery**
- **1 c. catsup**
- **½ c. water**
- **¼ c. lemon juice**
- **4 Tbsp. honey**
- **3 Tbsp. Worcestershire sauce**
- **2 Tbsp. vinegar**
- **1 Tbsp. mustard**
- **½ tsp. salt**
- **¼ tsp. pepper**

DIRECTIONS

Wipe chops with damp cloth, place in large casserole dish so that chops don't overlap. Mix remaining ingredients together for sauce. Pour barbeque sauce over them. Cover tightly with foil and bake at 375° for 1 hr. Remove foil, continue to bake for 45 min. longer, or until chops are brown and sauce very thick.

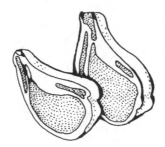

PORK WITH CORN
Lakeside Camping Inc. – Henderson, NE

Nebraska is in the great American desert where most crops are irrigated. The water comes from the Nebraska Aquaphor. Corn is the main farming product and there are many pig farms. Our park is noted for the many trees that we've planted through the years and for our peaceful surroundings.

INGREDIENTS
- **3 pork steaks cut in half**
- **salt & pepper to taste**
- **1 can cream style corn**
- **¼ c. milk**
- **1 egg**
- **¼ tsp. salt**
- **⅛ tsp. pepper**

DIRECTIONS

Salt and pepper steaks, place in baking pan and set aside. In mixing bowl, add all other ingredients. Mix well and pour over steaks, covering evenly. Bake 45 min. in 400° oven.

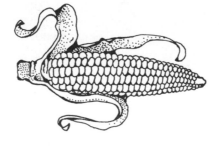

CHICKEN THIGHS A LA PAUL
College Courts & Trailer Park – Beaumont, TX

This recipe is a family favorite, named after my grandson.
Our park consists of large and grassy sites with patios. We offer full hookups, pull-thrus and reasonable rates. Mobile home rentals are also available.

INGREDIENTS
- **3 Tbsp. brown sugar**
- **3 Tbsp. Worcestershire sauce**
- **2 Tbsp. chopped onion**
- **¼ c. vinegar**
- **1 Tbsp. dry mustard**
- **8 chicken thighs**
- **3 Tbsp. oil**
- **¼ c. water**
- **½ c. chili sauce**
- **1½ tsp. salt**
- **½ tsp. pepper**

DIRECTIONS
Arrange chicken in baking dish. Mix other ingredients together in saucepan and simmer for 10 min. Pour half of sauce over chicken. Bake uncovered at 350° for 45 to 50 min. Baste with remaining sauce every 15 min.

CHEESE CHICKEN
Shady Acres — McLean, TX

This recipe is one of my family's favorites. Since it's so easy to prepare ahead of time and it makes an excellent leftover meal, I make it often for them. This dish is also good for get-togethers and church socials.

Shady Acres is located 15 miles west of Shamrock and 4½ miles east of McLean right off I-40. Our campsites are in a quiet, shady area, away from highway noise. Turkeys and peacocks are raised here on our premises, and this area is a favorite with birdwatchers. We also offer a swimming pool, hot showers, playground, laundry facilities and an overnight horse corral.

INGREDIENTS
- **1 fryer chicken**
- **1½ sticks margarine, melted**
- **bread crumbs**
- **salt and pepper to taste**
- **1 can parmesan cheese**

DIRECTIONS
Dip cut-up fryer in melted margarine, roll in mixture of bread crumbs, parmesan cheese and salt and pepper. Place pieces in baking dish. Bake at 350° for 1 hour. For moister chicken, cover for last 15 min. of baking.

MASSANUTTEN CHICKEN
KOA-Harrisonburg/New Market – Broadway, VA

We use this recipe for our spring "Thank you" barbeque. This is a very heavy poultry producing area. Our campground is located in the beautiful and historic Shenandoah Valley of Virginia. The park is located in "Mountain Valley" at the foot of the Massanutten Mountains bordering George Washington National Forest. Our guests take advantage of the poultry produced in the area and this recipe is one of their favorites.

INGREDIENTS
- 12-half chickens
- 1 qt. salad oil
- ½ gal. cider vinegar
- 1 pt. tomato juice
- ¼ c. onion salt
- ¼ c. pepper
- ½ oz. garlic salt
- ½ oz. poultry seasoning
- 1 sm. bottle hot sauce
- ¼ c. salt

DIRECTIONS

Mix all ingredients together and pour over chicken halves to marinate overnight. Brown chicken slowly over campfire. Brush with marinade every 10-15 min. Turn chicken occasionally to cook evenly for 2 hrs.

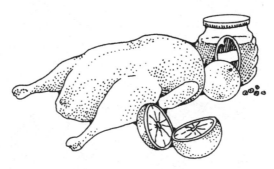

CHICKEN IN ORANGE JUICE
American Campground — Del Rio, TX

I came up with this recipe years ago. It has become a family favorite for a variety of reasons. It's easy to prepare and clean up after, and it's delicious. Our winter Texans particularly like this dish as it's low in calories and easy on the pocketbook.

While at American Campground, enjoy our full and partial hookups, clean bathhouse and laundry, camping cabins, mini-golf, horseshoes, swimming pool, boat rentals, watersports center and more. Or take advantage of all that the area has to offer — historic Del Rio, Amistad Dam, Amistad Lake, shopping, special tours and sporting events.

INGREDIENTS
- 1 fryer chicken, skinned
- orange juice, fresh or frozen (if frozen, dilute with half of water required)

DIRECTIONS

Place chicken in deep pot. Cover chicken completely with orange juice. Bring to a boil. Reduce heat and simmer uncovered for 1½-2 hrs. or until juice becomes a light brown gravy and chicken appears glazed. Serve hot with rice or baked potato and salad.

UTAH'S OVEN FRIED CHICKEN
Mineral Springs Junction – Draper, UT

Utah is known for its Pioneer Heritage. Delicious recipes are handed down from generation to generation. This recipe was handed down through generations to one of our employees. Our park has a quiet and relaxing atmosphere with a great view of the mountains. We are located within minutes of Salt Lake City and its historical sites.

INGREDIENTS
- ¾ c. flour
- 2 tsp. salt
- ⅛ tsp. pepper
- 1 Tbsp. paprika
- 2½-3 lb. chicken
- ½ c. butter or margarine
- spices to taste (cayenne, garlic, etc.)

DIRECTIONS
Preheat oven to 400°. In a bag or bowl combine flour and spices. Shake pieces of chicken to coat well. Melt butter in shallow baking pan. Arrange chicken skin side down in single layer. Bake at 400° for 45 min. to 1 hr. or until tender. Turn chicken once after 30 min. of baking.

LEMON HERB CHICKEN
Sun Valley RV Resort – Ketchum, ID

It is easy to prepare and many people in the camp also use this for the fish that they catch.
Sun Valley RV Resort is located on the Big Wood River, where fishing is a very popular activity. Our area is lush and green, and countless activities the whole family can enjoy await you. Enjoy swimming, mini golf, jacuzzi, bicycling, cross country skiing and more!

INGREDIENTS
- 3-4 lbs. cut up chicken
- 1 c. lemon juice
- 1 whole lemon, sliced
- lemon & herb spice
- 6 Tbsp. Dijon mustard
- olive oil

DIRECTIONS
Fry chicken in olive oil lightly on both sides; do not cook too long, just enough to brown. Remove excess oil and mix Dijon mustard with lemon juice and pour over chicken. Add sliced lemons and simmer for 45 min.

"BUSY-DAY" CHICKEN
Edgewater Resort & RV Park – Kelseyville, CA

This is a quick, easy dish to prepare when I have a busy day out on the resort. I serve it with rice as a one-dish meal. It is excellent when re-heated and is low in cholesterol.

We are located in a rural area right on Clear Lake with lots of shade under beautiful mature oaks. On a hot summer afternoon, you will find most of us by the edge of the lake on the large, grassy area adjacent to the private beach. Clear Lake is California's largest natural lake and may be the oldest lake in North America.

INGREDIENTS
- **18¾ oz. can solid pack tomatoes**
- **1 lg. chopped onion**
- **4 minced garlic cloves**
- **2 bay leaves, optional**
- **2 tsp. ground cumin**
- **1½ tsp. crumbled dry oregano**
- **2 Tbsp. wine vinegar**
- **salt & pepper to taste**
- **2½ to 3 lb. chicken, skinned and cut into eight pieces**

DIRECTIONS

After cutting tomatoes into pieces, place in large ovenproof casserole with juice. Add all other ingredients except chicken and simmer on top of stove, stirring occasionally, for 30 min. Add skinned chicken pieces, pushing them down into the sauce. Cover and bake at 350° for about 1 hr. Serves 4. Serve with rice or noodles.

CHICKEN SUPREME
Peachland Trailer Inn – Peachland, BC

This is my family's favourite chicken recipe. It's easy to prepare and looks and tastes fantastic. I make this dish every year for my husband's fishing trip in May. I have yet to tell him how easy it is to prepare!

Peachland is centrally located in the fruit-filled Okanagan Valley in beautiful British Columbia, Canada. Our park is set amidst orchards with large shade trees on the shores of Okanagan Lake. We at Peachland Trailer Inn hope you and your family enjoy this recipe as much as we do!

INGREDIENTS
- **4 chicken breasts, boneless**
- **6 oz. crab or shrimp**
- **asparagus or broccoli**
- **1 pkg. bearnaise sauce (prepared as directed)**

DIRECTIONS

Bake chicken at 350° for 20 min. Drain off excess fat and remove skin. Top chicken with crab or shrimp, then asparagus or broccoli. Pour bernaise sauce over the top and bake at 350° for 30-40 min.

CHICKEN PIE WITH PUFF CRUST
Jim's Travel Trailer Park – Zephyrhills, FL

Jim's Travel Trailer Park is an adults only RV Park located in the friendly city of Zephyrhills. We offer full hookup sites with a variety of amenities and plenty of planned activities that keep our guests busy. It seems everytime this dish is served at a potluck dinner, it's always gone. All that's left is an empty dish to wash!

INGREDIENTS
5 c. chicken, boned & diced
¾ c. carrots, sliced
¾ c. celery, sliced
¾ c. onion, chopped
2 chicken bouillon cubes
½ tsp. poultry seasoning
5 c. water
5 Tbsp. cornstarch
salt & pepper to taste
Crust:
3 eggs
½ c. biscuit mix
¼ tsp. salt
½ tsp. paprika
1 Tbsp. vegetable oil
¼ c. milk

DIRECTIONS
Mix chicken, vegetables, bouillon, poultry seasoning, salt & pepper, and water together. Cook until tender. In separate pan add water to cornstarch and cook until thickened. Pour over chicken and vegetable mixture. Be sure this mixture is hot before adding crust.

Puff crust: Beat egg whites until soft peaks form. Set aside. Beat egg yolks until thick. Add salt, paprika and oil. Beat again. Add milk and flour and fold in egg whites. Pour over vegetable mixture. Bake at 375° for 20 min. or until golden brown. Let stand for 5 min. then cut into squares.

CHICKEN BARBECUE
Camp Bell Campgrounds – Campbell, NY

We did our first barbecue in 1973 as a "thank you" for our customers (about 50 dinners). One camper mentioned that we should make it an annual event. Word got around and we now do 3 to 4 a year and at times have had to cut off reservations at 300. Many people asked for our recipe so we pared it down to accommodate 10 chicken halves.

Camp Bell Campground is located in the heart of New York's Finger Lake Region. It is a modern, clean family campground within minutes of Corning Glass Center, Wine Country, Watkins Glen, The Soaring Capital of America, glider rides and museum, and many other attractions.

INGREDIENTS
1 egg
1 c. salad oil
2 c. vinegar
3 Tbsp. salt
1 Tbsp. poultry seasoning
2 Tbsp. garlic salt
1 tsp. pepper
10 chicken halves
10 lb. charcoal

DIRECTIONS
In large mixing bowl, beat egg until frothy. Slowly add ¼ cup of the oil. Slowly add the dry ingredients beating constantly, then add remaining oil and vinegar. Place chicken halves on grill over charcoal fire. When chicken is warm, baste with sauce, then baste with sauce every time you turn the chicken. Takes approximately 2 hrs. Chicken is done when the leg turns easily.

CHICKEN LA JOIE
Willits-Ukiah KOA — Willits, CA

I like this recipe for two reasons. One is because it's a great meal served with rice and a salad. The other reason is because you can make it ahead of time, reheat and serve this hearty meal after a busy day at the campground.

Nestled at the western edge of Little Lake Valley, our campground has a real country atmosphere with large oak trees and grassy tent sites. You can board the famous "Skunk Train" right here at our depot for a fabulous ride through the redwoods to the coast. We're open all year and offer large pull-thru sites with full hookups, a swimming pool and playground for the kids.

INGREDIENTS
6 chicken breasts, skinned
1 can cheddar cheese soup
1 can cream of mushroom soup
1 can water
½ bag frozen green beans
3-4 Tbsp. butter or margarine
1 med. onion, cut lengthwise
1 sm. garlic clove, minced
½ bag frozen sliced carrots
1 sm. can mushroom pieces
pepper to taste

DIRECTIONS
In a large skillet or frying pan, brown chicken with onion, garlic and margarine. In a large bowl, mix together mushroom soup, cheddar cheese soup, water, mushrooms and pepper. Pour over chicken in skillet. Stir in green beans and carrots. Cover and simmer for 30 to 45 min. until chicken is tender. Serve over rice.

SMOKED STUFFED CHICKEN BREASTS
Morningside Park – Loch Sheldrake, NY

Throughout the season we hold potlucks for our guests. Often this is the entree we serve and our campers always ask for the recipe. We are located in the Catskill Mountains on an excellent large-mouth bass lake. We have hiking trails, swimming pool, tennis courts, baseball field, staff naturalist for guided hikes, primitive sites as well as water and electric hookups for trailers.

INGREDIENTS
6 chicken breasts pounded flat
1 box frozen creamed spinach
3 oz. crumbled pecans
6 oz. Monterey jack cheese
**   with jalapeno peppers**
Frangelico liqueur

DIRECTIONS
Lay chicken breasts flat. Place a layer of spinach and crushed pecans on breasts, sprinkle with liqueur and place thin slices of cheese on top. Carefully take the breasts and roll them, holding them together with toothpicks. Place them on your grill using hickory chips, smoke them and serve hot.

CHICKEN AND SAUSAGE JAMBALAYA
Baton Rouge-KOA – Denham Springs, LA

We like this recipe because it's easy to prepare. Occasionally we even prepare this and serve it to our guests.

Our campground is located in the heart of "Plantation Country" where some of the best food in the world is served. We offer daily tours going to the plantation homes as well as New Orleans. Our KOA has shady, wooded sites in a quiet atmosphere, with a rec hall, swimming pool, playground and more.

INGREDIENTS
- 1½ c. vegetable oil
- 2 chickens, cut up and seasoned
- 2 lb. sausage, cut in 1½" pieces
- 2-1 lb. cans tomatoes
- 5 c. long grain rice *
- 10 c. water
- 4 lbs. onions
- 5 cloves garlic
- 1 bunch shallots (green onions & tops)
- 1 bell pepper
- salt, black pepper & red pepper to taste

* proportion of water to rice is always 2 to 1

DIRECTIONS

Brown seasoned chicken in hot oil, preferably in 12-qt. black iron pot, or at least a cast aluminum pot. Next, brown sausage well. Remove meat and most of the oil, and add onions, garlic, bell pepper and shallots. It is extremely important to brown these vegetables well. You may have to add a little water from time to time to keep them from sticking.

Put chicken and sausage back in the pot along with all the water and tomatoes. Add salt and pepper. When the mixture comes to a rolling boil, add the washed rice. When this reaches a good boil again, lower the fire a little and let all the water boil out. Stir well, lower the fire, and cover. After 15 min., uncover, stir well once more and then cover again. Do not keep stirring, but leave undisturbed over a low fire for 45 min. Excess stirring makes the rice mushy. Serves 16 to 20 people.

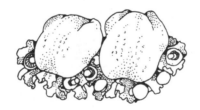

CHICKEN ROLL
Lakeview Marina & RV Resort – Taylor, AR

This dish is a favorite here. And best of all, it's quick and easy to prepare.

Lakeview Marina is located on beautiful Lake Erling. Boating, fishing, swimming and picnicking are favorite pasttimes here. We offer furnished cabins, RV hookups, boat rentals, sporting goods store and gift shop. Come visit us where you'll find great southern fishing all year 'round.

INGREDIENTS
- 6 chicken breasts
- 2 cans crescent roll
- cheddar cheese, grated
- 1 can chicken broth

DIRECTIONS

Boil or bake chicken breasts until tender. (Save the broth from the chicken.) Unroll crescent dough individually. Place pieces of chicken and grated cheese on each one and roll the dough back up. Pour chicken broth and can of chicken broth over the rolls. Then cover with grated cheese and bake at 350° until brown.

CHICKEN A LA KING MICROWAVE STYLE
Scottyland Camping Resort & RV Sales-Rockwood, PA

This is a favorite because my husband thinks I have slaved over it; however, it is extremely easy and quick. You can make it in the microwave or on the stove. It's even a breeze to prepare while camping, which I always do.

Scottyland is rated 5W by Woodall's and focuses on family fun. We have a constant activities program that is free of charge. We offer fishing in a stocked lake and state-stocked trout stream. Scottyland has a swimming pool, skating rink, live entertainment, restaurant and more. All on 300 acres of mountainous beauty. Come enjoy a fun-filled vacation with us.

INGREDIENTS
- ¼ c. margarine
- ¼ c. shredded carrots
- ¼ c. chopped celery
- ¼ c. chopped onion
- ¼ c. all purpose flour
- ½ tsp. salt
- 1 c. chicken broth
- 1 c. milk
- 2 c. cooked chicken
- 2½ oz. mushrooms, fresh or canned
- frozen patty shells

DIRECTIONS

Preheat oven to 400°. Bake puff pastry shells on cookie sheet for 20 min. In a deep 2-qt. casserole dish, combine margarine, carrots, celery and onion. Microwave on high for 5 min. or until vegetables are tender. (Stir after 2½ min.) Blend in flour and salt. Microwave on high for 30 seconds. Stir in broth and milk. Microwave on high for 4-5 min. or until thickened and bubbly. Stir every minute. Mixture should be thick and smooth. Stir in chicken and mushrooms. Cover and microwave on high for 3 min. or until heated through. Stir. Serve in patty shells or over toast triangles or mashed potatoes. Makes 4 servings.

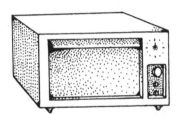

BROWN BAG CHICKEN
Heceta Beach RV Park – Florence, OR

Brown Bag Chicken is easy to prepare, juicy, tender and easy to clean up. It's great for RVers.

Our park offers large, wooded sites. We're only three blocks from the beach so you can enjoy fun in the sun. Come and stay with us and experience the peace and quiet we have to offer.

INGREDIENTS
- celery salt
- paprika
- garlic salt
- onion salt
- pepper
- chicken

DIRECTIONS

Make a shaker of equal parts of first four spices. Add pepper to taste. Cover chicken with mixture. Put chicken in brown grocery bag and place in pan to catch drippings. Bake at 375° for 1½ hrs.

CHICKEN SPAGHETTI
Spring Oaks Mobile Home Community – Spring, TX

We all enjoy sitting together for our potluck dinners and the special request is always my chicken spaghetti. We serve this with all different kinds of salads and garlic bread. It's even better warmed over the next day, that is, if there are any leftovers (usually there aren't any).

Our park is located in the Spring area, outside of the hustle and bustle of Houston living. We are located 3 miles west off of Interstate 45 at the Tomball Exit (#70A). We offer quiet, country living with full hookups. Our park is a great place to stay when away from home. We're only 3½ miles from old Town Spring with 85 craft and gift shops. We are also close to Splash Town and many other sites of interest. We offer activities to keep the whole family busy.

INGREDIENTS
- 1 chicken
- 2 eggs
- 1 can cream of mushroom soup
- 1 lb. long spaghetti
- 1 lb. Velveeta cheese
- 2 c. chicken broth
- butter
- salt and pepper to taste

DIRECTIONS
Boil chicken in large pan with salt, pepper and butter until tender. Remove 2 cups of broth and set aside. Grate cheeses. Bone and skin chicken. Cut chicken into small pieces. Beat eggs well and add soup, broth, cheese and chicken pieces. Boil spaghetti. Drain and pour creamy mixture into spaghetti and mix well. Serve with salad and garlic bread.

EMERGENCY CHICKEN DELIGHT
The Landing Campground – Sylvan Beach, NY

Being self-employed and very much involved with CONY (Campground Owners of New York), I have very little time for the kitchen. This recipe was born when I remembered at 4:00 p.m. that our monthly CONY pass a dish dinner meeting was at 6:00 pm. It was a great success.

The Landing Campground, located on Fish Creek is a major tributary to Oneida Lake, the largest inland lake in New York state. The campground is a 15 acre peninsula bordered on one side by a beautiful sandy beach, giving us some of the best swimming in the area. The other side accommodates our boat launch and docks. The fishing is great!

INGREDIENTS
- 1 16 oz. bag frozen broccoli pieces
- 8 regular slices swiss cheese
- 6 thin slices boiled ham
- 1 10¾ oz. can condensed cream of celery soup
- 2 lb. fresh boneless, skinless chicken breast strips

DIRECTIONS
Spread frozen broccoli in a two qt. oval baking pan. Cover with cheese, then ham, and top with chicken breast. Spread cream of celery soup to cover contents. Bake approximately 1 hr. at 375° until chicken is tender. Serve with a seasoned rice. Makes 4 servings.

CHICKEN HAWAIIAN
Indian Rock RV Resort & Campground-Jackson, NJ

This is a favorite recipe at Indian Rock Campground. We serve it at our Luau Weekend and various other times during the season. It's light and easy to make. Summertime is the perfect time to cook using fresh fruit and we think Indian Rock RV Resort & Campground at Luau Weekend is the next best thing to Maui!

We're located in central New Jersey, about ½ hour from the Jersey Shore and in the peaceful New Jersey Pinelands. It's a very tranquil campground, but with lots of activities and great family fun.

INGREDIENTS
4 boneless and skinless chicken breasts
juice of 1 lemon
1 fresh pineapple
fresh fruit, any type, we recommend a bunch of grapes, 1 apple, 2 bananas
8-10 cloves
4 Tbsp. butter
½ c. sugar
1 tsp. cornstarch
1 c. water

DIRECTIONS
Cut chicken breasts in slices. Saute in butter over low flame. Cut fresh fruit and squeeze ½ of the lemon juice over the fruit. Set aside. Mix sugar, cloves, water and rest of lemon juice. Cook until thickened. Remove juice from fresh fruit, which has been sitting, and add to cooked sugar mixture. Blend well. Take chicken breast and cook in fruit mix for two minutes. Turn onto platter. Decorate with pineapple rings, bananas and grapes. We serve this dish with white rice. Cooking time is about 10 min. Serves 4.

CHICKEN CORDON BLEU
Colonial R.V. Resort – Four Oaks, NC

This recipe is dished up at our potluck get togethers. Colonial RV Resort offers level pull-thru sites, spotless restrooms, swimming and mini golf. We try our hardest to keep our customers happy.

INGREDIENTS
6 chicken cutlets — split and pounded
Italian flavored bread crumbs
1½ lb. boiled deli ham
1 lb. swiss cheese sliced thin

DIRECTIONS
Lay out chicken cutlets on counter top. Place a piece of cheese and a piece of ham on top of each cutlet. Roll all of it to the end, so it looks like a roll. Then wrap and tie with string. Dip in water and bread crumbs and fry in butter until golden and cheese melts.

ROAST DUCK & APPLE RAISIN STUFFING
Smokey Hollow Campground – Lodi, WI

Roast duck is a nice main dish to prepare in an RV oven or on a grill. Lodi, Wisconsin has been named after "Susie the Duck". In Lodi, you will find Susie downtown with her family greeting passers by along the creek and road. We have "Susie the Duck" days with many activities for Susie and her friends. Our campground consists of 100 sites, hills, recreation room, groceries, RV parts and clean restrooms. We're a camper's campground, open all year for winter and summer sports by Lake Wisconsin.

INGREDIENTS
- 1 3-6 lb. duck
- 1 c. margarine
- 3 apples, finely chopped
- ¾ c. raisins
- 1½ c. chopped celery with leaves
- ¾ c. chopped onion
- ½ tsp. sage
- 1 tsp. salt
- ½ tsp. thyme
- ¼ tsp. pepper
- 9 c. soft bread cubes

DIRECTIONS

Wash duck. Mix all ingredients except margarine to make stuffing. Fill duck with stuffing. Cross duck legs. Cook 3½ lb. duck for 2 hrs. or 5½ lb. duck for 3 hrs. at 350°. Baste occasionally. Brush with margarine. Do not cover.

ROAST DUCK DRESSING
Mom & Pop RV Park – Farmington, NM

We are located at the southeast end of Farmington on Highway 64. We are the central point for 16 Indian and historical day trip tourist attractions in our area, plus home of the world famous Anasazi Indian Pageant. All of our sites are paved and the pull-thrus will handle the longest of rigs. Our gift shop contains original, handcrafted Christmas decorations, and metallic, handcrafted toy soldier chess sets, plus toy soldier museum. Gramma brought this recipe from Germany. This recipe is often standard fare at holidays. One bite and you'll be going back for more.

INGREDIENTS
- 2 regular ducks
- ¼ lb. pork sausage
- ¼ med. head of cabbage
- 1 Tbsp. butter or margarine
- 1 tsp. salt
- 2 med. onions
- ¼ tsp. nutmeg
- 1 loaf of bread
- 2 eggs
- 3 bacon strips

DIRECTIONS

Put sausage, onions, and cabbage through food processor. Soak bread in milk, squeeze dry. Mix all ingredients together except bacon. Salt inside of duck. Fill both ends of duck with stuffing and truss. Place bacon strips on top of duck and wrap in foil. Place on rack inside of roasting pan. Roast duck at 350° for 2 hrs. or until done. Remove grease from bottom of pan as needed. Remove foil and brown duck as desired.

"GARBAGE CAN" TURKEY
Lakewood South Campground – Davenport, FL

We at Lakewood South pride ourselves on being a very personalized and sociable park. We create a "one big family" atmosphere here, thereby providing a comfortable "home away from home" for our winter guests. Our return rate is very high and we feel it is due to the caring with which we treat each and every one of our guests. One of the tools with which we work is man's favorite pastime, EATING. We have several large park dinners per season in addition to weekly potlucks and frequent get-together meals for invited guests. One of the special meals we enjoyed recently was "Garbage Can" Turkey.

INGREDIENTS
- **1 10 gal. galvanized garbage pail**
- **1 2″ x 2″ wooden stake — 2 ft. long**
- **10 lb. charcoal brickettes**
- **heavy duty aluminum foil — 18″ wide**
- **10-12½ lb. turkey, thawed, washed & dried**
- **1 shovel**

DIRECTIONS

Light entire 10 lb. charcoal in a pile. Let burn for about 20 min. until white. While coals are heating, drive stake into ground, leaving about 12″ extending above ground. Wrap stake with aluminum foil. Spread additional foil on ground around stake to make an area about 3 ft. Place turkey on stake through open butt end with the neck up. Invert a metal garbage can over turkey. Make sure top and sides of container *do not* touch bird. Shovel one layer of burning coals over top area of garbage can. Shovel remainder of coals evenly around base of can, touching can all the way around. Let cook 90 min. undisturbed. After 90 min. carefully remove hot ashes from top and sides of can. Lift off can carefully and remove turkey from stake. Carve and serve.

CHOW MEIN DINNER
The Alamo Rec-Veh Park – Alamo, TX

The Alamo Rec-Veh Park consists of 375 spaces offering full hookups, blacktop parking and concrete patios. We offer a large variety of amenities and there's always something to do here. Take advantage of our stocked 8 acre fishing lake, indoor swimming pool and therapeutic spa or reading room with a color TV. Residents can take part in our near limitless activities including arts & crafts classes, square and ballroom dancing, physical fitness classes, shuffleboard courts, costume parties, talent shows, potlucks and much more! Come and join the fun!

INGREDIENTS
- ½ c. oleo
- 5 c. cooked turkey, chicken or pork
- 2 c. chopped onion
- 6 c. cut celery
- 2 Tbsp. salt
- ½ tsp. msg
- ½ tsp. pepper
- 3½ c. broth
- 3 c. Chinese vegetables
- soy sauce to taste
- cornstarch
- rice or noodles

DIRECTIONS

Saute onions and celery in oleo. Add rest of ingredients, except vegetables and cook. Stir in vegetables. Thicken mixture with cornstarch. Serve over rice or chow mein noodles. Serves 12.

BEEF STRIPS ORIENTAL
Creekside Mobile Estates – Shingletown, CA

This recipe is easy to prepare whether it's in the kitchen of your RV or over a campfire.

We are located about 30 miles east of Redding on Hwy. 44. There is a variety of nice lakes in our area for fishing in addition to a creek filled with brown trout that runs through our property. Lassen Park is also nearby with trails for hikers. If you like country air and water that tastes like spring water, we have it here at our park. We also provide laundry and shower facilities for our guests. Come and join us in the beautiful Lassen Mountain area.

INGREDIENTS
- 1 lb. round steak, ¾" thick
- 1 c. water
- 2 Tbsp. soy sauce
- 1 clove garlic
- 2 c. green pepper, cut into strips
- 1 c. carrot, cut into strips
- 2 c. mushroom halves
- ¼ c. cold water
- 2 Tbsp. cornstarch
- ½ c. parmesan cheese, grated

DIRECTIONS

Cut meat into 3" strips. Brown in oil. Add water, soy sauce and garlic. Cover and simmer for 30 min. Add vegetables, cover and simmer for 20 min. Combine ¼ c. water and cornstarch; add gradually to mixture. Boil and stir until thick. Stir in cheese. Serve over hot rice.

SEAFOOD ENCHILADAS
Campland On the Bay – San Diego, CA

San Diego is only twenty minutes from the Mexican border and is located on Mission Bay of the Pacific Ocean. This makes the availability of seafood not only easy, but it gives us a great variety. Along with the influence of our southern neighbors, this combination makes an excellent entree which is easy to prepare.

Campland On the Bay is a complete destination RV and tenting resort. Facilities include, but are not limited to: sand swim beach, pools, jacuzzi, marina, boat launch, market, restaurant, and much more. A combination of all things the "Finest City in America" has to offer and the facilities of a top rated campground make Campland On the Bay perfect for family vacations, banquets or club gatherings.

INGREDIENTS
- **1 lb. mixed seafood (shrimp, crab, fish)**
- **1 c. sour cream**
- **1 c. shredded jack cheese**
- **½ tsp. salt**
- **½ tsp. white pepper**
- **¼ tsp. garlic powder**
- **12-inch flour tortillas**
- **1 c. hollandaise sauce**
- **1 avocado**

DIRECTIONS

Mix all ingredients except tortillas, hollandaise, and avocado. Place approximately ½ cup of mixture in each tortilla, folding ends. Bake at 350° for 15 min. Place on serving dish, cover with hollandaise and place avocado fanned out over top. Serve.

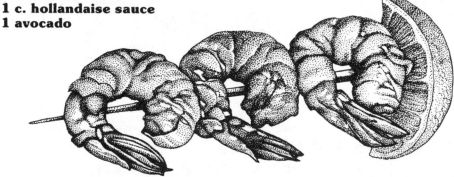

BOILED SHRIMP
Island RV Resort – Port Aransas, TX

Shrimp is found in abundance here and as such it's a favorite of the locals as well as our guests. This recipe is so easy to prepare and it calls for ingredients most campers have on hand.

INGREDIENTS
- **whole shrimp (with heads still on if possible)**
- **water**
- **lemon butter**

DIRECTIONS

Bring water to a boil. Toss in shrimp, stirring gently. Cook for 3 min. (don't return to a boil). Drain and immerse shrimp in cold water to prevent overcooking. Remove the heads but leave in shell until ready to serve. This process allows shrimp to cook in their own juices and not dry out. Serve with lemon butter.

CRABBIES
Big Oaks Family Campground – Rehoboth Beach, DE

Rehoboth Beach is known as the nation's summer capital with plenty of fish, delicious blue claw crabs, and clams for the taking.

Big Oaks is located three miles from the ocean and bays, nestled in a quiet wooded area. Our campers love to eat the seafood they catch and this recipe is one of many taking advantage of the excellent fish and seafood in our area.

INGREDIENTS
- **1 stick butter or margarine**
- **1 jar cheese spread**
- **1½ tsp. mayonnaise**
- **½ tsp. garlic salt**
- **½ tsp. seasoned salt**
- **6-7 oz. crabmeat, fresh or frozen**
- **6-8 English muffins, split**

DIRECTIONS
Soften butter and cheese at room temperature. Mix together with mayonnaise. Add salts and crab meat. Spread mixture on split muffins. With sharp knife cut into quarters. If serving immediately, freeze 10 minutes, then broil until bubbly and crisp. If preparing ahead of time, wrap crabbies in plastic cling wrap and freeze until needed. No need to thaw before broiling.

EASTERN SHORE CRAB CAKES
Cherrystone KOA – Cheriton, VA

We have an abundance of Chesapeake Bay Crabs to be caught from our four piers. Our park is on 300 wooded acres on the Chesapeake Bay — a complete destination resort campground of 700 sites.

INGREDIENTS
- **1 lb. crab meat**
- **1 tsp. Old Bay seasoning**
- **¼ tsp. salt**
- **1 Tbsp. mayonnaise**
- **1 tsp. Worcestershire sauce**
- **1 Tbsp. chopped parsley**
- **1 Tbsp. baking powder**
- **1 egg, beaten**
- **2 slices bread (crust removed)**

DIRECTIONS
Break bread into small pieces and moisten with milk. Mix ingredients and shape into cakes. Fry quickly until brown.

FIESTA KEY SHRIMP
KOA-Fiesta Key – Long Key, FL

This tasty dish is served in our restaurant in season. Catch your own shrimp off the docks or in the Gulf on our boats.

Fiesta Key KOA is a resort campground located on its own island surrounded by warm ocean waters. We are truly a camping resort nestled in the heart of the Key's tropical paradise. The park offers a gigantic swimming pool, two hot tubs, boat rentals, full-service marina, waterfront pub and restaurant, motel units, waterfront sites, tent village, a paved dog run, convenience store and more.

INGREDIENTS
- **2 lbs. fresh shrimp, unshelled**
- **1 lb. butter**
- **1 lb. margarine**
- **salt & pepper to taste**
- **sprinkling of minced parsley**

DIRECTIONS

Wash shrimp, leaving shell on. Pat dry and arrange in glass baking dish. Sprinkle with salt and pepper to taste. Add parsley sprinkles. Cut butter and margarine into ½ inch chunks. Add to other ingredients in dish. Bake at 375° for 35 min. Serve with French bread and lots of napkins.

SHRIMPLY DELICIOUS
Hub Total RV Park – Fallon, NV

Being a manager doesn't give me much time to cook. This recipe is quick and easy and tastes so good. It really is shrimply delicious.

We are 3 miles west of Fallon, Nevada, which is known as the Oasis of Nevada. You'll find lots of fun at our park as well as lots of smiles. We treat you like family because we believe each customer is special!

INGREDIENTS
- **1½ lb. raw, deveined shrimp**
- **2 Tbsp. lemon juice**
- **½ c. butter**
- **½ c. bread crumbs**
- **½ tsp. minced garlic or onion**
- **2 Tbsp. chopped parsley**
- **1 Tbsp. Parmesan cheese**
- **1 Tbsp. oregano**

DIRECTIONS

Arrange shrimp on a 9″ buttered pie plate. Sprinkle shrimp with lemon juice. Combine butter, bread crumbs, garlic or onion, and parsley. Spoon over shrimp. Bake at 350° for 15 min. Broil 3 min. to brown crumbs. Garnish with parsley and lemon.

POOR MAN'S LOBSTER
White River Campground – Montague, MI

White River Campground has many unique features. You'll be impressed by the rustic, secluded, natural setting. We're in the Manistee National Forest on the banks of the White River. To further enhance your stay with us, our campground offers a heated swimming pool, a sandy beach, picnic shelter and more. We're close to Lake Michigan, known for its abundance of salmon during the fall. This recipe offers another way to prepare your catch. It's simple to prepare and serve; all you need to add is a salad and dessert and you have a complete meal. And it really does taste like lobster.

INGREDIENTS
  fish *
  salt
  onions, quartered
  potatoes, quartered
  melted butter or margarine

  * coho, chinook salmon or
    large lake trout

DIRECTIONS
  Fill pot about ½ full of water and bring to a boil. Fill bottom with onions and potatoes; bring water back to a boil. Sprinkle in salt, do not lose boil (4 cups salt for large pot or 1 cup for small pot); boil 13 min. and add fish. Bring back to a boil and boil 12-13 min. Fish should be white in color and flakey. Serve with melted butter or margarine.

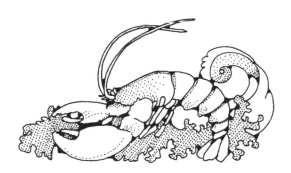

CLASSIC NEW MEXICO RED ENCHILADAS
Hunt's Trailer Park – Tucumcari, NM

Tourists coming to our park often want to sample authentic Mexican food. Tucumcari has many restaurants that serve good Mexican dishes and this recipe is just one of our many favorites. Our park is located in Tucumcari and we offer full hookup sites with modern restrooms.

INGREDIENTS
  12 corn tortillas
  ⅓ c. vegetable oil
  3 c. red chile sauce (picante)
  3 c. grated longhorn cheese
  2 sm. onions, minced
  4 eggs (optional)
  pinto beans

DIRECTIONS
  Fry tortillas in oil until soft and drain on paper towel. Heat chile sauce. Layer tortillas on serving plates, topping each with grated cheese and minced onions and sauce. Stack 3 per serving plate and top with cheese and sauce. Put plates in oven to allow cheese to melt. Meanwhile, fry eggs in remaining oil. Top each enchilada stack with a fried egg. Serve immediately with a bowl of pinto beans.

OLE FASHION DOWNEAST LOBSTER BAKE
Virginia Park Campground—Old Orchard Beach, ME

Our park, located in the quiet Ocean Park section of Old Orchard Beach, has 130 sites with 95 hookups. We offer clean and quiet family camping under the pines or hardwood trees. We also have a pool, playground, convenience store, clean restrooms and a warm family atmosphere. Lobster bakes are a weekly event.

INGREDIENTS (per person)
- 1 lobster
- 1 lb. clams
- 1 egg
- 1 onion
- 1 ear of corn
- 1 potato
- seaweed

DIRECTIONS

Place a bed of seaweed in a 4″ x 8″ pan. Place live lobster on the seaweed. Place cheesecloth bag containing the clams, egg, corn, onion and potato over the lobster. Cover with seaweed. Cover it all with burlap bag and a canvas topping tucked tightly beneath the lower seaweed bed. Cook over fire for 45 min. Serve and enjoy.

BOILED LOBSTER
Meadowbrook Camping Area – Bath, ME

During the summer we cook lobsters and clams each night here at our campground. Fresh lobsters and clams are always available here and this recipe is easy to prepare. Everyone loves it.

Meadowbrook Camping offers natural spacious RV and tent sites on 60 acres. We provide a swim pool, mini golf course, laundry facilities, dump station, seasonal sites, bathhouse and more. Come visit us and feast on fresh lobster and clam to your heart's content.

INGREDIENTS
- 1-2 lb. lobster
- salt

DIRECTIONS

In a deep kettle, have enough boiling water to cover lobster. Add 2 tsp. of salt per 1 qt. of water. Put lobster in boiling water head first. Cover and boil for about 5 min. Remove cover and simmer about 20 min.

BBQ SALMON – INDIAN STYLE
Capilano RV Park – Vancouver, BC

During season, fresh salmon is abundant in our area. For a different way of preparing salmon, try it Indian style.

Our park is located at the northwest end of Lions Gate Bridge in northern Vancouver. We offer full hookups, dumping and propane stations, clean restrooms and laundry facilities to satisfy your creature comforts. For your entertainment needs, we offer a swimming pool, jacuzzi room, playground and game rooms. Since we're only 5 min. to downtown Vancouver, you can also enjoy all the attractions the city offers.

INGREDIENTS
   fresh salmon, sockeye or chum
   salt
   brown sugar

DIRECTIONS

Dig a pit 4 x 12 feet and fill with rocks. Place firewood (alder wood works best) the length of the pit. Put a large cedar stick upright in the ground at each end of the pit. These support sticks should be split halfway down the center so that fish will be suspended four feet above alder fire.

Make an incision along the top backside on each side of the bone of the fish. Remove backbone and entrails. Do not scale the fish. Soak salmon in salt and brown sugar.

Spread salmon on cedar sticks along each side and bind tips with wire. Insert a large cedar stick lengthwise all the way through the fish.

When fire has burned down to coals and the rocks are hot, place large cedar stick holding the salmon onto the "Y" formation of the supporting cedar sticks. Rotate salmon over coals until salmon ceases dripping juices. Serve hot.

CRANBERRY COAST BARBEQUED SALMON
Kenanna RV Park – Grayland, WA

Our park is located near Westport, the salmon capital of the world, and this salmon recipe is often prepared by our guests.

We are located on the coast in the middle of the Cranberry Coast, so called for the berries raised in the area. We are near Westport and Tokeland, both great for all kinds of fishing. We have 100 sites, a barbeque, recreation hall, and all the amenities necessary for comfortable camping. When people get tired of fishing, there are historical buildings, unique gift shops and studios, and 14 miles of beach to enjoy.

INGREDIENTS
   3 lbs. salmon fillets
   ½ tsp. salt
   ½ tsp. garlic salt
   ⅓ c. salad oil
   ⅓ c. soy sauce
   ⅓ c. bourbon

DIRECTIONS

Sprinkle salmon with salt and garlic salt, and let set 30 min. Combine oil, soy sauce and bourbon. Have charcoal burned down to grey, and coals about 1 inch apart. In wire basket or hinged broiler, put salmon about 5″ or 6″ above coals. Baste frequently with soy mixture. Remove when fish flakes — about 20 min. Serves 4 to 6.

BBQ SALMON
Eureka KOA – Eureka, CA

The Eureka KOA is located on the north coast of California on Hwy. 101, just 4 mi. north of Eureka. We have the Redwoods nearby along with sandy beaches, rivers and lots of sightseeing opportunities. My husband prepares this dish during the salmon season and we put it out near our registration counter for our customers to enjoy. It's always a big hit — in fact there just never seems to be enough.

INGREDIENTS
- **part or whole sm. salmon**
- **1 celery stalk, finely chopped**
- **1 can smoked oysters, drained & minced**
- **½ med. green apple, pared & diced**
- **1 sm. bag stuffing mix, seasoned**
- **¼ c. bacon fat**
- **lemon juice**
- **lemon pepper**
- **salt & pepper to taste**

DIRECTIONS

Preheat BBQ. Clean salmon and pat cavity and outside dry. Sprinkle inside with lemon juice and lemon pepper. Set aside. Mix the rest of the ingredients thoroughly, then pack the cavity. Place the salmon on heavy duty foil. Put remaining ingredients around outside of salmon. Sprinkle outside with lemon juice and lemon pepper. Seal foil tightly. Place on medium hot BBQ for 30 to 45 min. Open top of foil and let cook at low for another 30 min. After salmon has been removed from BBQ, let cool for a few min. Then remove all dressing from salmon and throw away. Salmon should fall away from bones and skin.

SMOKED SALMON
Heriot Bay Inn & Marina – Quadra Island, BC

Fishing is a favorite camper activity — then the afternoons are often spent sharing smoking and canning ideas with new friends. The Heriot Bay Inn is a historic guesthouse surrounded by 7 acres of beachfront R.V. park. Its marina served for many years as a Union Steamship dock, servicing the many small island communities accessible only by water even today. Rental boats or marina space are available to guests for exploring this lovely wilderness area and catching their supper at the same time!

INGREDIENTS
Brine:
- **1 qt. water**
- **½ c. canning salt**
- **½ c. brown sugar**
- **½ tsp. liquid garlic**
- **½ tsp. liquid onion**

DIRECTIONS

Mix brine thoroughly in a non-metal container. Soak fish for at least 12 hr., turning several times. Then dry fish in smoker 6-8 hr. using favorite wood such as alder or cherry chips.

TROUT COOKED IN FOIL
Yogi in the Smokies – Cherokee, NC

Our park consists of 210 sites on 100 heavily forested acres in the heart of the Smokey Mountains. A trout stream/river runs the entire length of the campground and a fish farm is nearby. Everyone wants trout!

INGREDIENTS
  2 fresh trout
  lemon to taste
  salt & pepper to taste
  1 Tbsp. butter

DIRECTIONS
  Place cleaned trout on heavy aluminum foil. Fill cavity with slices of lemon and butter. Salt and pepper to taste. Wrap foil around trout and cook over fire until done — about 15 minutes on a hot fire. Turn every few minutes.

STEELHEAD, DEAN CREEK STYLE
Dean Creek Resort – Redway, CA

Our park is noted for its fine Salmon and Steelhead winter fishing. We bring in our share of beauties which we enjoy or give away to the "no-luck" fishermen. This recipe is my favorite and one that I often share with our campers. We're located on the banks of the South Fork of the Eel River in northwest California, close to the beautiful state redwood parks. We boast full and partial hookups (cable TV to all sites) and a motel (some units have kitchens). We have a fish cleaning area, take Polaroid pictures of the ones that didn't get away and have freezer space available for your fish.

INGREDIENTS
  fresh Steelhead, skinned &
    filleted
  Avocado oil
  Shoffeitt's Flavor Crystals*
  3-6 garlic cloves
  dry dill weed
  dry white wine

  ***California product**

DIRECTIONS
  Heat about 3 Tbsp of oil in electric fry pan. Add 3-6 whole peeled garlic cloves and fry until golden brown. Remove from oil. Add serving size pieces of steelhead, sprinkle with flavor crystals and dill weed. Fry about 3 min. or until lightly browned. Turn and sprinkle again with seasonings. Add 3 to 5 Tbsp. of wine, cover and poach about 5 min., depending on thickness of fish. Be careful — don't overcook! Serve with lemon wedges and white wine.

FISH BAKED IN FOIL
Pine Acres Resort and Campground – Orr, MN

We are located on Pelican Lake in northern Minnesota. Many fishermen camp with us. They are always looking for a new way to cook all the fish they catch and this is a great one.

We have over 100 campsites in this rocky, wooded area of northern Minnesota. It is beautiful country with many lakes and wildlife all around us.

INGREDIENTS
3 lb. fish fillets
salt & pepper to taste
dash of red pepper
2 Tbsp. flour
4 Tbsp. salad oil
2 cloves garlic
½ lg. green or red pepper
¼ lb. mushrooms
½ c. onion diced
½ c. white wine
1 med. tomato, peeled & diced
1 Tbsp. lemon juice
1 tsp. minced parsley
1 tsp. tarragon

DIRECTIONS
Dredge fish in flour, salt and peppers. Heat oil in skillet and add garlic. Quickly brown fish on both sides. Place fish in center of large piece of foil. Saute peppers, onions, and mushrooms and place on top of fish. Add wine to remaining ingredients in pan and bring to boil. Pour mixture over fish. Seal foil edges tightly around the fish and place in shallow baking dish. Bake 20 minutes at 425°. Or you may grill over medium heat for 30 minutes, flipping carefully once or twice. Makes 4 servings. Delicious!

MY FAVORITE FISH DISH
Bell's Trailer Park – Wilbur, WA

Our park is situated near several large bodies of water including Roosevelt Lake which is 55 miles long. A variety of fish can be caught in our area and this recipe is great for whatever you catch. We have 30 level, grassy spaces with full hookups, laundry, hot showers, picnic tables with patios, ice and telephones.

INGREDIENTS
2 lb. fillets
¼ tsp. salt
¼ tsp. pepper
¼ tsp. paprika
4 Tbsp. lemon juice
2 Tbsp. margarine
2 Tbsp. flour
1 Tbsp. mustard
1 c. milk
½ c. buttered bread crumbs
1 Tbsp. minced parsley

DIRECTIONS
Arrange fillets in greased baking pan. Sprinkle with salt, pepper, paprika and lemon juice. Melt margarine and blend in flour and mustard. Add milk slowly, making a white sauce. Season with salt and pepper. Pour over fillets. Combine bread crumbs and melted butter. Sprinkle crumbs and parsley over fillets. Bake uncovered at 350° for 30 min.

BAKED FISH
Ocean Gate Resort – Grayland, WA

Enjoy this easy, no-mess recipe using your catch of the day.
We're an oceanfront RV park and offer full and partial hookups. We have access to the beautiful Pacific Ocean where you can surf, swim, clam or just relax in the sun on the beach. Come enjoy yourself Ocean Gate style.

INGREDIENTS
pan fish, fresh or saltwater
margarine or butter
lemon pepper
garlic or garlic salt
aluminum foil

DIRECTIONS
Butterfly fish. Butter and season the meat to your taste. Close fish and wrap in foil. Bake at 400° for 5-7 min. each side.

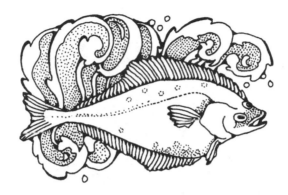

DOOR COUNTY FISH BOIL
Wagon Trail Campground – Ellison Bay, WI

We have a couple of "work weekends" every year where we offer free camping and a fish boil for a ½ day of your time in helping us with projects.
The Door County Peninsula is surrounded by water. Many of the early Scandinavian settlers were fishermen. As the fishing tugs they used did not have galleys, they would cook some of their catch on a pot bellied stove or in a pot on the beach over an open fire. Our campground is located near the end of this peninsula close to some of the fishing villages and we serve the fish boil to tie in with the local tradition. The Viking Restaurant, the "home" of the fish boil is only 3½ miles from our campground.

INGREDIENTS
16 chunks of whitefish (2-inch slices)
16 sm. red potatoes with ends cut off
16 peeled sm. onions
½ lb. salt
2 gal. water

DIRECTIONS
Add ¼ lb. of salt to water and bring to a boil. Add potatoes to water and boil for 16 min. Add onions and boil for 4 min. more. Add fish and ¼ lb. salt. Boil for 10 min. then drain into colander. Yields 8 servings. Serve with melted butter, lemon, cole slaw and bread or rolls. Add a slice of Door County cherry pie for dessert.

GRILLED TROUT
White River Campground – Cotter, AR

The White River system of Arkansas, situated below the Bull Shoals Dam, has become a favorite of fishermen for world record Rainbow and Brown Trout. White River Campground is at the edge of Cotter, a small town boasted as the "Trout Capitol of the World." Different ways of preparing these fine eating fish have always been fun and rewarding for the fishermen that travel from all over the world to fish these waters. This tasty recipe is designed especially for our angler campers.

INGREDIENTS
- **6 or 8 trout fillets**
- **4 c. water**
- **¼ tsp. salt**
- **2 tsp. sugar**
- **3 Tbsp. lemon juice**
- **paprika**
- **lemon salt**
- **1 sm. onion**
- **1 stick butter, melted**

DIRECTIONS

Fillet and skin several large trout. In bowl of water, add salt, sugar, lemon juice and fillets. Let soak in for 1 hr. Cover grill with aluminum foil and place the fillets on the grill and baste with melted butter. Season fillets with paprika, lemon salt, salt and pepper. Slice onion and place slices on fillets. Grill until fillets turn solid color and edges become slightly brown.

CAJUN TROUT
LoBo Landing Resort – Heber Springs, AR

Our park is located on a trout stream called the Little Red River. We have 25 acres of land in the foothills of the Ozarks in north central Arkansas.

INGREDIENTS
- **Rainbow trout, skinned**
- **Tabasco sauce**
- **seasoned salt**
- **yellow cornmeal**
- **cooking oil**

DIRECTIONS

Marinate skinned trout in Tabasco sauce for 30 min. Roll in salted cornmeal and deep fry until brown and floating in the oil. Note: trout cooks quickly, do not overcook.

PAW PAW WOOTSIE'S REDFISH & BROCCOLI FEAST
Carriage Cove Mobile Home Park – Houma, LA

This recipe was created here and offers an original but authentic way to prepare Louisiana Redfish in true Creole style.

We're a 300 unit mobile home park on over 40 acres. Our amenities include RV facilities, playground, picnic area, and swimming pool. We're located in the heart of "Cajun Country."

INGREDIENTS
- 3-4 lb. redfish fillets (enough to form single layer in 11 x 17-inch pan
- 2 10-oz. pkg. frozen broccoli spears
- 1 10¾-oz. can cream of mushroom soup
- 1 10¾-oz. can cream of celery soup
- 1 10¾-oz. can cream of cheese soup
- 4 Tbsp. liquid margarine
- 1 Tbsp. garlic puree
- creole seasoning
- paprika
- 4 lemons
- 1½ c. water
- 1 Tbsp. salt

DIRECTIONS

Wash and dry fish fillets. Season to taste wtih creole seasoning, saving a tsp. to use later. Place in mixing bowl and put in refrigerator. Marinate for several hrs.

Preheat oven to 400°. In saucepan, add salt to water and bring to boil. Add frozen broccoli spears and bring to second boil. Reduce heat and simmer for five min. Drain in colander.

In mixing bowl, mix the three cans of soup thoroughly. Add 1 tsp. of creole seasoning. Do not add water to soup. Set aside.

Remove fish from refrigerator. Mix liquid margarine and garlic puree together, and pour over fish in mixing bowl. Toss fish fillets until well coated with margarine and garlic mixture. Add more margarine if necessary. Arrange fish fillets in baking pan in single layer. Place in oven and bake at 400° until fish is lightly browned, about 20 min.

While fish is browning, cut three thin slices from center of each lemon. Put aside. Remove fish from oven and squeeze remaining lemon over fish. Do not turn fish. Arrange broccoli spears on top and between fish fillets. Pour enough soup mixture over fish and broccoli to completely cover. Return to 400° oven and bake until soup is bubbling, about 20 min. Remove from oven, place reserved lemon slices on top and return to oven for 15 min. Remove from oven and sprinkle lightly with paprika. Let cool about 5 min. before serving. Garnish with fresh parsley sprigs. Serves 6.

PAN FRIED MOUNTAIN TROUT
North Carolina High Country – Linville, NC

The North Carolina High Country is an excellent destination for trout fishermen. Fresh ground cornmeal is available daily from the grist mill at the Old Hampton Store in Linville. The 6,000-foot Grandfather Mountain is the site of headwaters for hundreds of pristine mountain streams feeding dozens of scenic mountain lakes that make the North Carolina High Country one of the best trout fishing destinations in the east. Enjoy a variety of recreational opportunities and family attractions in this four season vacation destination.

INGREDIENTS
1 fresh trout, 12"-15"
½-1 c. freshly ground cornmeal
salt & pepper to taste
2 eggs
2-3 Tbsp. butter or margarine
1 fresh lemon

DIRECTIONS
Clean and rinse fresh trout. Dredge through beaten eggs and roll in cornmeal. Salt and pepper to taste. Melt butter in skillet over medium heat and add trout. Cook over medium heat about 10 min. per side, allowing more time for larger trout. Skin should be crispy brown when done and meat should pull easily from bones when well done. Be sure to turn the trout frequently to cook evenly. Squeeze lemon juice over trout before serving.

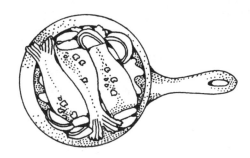

CAMPFIRE TROUT
Rainbow Springs Campground – Franklin, NC

The western North Carolina mountains and rivers attract many visitors, especially in the spring, summer and fall. One attraction is fresh mountain trout. At Rainbow Springs Campground there is many a trout cookout, since we are located on the Nantahala River. We chose this recipe as most campers will have the ingredients on hand. And if by chance you don't have any luck in the river, we have trout ponds, so either way you can still enjoy fresh mountain trout.

INGREDIENTS
fresh mountain trout
salt & pepper to taste
diced onion (optional)
butter or margarine

DIRECTIONS
Clean and gut trout (removal of head is optional). Open trout, place butter, diced onion, salt & pepper to taste. Wrap in aluminum foil. On grate over good hot coals, cook approximately 6-8 min. on each side, depending on size of trout.

BEER BATTER FISH
Lake Corpus Christi KOA – Mathis, TX

We consider ourselves the catfish capitol of the world. Located on Lake Corpus Christi, the KOA is a busy winter Texan haven from October until April 15. Fish fries are a favorite get together, with winter Texans supplying the fish.

INGREDIENTS
- 2½ c. biscuit or pancake mix
- 1 well beaten egg
- ½ tsp. salt
- 1 can beer–room temperature

DIRECTIONS

In a medium bowl mix biscuit mix, salt, egg and enough beer to make a medium batter.

Drain fish fillets on paper towel. Pat dry. Cut into 2-inch cubes or strips. Dip in batter and drop into hot oil. Cook 3 – 5 minutes or until golden brown.

BLACK HILLS TROUT PAN FRIED
Spear Fish City Campground – Spearfish, SD

Our park is located in the beautiful Black Hills of South Dakota. The highest quality trout stream in South Dakota, Spearfish Creek, flows through the campground. Many of our campers fish for trout and catch and eat them right next to their camp.

We are located in the city of Spearfish, shaded, well-maintained; adjacent to Historic Fish Hatchery.

INGREDIENTS
- 1½ lbs. trout
- ¼ c. salad dressing
- ½ c. frying fat
- ½ c. corn meal
- 1 tsp. salt
- ½ tsp. pepper

DIRECTIONS

Clean fish (may be skinned if desired). Dip lightly in salad dressing, dip in mixture of corn meal, salt and pepper. Fry in hot fat until brown. Don't overcook. Other fish may be substituted.

FISH CAKES
Bill & Bev Hoffman Lake Camp – Warsaw, IN

Our 135 site campground is located on Hoffman Lake, just one of the 99 lakes in the county. The lake is ideal for fishing and this recipe was created by one of our seasonal guests who has stayed with us for 23 years. Besides great fishing, our guests also spend time in the Amish area near Nappannee.

INGREDIENTS
- 1 c. Jiffy Mix or Bisquick
- 1 egg
- ¼ c. chopped green pepper
- ¼ c. chopped onion
- ½ tsp. salt
- ⅜ c. milk
- ½ c. chopped fish

DIRECTIONS

Combine all ingredients. Drop by spoonfuls into hot oil or shortening. Turn and flatten when brown.

CATFISH CURLS
Palisades RV Park — Albuquerque, NM

Natives and guests alike fish in the surrounding areas and bring their catch in for a fish fry. This recipe is a delicious way to prepare the catch of the day while bragging about the one that got away.

Palisades Park is a clean, quiet park on the outskirts of Albuquerque. We're near Old Town and other historic areas. In addition to this, there are three lakes within 60 mi. of us all filled with fish just waiting to be hooked.

INGREDIENTS
  catfish, cubed
  half & half
  2 eggs
  lemon juice
  flour

DIRECTIONS
  Combine eggs, half & half, and lemon juice in blender. Thicken mixture with flour. Dip catfish into egg mixture. Deep fat fry until golden brown.

STEAMED TROUT A LA OTTAWA VALLEY
Ryan's Campsites — Deep River, ONT

Ryan's Campsites has trout ponds that our campers enjoy fishing in. This recipe is one way they can prepare their catch. Our park is located on the sandy shores of the Ottawa River, beneath towering pines. We have 100 sites with electric and water hookups, modern conveniences, dock, boat ramp, wildlife museum, playground and air service.

INGREDIENTS
  trout
  5 whole cloves
  2 bay leaves
  2 Tbsp. white vinegar
  melted butter
  lemon (optional)
  onion (optional)

DIRECTIONS
  Combine cloves, bay leaves and vinegar in a saucepan. Place trout on rack above the water line. Bring to boil and cover saucepan. Steam for 15-20 min. depending on size of fish. Serve with a sauce of melted hot butter, lemon or chopped onion.

DEEP FRIED CLAM STRIPS
Riverside RV Resort – Copalis Beach, WA

Every spring during clam season we have a "clamoree". It's a potluck dinner for all our guests staying at the park. Everyone brings their favorite dish. We usually share clam strips or clam chowder.

We are located on the Copalis River, which is great for salmon and perch fishing. We're about 5 blocks from the ocean, where we dig for clams in season. We have a nice recreation room for club meetings, billiards, and a patio with a firepit for beautiful group campfires or barbeque parties. We have many activities for all ages. Come and join in the fun.

INGREDIENTS
6-8 lg. clams (5"-6")
4 Tbsp. flour
2 eggs, beaten
¼ tsp. pepper
½ tsp. onion, grated
shortening

DIRECTIONS
Cut clams into ¼" wide strips (save the necks for chowder). Mix flour, eggs, pepper, and onion. Wash clam strips, shake off excess water and roll in flour mixture. Drop into hot shortening in a large frying pan. When golden brown all over, take out and drain on paper towel. Serve hot with brussel sprouts and herb rice.

BEER BATTER STRIPER
Sandpoint Marina & RV Park – Lake Havasu City, AZ

Located on the south shore of beautiful Lake Havasu, Sandpoint is the finest fishing resort on the Colorado River, where anglers fish for their favorite striped bass (striper) fish. Sandpoint is a public resort, a concession of Arizona State Parks. We are located on the south shore of Lake Havasu (that's Indian for "blue"), 15 miles south of London Bridge. Amenities include 175 full hookup sites, planned activities, general store and cafe, tackle shop with fishing guide service available, auto and marine fuel, dump station, boat and slip rental, dry storage and complete main repair service.

INGREDIENTS
1 c. flour
1 tsp. baking powder
salt & pepper
1 egg
1 c. beer
¼ tsp. paprika
1 lb. striper fillets

DIRECTIONS
Blend together flour, baking powder, salt and pepper, egg, beer and paprika. Coat fillets with mixture and bake 20-25 min. at 325°.

CHARCOALED MULLETS
Cedar Creek Campground & Marina — Sealevel, NC

Each Labor Day we invite all of our campers to our fish fry. We provide the fish and this recipe is always a success. It's excellent!

Cedar Creek is a family-oriented campground. We offer shady sites, swimming pool, boat ramp and excellent fishing. We're located on SR 1376 in Sealevel. Hope to see you soon!

DIRECTIONS

Prepare charcoal grill at least 1 hour before you begin cooking mullets. Split, but do not scale, enough medium- to large-size mullets for number of people you wish to feed. Remove gut and head. Rinse well and drain; pat dry. Lay fish out on waxed paper on counter or table.

Salt, medium to heavy, on both sides of fish. You may wish to use paper towels under fish to help absorb moisture. Turn fish over after 2 hours; let stand 2 hours more. Turn fish over again; let set 2 hours more. This time may vary according to size of fish and how salty you want the fish.

Rinse salt off fish and lay on paper towels to dry. Spray both sides of fish with Pam before cooking; also spray grill. Cook fish meat side first, until golden brown; turn fish over and finish cooking scale-side down. Cooking time should be about 30-40 min. for each side.

Serve with coleslaw, baked beans, fresh cucumbers and tomatoes and hush puppies.

HOMEMADE BLUEBERRY PANCAKES
Branch Hollow MH & RV Park – Benton, AR

People are always amazed when they learn we make our own homemade blueberry pancakes. Someone always comments that you buy blueberry pancakes because they are so hard to prepare. This easy and delicious recipe proves just how wrong they are.

Branch Hollow offers country living with city conveniences. Just off I-30, we're conveniently located and offer shaded, grassy, full hookup sites.

INGREDIENTS
- 3½ c. flour
- 4 Tbsp. sugar
- 1 tsp. baking soda
- 1 heaping tsp. baking powder
- 1 cap of vinegar
- 1 cap of vanilla
- pinch of salt
- 2 Tbsp. vegetable oil
- 2 eggs
- 1½ c. blueberries
- 2 c. buttermilk or dry milk
- water (for texture)

DIRECTIONS

Mix together all dry ingredients. Add remaining ingredients and mix. Pour batter on greased hot griddle or frying pan. Flip cakes and cook. Serve warm.

SOUR DOUGH PANCAKES W/FRESH FRUIT
Frost Ridge Campground – LeRoy, NY

For over 15 years now, we have been serving our guests breakfast on Sunday as an expression of our thanks for choosing our park.

We are located in an old apple orchard at the base of the ski slopes. Most of our fruit comes from local farmers. We offer wooded sites with a variety of hookups, modern restrooms and lots of recreation. We also enjoy a swimming hole with tubes in a nearby creek.

INGREDIENTS
- 1 c. flour
- 1 c. milk
- 1 Tbsp. starter (yeast culture)
- 1 egg
- 1 tsp. sugar
- 1 pinch bicarbonate of soda
- 1 pinch salt
- 1 tsp. oil
- fresh fruit, in season

DIRECTIONS

A day before combine flour, milk and starter. Let set overnight — do not refrigerate. In the morning, replenish your starter and combine eggs, sugar, soda, salt, and oil in that order with the flour mixture. For thinner batter, add milk. Cook on a hot grill. Sprinkle with raspberries, strawberries, blueberries, apples, or peaches (we've tried them all) before flipping.

CRAB-SPINACH SOUFFLE
Cherry Hill Park – College Park, MD

This easy recipe for a main dish, using Maryland crabmeat, is a family favorite. We are happy to share it and hope you enjoy it.

Cherry Hill Park, the closest RV park to Washington, DC is an all new facility offering complete camping. Located just off I-95, Cherry Hill is the ideal center for families, groups and rallies visiting the Nation's Capital, Baltimore, Annapolis and the Chesapeake Bay area. We offer full hookup sites, tenting areas, heated swimming pool, sauna, hot tub, cable TV, public transportation to Washington, DC, guided bus tours and activities for the whole family. Opening 1989, Cherry Hill Park is designed for the RV of today and the future.

INGREDIENTS
- 1 pkg. frozen, chopped, spinach souffle, defrosted
- 2 lbs. small curd cottage cheese
- 6 Tbsp. flour
- 6 eggs
- 5 Tbsp. butter, diced
- ½ lb. sharp cheddar cheese, diced
- 12 oz. fresh crabmeat

DIRECTIONS
Beat eggs. Add all ingredients and mix together. Bake in a greased 9" x 13" pan at 350° for 1 hr.

SAUSAGE EGG SOUFFLE
Rio Bend RV Resort — El Centro, CA

This dish is delicious and it's easy — prepare it the day before, and you're ready for early guests. It makes a marvelous buffet dish for the many brunches we have.

We are in the desert of Southern California where the sky is huge, clear and beautiful. We're away from the cities' noises with only the coyotes, pelicans and egrets here to share Nature with us. We have so many places to explore and lots of planned activities to share. Do come.

INGREDIENTS
- 6 eggs
- 6 slices bread, cubed and no crust
- 1 lb. mild sausage
- 1 c. grated cheddar cheese
- 2 c. milk
- 1 Tbsp. dry mustard
- ½ tsp. salt

DIRECTIONS
Brown sausage, crumble and drain. Beat eggs, add milk, salt and mustard. Add bread, cheese and sausage. Put in 8" x 8" glass baking dish. Refrigerate overnight. Bake at 350° for 45 minutes.

BACON & EGGS IN THE ROCK PIT
Shallow Lake Tent & Trailer Park Camping-Hearst, ON

In the past, we have received girl scouts here and we experimented with this recipe as part of the scouts activities. Since then, many of our campers have heard and talked of our park as a fun place to stay.

We offer 163 acres of trees, trails, roads, and a lake with a private beach. Lots of wilderness trails and good fishing as well as good accommodations, laundry facilities, arcade, lots of fire wood and boat rentals make your stay at Shallow Lake a pleasant one.

INGREDIENTS
country bacon cut into thin
    sections 4″ long
1 egg
a big fire in a pit surrounded
    by rocks
lots of paper bags and red
    hot coals

DIRECTIONS
Open brown paper bag. Put pieces of bacon inside. Break egg over bacon inside the bag. Fold top of the bag and make a hole in it. Place a branch through hole to hold the bag. Alternate the coals around the fire. Cook bacon and eggs in bag over coals.

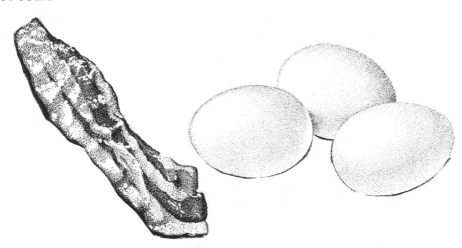

FLUFFY SCRAMBLED EGGS
Mountain View Park RV & Camping – Idanha, OR

This recipe is quick to prepare and is great for outdoor cooking. Start your day off right with this nutritious and delicious breakfast.

We're located near Detroit Lake on the Santiam River. We offer a quiet, relaxing atmosphere with beautiful scenery and river frontage. We welcome RVs, mobile homes, and tents.

INGREDIENTS
6 well beaten eggs
⅓ c. light cream
¾ tsp. salt
¼ tsp. Worcestershire Sauce
dash of pepper
bacon strips
buttered toast

DIRECTIONS
Combine eggs, cream, and seasonings. Cook in double boiler until eggs set, stirring frequently. Serve on toast with bacon.

COUNTRY BISCUITS AND GRAVY
Follow's Camp – Azusa, CA

This recipe was a favorite of the early miners from this region. This hearty, stick to your ribs meal provides energy so you can go all day long.

Follow's Camp is an authentic gold mining camp located in Los Angeles County. We're a rustic campground with river access for fishing or gold panning. Follow's Camp hosts two gold and treasure shows as well as two bluegrass festivals each year. Located in the Angeles National Forest, we also offer excellent hiking and backpacking trails.

INGREDIENTS
- ½ lb. bacon
- ½ lb. crumbled sausage
- 6 Tbsp. flour
- 2 Tbsp. fresh ground nutmeg
- 3 Tbsp. salt
- 2 c. boiling water
- 3 c. milk

DIRECTIONS

Cut bacon in one-inch strips. Brown bacon and sausage thoroughly in skillet. Add flour. When it is brown, add boiling water, milk and seasonings. Stir well over low fire until gravy thickens. Serve over hot country biscuits.

POTATO PANCAKES
Pine Springs Resort – Goldendale, WA

This recipe is a favorite here because it offers a different way to make pancakes — a nice change of pace. These pancakes are also easy to prepare while camping.

Pine Springs Resort is located 25 miles north of the Columbia River, on US 97 in eastern Washington. We are in the Simcoe Mountains and our park is shaded by huge Ponderosa pine trees. We are a popular resort for family reunions as we're centrally located between the tri-state area and close to the interstate. We offer all sorts of recreational opportunities for adults and children alike.

INGREDIENTS
- 3 c. shredded potatoes
- 2 eggs
- 1 sm. onion
- 1½ tsp. salt
- ¼ tsp. pepper
- ¼ tsp. nutmeg
- 1 Tbsp. flour
- shortening

DIRECTIONS

Beat eggs in large bowl and mix in remaining ingredients. Drop by ¼ cup spoonfuls into ¼ inch hot shortening. Flatten to make thin pancakes. Fry 3-5 min.

BREAKFAST FOR 2 – 200
Ventura Beach RV Resort – Ventura, CA

My mother made this dish during the Depression because it would feed everyone and it cost very little. I have used it as a breakfast menu many times.

Ventura Beach RV Resort is next to the blue Pacific Ocean and features 144 full hookup sites complete with cable TV at each site. Ventura is a mission town and is considered one of the most charming small cities in California. Come stay with us.

INGREDIENTS
- steamed rice
- bacon
- eggs
- lots of TLC

DIRECTIONS
Fry or broil bacon until crispy brown, set aside. Scramble eggs (number depends on how many are to be served or how many eggs you have.) Crumble bacon into bits and add to cooked eggs. Slowly add steamed rice. Stir until all is warm.

BAKED COUNTRY OMELET
Meadow Lake Resort – Urbana, OH

This is a great one dish meal. We serve this dish at many of our camp brunches.

We are located about 8 mi. NW of Urbana in a wooded, country setting with rolling hills. Our 41 acre resort offers something for everyone; from a well stocked fishing pond to a beautiful 4 acre swimming lake with sandy beaches and many interesting and uniquely designed aquatic equipment. Relax awhile in our spacious lodge overlooking the lake or enjoy a snooze after indulging in Baked Country Omelet.

INGREDIENTS
- 1 pkg. au gratin potatoes
- 3 c. very hot water
- ½ lb. bulk sausage
- ¼ c. chopped onion
- ¼ c. chopped green pepper
- 4½ oz. jar sliced mushrooms

Topping:
- ½ c. very hot water
- ½ c. milk
- 6 eggs

DIRECTIONS
Heat oven to 350B Grease 8Nx 12Npan. In large bowl, cover potato slices with 3 c. hot water; let stand while frying sausage and onion (fry sausage until meat is crumbly and loses pink color); drain. Drain potatoes and add with green pepper and mushrooms to sausage mixture. Stir well. Spoon into pan. In bowl, combine au gratin seasoning envelope with ½ c. water. Beat in milk and eggs and mix well. Pour over sausage mixture. Bake 35-40 min. To serve, cut into squares. Serves 8.

DUTCH OVEN SORE TUMMY BREAKFAST
Avila Hot Springs Spa & RV Resort-San Luis Obispo, CA

This recipe is always a hit since everyone gets to eat at the same time and they can eat as much as they want, maybe more. Also, your third helping is as hot as your first. But, best of all, you only have one pot to clean.

We are located 8 miles south of San Luis Obispo. The hot springs, spa and RV resort are nestled between oak-covered foothills. We are open 7 days a week year round. The comment we most often hear from our guests is "What friendly, helpful employees you have." Stop by and take advantage of all we have to offer.

INGREDIENTS
- **8 to 12 oz. link pork sausage, cut into bite size pieces**
- **1 lg. onion, halved & sliced**
- **2 med. potatoes, chunked**
- **8 eggs, beaten**
- **¼ c. water**
- **1 c. sliced mushrooms, optional**
- **1 bell pepper, chopped, optional**
- **1½ c. grated cheddar cheese, optional**
- **season to taste**

DIRECTIONS

On top of stove or over charcoal, brown sausage in open Dutch oven. Add onions, cover and cook until tender, about 10 min.; if using kitchen oven, bake at 375°; if cooking over charcoal, add charcoal to top of camp type Dutch oven. Add potatoes and continue to cook until almost tender. Add mushrooms and bell peppers and cook until potatoes are fully cooked, 10-15 min. Add water and seasonings to eggs and beat well. Pour the egg mixture over the top of sausage mixture and continue to cook for approximately 5 min. Stir, sprinkle cheese over the top, cover and cook for another 5 min. or until eggs are set. Serve directly from the Dutch oven. This recipe will serve 4 hungry people.

Note: There is always more than you can eat and it tastes so good that most people will eat until they get a "sore tummy".

VEGETARIAN SPAGHETTI
Hidden Valley Recreational Park – Von Ormy, TX

This dish is easy to prepare and amounts can be varied to fit any taste and number served. It is a particular favorite with the Mountain Bike Racers as well as friends and family.

We're a 100-acre park on the Medina River with two stocked lakes. Bass, catfish and crappie fishing attract anglers from all over. We're located southwest of San Antonio and offer plenty of activities to keep you busy. Enjoy hay rides, river swimming, hiking and bike trails, playground and much more!

INGREDIENTS
bell pepper, diced
garlic
celery
onion
green onion tops
mushrooms, optional
pimento olives, optional
olive oil
red wine, optional
tomato sauce
canned peeled tomatoes
chili powder
leaf oregano
Italian ground spice

DIRECTIONS
Saute diced bell pepper, celery, onion, green onion tops, and garlic in olive oil until tender. Add mushrooms, olives, wine, tomato sauce, and canned tomatoes. Simmer 1 to 2 hrs.

STUFFED PEPPERS
R.C.A. Campground – Oklahoma City, OK

Even though we don't serve this dish at our campground, I still wanted to share it with you. It's one of my favorites and I'm sure you'll enjoy it.

Our park has 39 acres, with lots of shade trees, grass, asphalt pads, a swimming pool, picnic tables, full hookups, pull-thrus, bathrooms, hot showers, coin-op laundry and tent sites. We're convenient to nearby restaurants, service stations and Remington Racetrack.

INGREDIENTS
1 beef bouillon cube
1-6 oz. can tomato paste
1 c. water
½ lb. ground beef
½ c. chopped onions
1 clove garlic, minced
1 c. cooked rice
1 tsp. herbal seasoning
¼ tsp. salt
1 c. shredded mozzarella
   cheese
4-5 med. bell peppers

DIRECTIONS
Dissolve bouillon cube in tomato paste and water. Set aside. Brown ground beef, onion and garlic together. Drain. Add rice, seasoning, salt, 1 cup of the tomato mixture and ½ cup of cheese. Slice peppers in half lengthwise and cook in boiling water until almost tender. Drain and immerse immediately in ice water. Fill peppers with meat mixture. Place in lightly greased baking dish. Pour on remaining tomato sauce. Sprinkle with remaining cheese. Bake in preheated 375° oven for 25 to 30 min.

ITALIAN RAVIOLI
Missoula/El Mar KOA — Missoula, MT

This is an old family recipe passed down in our family. It is tedious to make but the results are just compensation. We enjoy this ravioli treat on holidays and special occasions.

Our park is family oriented with special emphasis on children with our farm animal petting zoo. We have lots of trees and grass, shade and picnic tables, 13 Kamping Kabins, a mini-golf course and two hot tubs. We are mid-way between Yellowstone and Glacier National Park and frequently find one-nighters extend their stay by several days because of all the things to do in the area.

INGREDIENTS
Filling:
- **4 lb. roasting chicken**
- **4 lb. pork roast**
- **salt and pepper to taste**
- **3 or 4 eggs**
- **1 clove garlic, chopped fine**
- **1 lg. spoonful of dried parsley**
- **½ c. parmesan cheese**
- **2 slices dried bread, ground**

Dough:
- **4 c. flour**
- **1½ sticks margarine**
- **salt**

Sauce:
- **3 lg. cans tomato sauce**
- **¼ c. oil**
- **½ stick margarine, melted**
- **garlic to taste**
- **parsley to taste**

DIRECTIONS
Grind chicken and pork together, removing any fat, skin or gristle. Then mix all ingredients together plus dried bred. (This makes the mixture hold together.) If too dry, add a little broth.

Mix ingredients together as you would for pie dough, but work it as you do noodles; then roll out and make ravioli. Ravioli should dry 12 hours on a board or cookie sheet which has been dusted with flour. They should be turned once to dry on both sides.

In saucepan, add all ingredients together. Simmer very slowly until thick and dark (6-8 hours).

Boil ravioli slowly for 20 minutes. If frozen, boil another 10 minutes. Then, with slotted spoon, layer ravioli in a baking dish with sauce and parmesan cheese. (You may add mushrooms to the sauce if desired.)

All this preparation can be done ahead of time and then frozen, either as a finished casserole or by putting the individual ravioli in zip-lock bags.

SYLVIA'S GLOP
Riverview RV Park & Campground – Loveland, CO

Riverview RV Park & Campground is located between Estes Park and Loveland on US Hwy 34 — the route to Rocky Mountain National Park. Riverview sits at the mouth of the beautiful Big Thompson Canyon with shade trees and 1/4 mile of river frontage from which Rocky Mountain trout can be caught.

When our son, Eric, was three he was seated, cross-legged on a picnic table. Some neighboring campers asked what he was stirring and he replied, "It's called, it's called, it's called . . . Sylvia's Glop". Hence the name. Our campground store always carries these supplies and the recipe is printed on a large poster board hung on the campground store wall for the campers to copy the recipe

Not only is this a favorite family recipe, it's also popular with groups/clubs because they can use it for their group potluck dinners. It can be increased to serve any number of people.

INGREDIENTS
- 1 lb. hamburger
- 1 chopped onion
- 1 2-c. can sliced peaches (including juice)
- 1 6-oz. can tomato paste
- 1 2-c. can stewed tomatoes
- 1 Tbsp. cinnamon
- 1/2 tsp. salt
- 1/2 tsp. pepper

DIRECTIONS

Brown hamburger and onions. Add remaining ingredients. Simmer slowly 15 to 20 min. Serves 4-6 people. Freezes well.

Note: When increasing the amount of this recipe a quick rule of thumb is 1 Tbsp. cinnamon per 1 lb. hamburger. The other ingredients can vary according to what you have on hand.

BAKED ZITI WITH SAUSAGE
Sprawling Hills Park – Brewster, MA

We occasionally have this dish at our weekly cookouts and everybody loves it. Sprawling Hills Park offers facilities and recreation sure to please the entire family. Come visit our park with rolling hills on a sparkling spring fed lake.

INGREDIENTS
Sauce
- 1 lg. can whole peeled tomatoes
- 2 sm. cans tomato paste
- 1 med. onion, chopped
- 1 clove garlic, minced
- 1 tsp. salt
- 1 Tbsp. sugar
- 1 tsp. basil
- 1 tsp. oregano
- 1 handful fresh parsley
- 1/4 c. oil
- 2 lb. Italian sweet sausage
- 1/2 lb. chopped beef

Ziti:
- 1 lb. ziti
- 1/2 lb. ricotta cheese
- 1/2 lb. mozzarella

DIRECTIONS

Place all sauce ingredients except sausage in a large pot. Blanche sausage in oven or skillet. Cook sauce 3 hrs. on low heat stirring occasionally. Be careful not to burn. Refrigerate overnight.

Remove sausage and slice in 1/8-inch pieces. Cook ziti noodles al dente. Remove from pot and cool with cold water. Return to a cool pot. Add ricotta cheese and sauce to the ziti to make desired consistency — not too wet. Mix in sausage slices. Place in baking dish and top with sliced mozzarella. Bake at 350° for 1 hr.

CREOLE GUMBO
Dunedin Beach Campground — Dunedin, FL

Every year our seasonal campers save all their aluminum cans. In the springtime, we cash 'em in and throw a big shrimp and oyster feast. A mug of beer cools off a balmy day, and a bowl of gumbo sasses it up again.

We are 8 scenic driving miles north of Clearwater, on Florida's west coast. Mangroves and long-legged seabirds share our roost beside the headwaters of Minnow Creek. Dunedin Beach, the mecca for local watersports, and Honeymoon Island are just a 10-minute tan away. After a hard day's play in the sun, nothing complements our shellfish-scented sea breeze more than chilled shrimp cocktail, roasted oysters, and a bowl of creole gumbo. Come on down and visit, you can taste it in the air!

INGREDIENTS
- 1½ c. water
- ½ tsp. salt
- ½ c. chopped onion
- 1 clove garlic
- 3 Tbsp. butter
- 3 Tbsp. flour
- 1 16-oz. can tomatoes
- 1 chopped green pepper
- 2 bay leaves
- 1 tsp. oregano
- 1 tsp. thyme
- ½ tsp. hot pepper sauce or cayenne pepper
- 10 oz. okra
- ½ lb. fresh shrimp
- 2 cans crabmeat
- white rice

THYME

DIRECTIONS

In a large soup pan, make tender the onion and garlic in butter. Blend in flour, stirring constantly until golden. Add undrained compressed tomatoes, green pepper, spices, hot sauce, water and salt. Boil, reduce heat, and simmer covered for 20 min. Remove bay leaves. Add sliced okra; boil. Simmer again. Cut up large peeled shrimps and throw shrimp and crabmeat in potion. Heat thoroughly about 5 minutes. Pour concoction over white rice. Garnish with a couple of steamed cherry-stone clams (optional).

MAIN EVENT CORNED BEEF
The Main Event – Quartzsite, AZ

This recipe has been handed down from generation to generation.

We're located on I-10 at milepost 17 in Quartzsite. We offer overnight RV parking with or without hookups; gasoline, groceries and gift store and laundry and restroom facilities. We're also home of the annual Gemboree — a shopping oasis for gems, jewelry, antiques, coins, crafts and much more. This 16 day Gemboree takes place at the end of January through early February. Come visit us at the main event and see what you've been missing!

INGREDIENTS
- 4 lb. corned beef brisket
- 1 12-oz. can beer
- 4 peppercorns
- 1 bay leaf
- ¼ tsp. thyme
- 6 sm. peeled potatoes
- 6 scraped carrots, halved
- 1 sm. cabbage, wedged

DIRECTIONS

Place corned beef in large, heavy kettle. Add beer and enough water to cover. Add peppercorns, bay leaf and thyme. Bring to boil. Reduce heat, cover and cook 3 to 3½ hr. until tender. If desired, add potatoes, carrots or cabbage 30 min. before meat is done.

BAKED LASAGNA
Reflections on Silver Lake – Avon Park, FL

We have luncheons and dinners at our park during different times throughout the season and this is one of the favorites.

Reflections on Silver Lake is an adult mobile home and RV park situated in the central part of Florida surrounded by orange groves and natural landscaping. Situated on a fresh water lake, we offer a variety of adult oriented recreational activities. We are close to shopping centers and golf courses.

INGREDIENTS
- 1 lb. lasagna noodles, uncooked
- 1½ lb. ground beef
- 2 lbs. Ricotta cheese
- ½ c. Parmesan cheese
- 1½ qt. spaghetti sauce
- 2 med. cans drained mushrooms

DIRECTIONS

Crumble and saute ground beef. Mix in mushrooms. Using a 9″ x 13″ pan, cover bottom of pan with thin layer of sauce, then a layer of uncooked noodles, layer of ricotta cheese, layer of ground beef and then cover with some of the sauce. Repeat each layer, covering the last layer with sauce. Store in refrigerator overnight. Bake at 350° for 1 hr., covered with foil. Remove foil and top with parmesan cheese until melted. Cool about 15 min. before serving.

BAKKEN FAMILY FAVORITE
Yogi Bear's Jellystone Park Camp-Resort - Shakopee, MN

This is a family favorite Mom made up one day. When I ask, "What should we have for a quick meal?", the answer is, "Hamburger and potatoes!"

We are located on the east end of Shakopee. Our campground is along the river in a wooded area. We are looking forward to our first full summer of camping. Come and visit us!

INGREDIENTS
- 1½ lbs. hamburger
- potatoes, cut in chunks
- onion
- celery, carrots (optional)

DIRECTIONS

Brown hamburger and onion in frying pan. Add raw potatoes and fry until golden brown. Note: you may add celery or carrots if you like. Serve with a salad.

BARBECUED RATTLESNAKE
Northwest River Park – Chesapeake, VA

We have rattlesnake barbecues here for the park staff every once in a while! Our park is 763 acres and is filled with many trails for horseback riding and hiking. We also have fishing, canoeing and row boating, along with an amphitheatre for our campers' enjoyment.

INGREDIENTS
- 1 rattlesnake, freshly skinned, head removed, 4′ or longer
- barbecue sauce
- salt & pepper to taste

DIRECTIONS

Cut snake into 4-6 in. sections. Marinate snake in barbecue sauce several hours. Wrap sections in tinfoil and barbecue over charcoal for 45 min. To keep meat from drying out, baste with barbecue sauce every 10 min.

HOT-DOG-ITO
San Lorenzo Park - King City, CA

This is quick, simple and delicious. It's a lunch staple for the park staff — or for at least for some of us.

Experience country living at its best by visiting the historical agricultural museum in San Lorenzo Park. We offer 116 campsites with partial and full hookups, modern restrooms and an RV dump station. Roast your hot dogs in a shaded eucalyptus grove where BBQ grills and tables are available. Located just outside King City, San Lorenzo Park is nestled along the Salinas River, in the foothills of the Santa Lucia Mts. Our park is as picturesque as the Salinas Valley which surrounds it. Take advantage of the nearby attractions including golf, missions, shopping, dining and wineries and vineyards. Or enjoy the variety of recreation located on the park's premises.

INGREDIENTS
- 1 lb. hot dogs
- 1 pkg. flour tortillas
- 1 c. picante sauce
- 1 sm. onion, chopped
- 1 c. grated cheese (optional)

DIRECTIONS

Place hot dog on tortilla, sprinkle with onion, add picante sauce to taste. Roll ingredients in tortilla and place on paper plate. Microwave for 1½ min. on high. Grated cheese can be added if desired.

MANASTA
South Fork Lodge – Lowman, ID

This recipe is different and delicious.

We're located on Highway 21 at milepost 72 in a beautiful mountain setting. Enjoy float trips down the river, hunting, fishing, horseback trails, cross country skiing and snowmobiling. No matter what the season, we offer plenty of activities to keep you busy.

INGREDIENTS
- 1½ lb. Italian pork sausage
- 1 Tbsp. basil
- 1 bag red beans
- 1 chopped onion
- 2 c. diced potato
- 1 c. Parmesan cheese

DIRECTIONS

Boil all ingredients except Parmesan until done. Add Parmesan cheese and serve hot.

PORK AND BEAN TACO
Big Bear Park — Waterford, CA

This is an easy dish to prepare and it works great for campouts.

Located 12 miles east of Modesto, we offer RV camping and day recreation. Along with tent camping and picnic areas, we have river fishing for our campers. We offer a laguana and sandy beach for swimming, along with our grizzly rapid waterslides. Little Bear's Water Wonder World is for the smaller children. Clean restrooms, large clubhouse, volleyball, horseshoes and snack car are also available. Come and see us and discover much more!

INGREDIENTS
1 lb. hamburger
fresh peppers
fresh onion
fresh garlic
1 lg. can pork & beans
1 sm. can salsa
tortillas
garnishes - tomatoes, onions, lettuce and cheese

DIRECTIONS
Saute peppers, onion and garlic; add hamburger. Fry together; drain. Stir in pork & beans and salsa. Put in taco shell and garnish with your favorite cheese, lettuce and tomato.

CHICKEN CHALUPAS (Cha-loop-us)
Four Seasons RV Resort — Gold Beach, OR

This recipe can be prepared a day ahead and can be served as an entree.

We are located 7 miles east of Gold Beach on the north bank of the Rogue River away from traffic. We have a boat dock and ramp for RVers staying in our park. Fishing licenses and guide service are available. The Jet Boats will pick you up and drop you off at our dock for trips up the beautiful Rogue River. We have potlucks nearly every month, the main ones being Memorial Day, Fourth of July and Labor Day. They are like one big family get-together. Hope you come and join us!

INGREDIENTS
1 pkg. small flour tortillas
4 lg. chicken breasts, cooked and cubed
2 cans cream of chicken soup
1 sm. can diced green chilis
1 pt. sour cream
¾ lb. monterey jack cheese, grated
¾ lb. sharp cheddar cheese, grated
1 bunch green onions, including tops
1 sm. onion, grated
1 sm. can diced black olives (optional)

DIRECTIONS
Mix soup, onions, sour cream, chilis and olives together. Add ½ of cheeses. Set aside 3 cups of mixture. Combine cubed chicken with remaining mixture. Fill tortillas with mixture and roll up. Place in greased 9" x 13" pan, rolled side down. Pour remaining mixture over top and sprinkle with remaining cheese. Sprinkle with paprika, refrigerate overnight. Bake at 350° for 45 min.

TEX-MEX SPECIAL
Arlington Kampground – Arlington, TX

This special recipe is a definite crowd pleaser — no matter what size group. Just increase the ingredients as you increase your group.

Arlington Kampground is located 1¼ miles north of Interstate 20 at exit 449 on South Cooper. We have 19 acres of country style camping in the heart of the Metro-plex. Feed our ducks, rabbits, birds and squirrels. Then go see Six Flags over Texas, Ranger Stadium, International Wildlife Park or Wet 'N Wild — all within 5 miles of us. Don't forget Big "D" and Cowtown. Stop by and enjoy our hospitality!

INGREDIENTS
- 2 lbs. hamburger
- 2 sm. onions
- 1 sm. can green chili peppers
- 1 lb. shredded cheese
- 1 lg. can tomatoes
- 1 pkg. corn tortillas

DIRECTIONS

Brown hamburger and onions. Add peppers and tomatoes. Layer in baking dish with one layer tortillas, one layer meat mixture and one layer cheese. Make as many layers as you want. Bake at 350° for 30 min. Top with sour cream.

SOUTHWEST TEXAS FAJITAS
Cedar Hill KOA – Junction, TX

In the hey-day of cattle raising of Southwest Texas, ranchers ate the high quality cuts of beef and the hired hands ate the rejected cuts of meat. They developed this dish and today it is served in fine restaurants from Dallas to Mexico City.

Our full service campground is nestled under large native pecan trees of the North Llano River in the western hill country of Texas.

INGREDIENTS (per person)
- ½ lb. beef skirt (flank) steak pounded
- unseasoned meat tenderizer
- soy sauce
- juice of fresh cut lemons
- Hunt's Natural Bar-B-Q Sauce

DIRECTIONS

Cut meat into 6 to 8-in. lengths and place in a large flat cake pan for marinating. Sprinkle with meat tenderizer, then sprinkle with soy sauce. Spray evenly with lemon juice. Let soak at least 2-3 hr. turning one time. Shortly before cooking, liberally cover meat with Bar-B-Q-Sauce. Cook over hot mesquite wood and charcoal fire until almost crusty on outside. Serve as steaks or slice into narrow strips and serve in flour tortillas with guacamole (mashed avocado mix). Add hot sauce if desired. Serve with pinto beans and other salad or hot bread.

HAZEL'S MEXICAN CHICKEN
Fort Clark Springs RV Park – Brackettville, TX

A fresh chicken dinner was cause for celebration during the frontier days of this original cavalry post. This recipe blends many tastes to provide the distinctive "Tex-Mex" flavor of our area.

"Where deer and armadillo roam," our RV park is located on the original cavalry/military post of Ft. Clark on US Hwy. 90, west of San Antonio in Brackettville. Just 30 min. from Mexico, the area around the tree-lined Las Moras Creek provides an oasis of spring-fed beauty for weary travelers, and those seeking an escape from winter's icy blast. We enjoy blending traditional Southern cooking with subtle Mexican seasoning for the "Tex-Mex" taste famous to this area of Texas.

INGREDIENTS
flour
buttermilk or milk and egg batter
boneless chicken breast
mild cheddar cheese
prepared picante sauce
fresh celantro

DIRECTIONS
Dip chicken in flour, then dip in batter. Press flour into chicken; repeat dip and press. Fry uncovered over medium high heat. Put chicken in baking pan, cover with picante sauce, sprinkle on celantro, cover with grated cheese and bake at 350° for 20 min. or until cheese is melted.

KATHY'S ENCHILADAS
Paradise by the Sea – Oceanside, CA

This recipe takes the trophy for best Mexican food from the Texans and places it with its rightful heirs — Californians!

Paradise by the Sea is 300 yards from the beautiful Pacific Ocean. Located in Oceanside, we're just minutes away from fishing, sailing and some of the finest restaurants anywhere. Visit Paradise and kick back for an enjoyable time.

INGREDIENTS
1 whole chicken
2 c. chicken broth
12 corn or flour tortillas
1 lg. onion, finely diced
4-6 c. cheddar or Monterey Jack cheese, grated
¼ c. butter
¼ c. flour
1 c. sour cream
1 can refried beans
jalapenos, optional

DIRECTIONS
Simmer chicken until tender, reserving 2 c. chicken broth. Debone and dice. Using a 9" x 13" pan, layer each tortilla with beans, chicken, onion and cheese. Roll tightly and place in pan. In a large skillet melt butter. Add flour and stir until bubbly. Stir in 2 cups of chicken broth until thickened. Blend in sour cream. Pour mixture over enchiladas. Top with cheese and jalapenos. Bake at 425° for 20 min.

CHICKEN TACOS
Leaf Verde RV Resort & Mobile Home Park - Buckeye, AZ

Eloise Dean's great grandparents homesteaded the Buckeye Valley, west of Phoenix, in 1898. Her grandfather rafted the first thoroughbred Guerney bull across the Aqua Fria River when Arizona dairymen used almost no breed of cattle except shorthorns. Eloise is now employed by the newest addition to the Buckeye Valley, Leaf Verde RV Resort and Mobile Home Park. One of the Dean's favorite recipes is this one for Chicken Tacos.

INGREDIENTS
4-5 c. cooked chicken,
   shredded or chopped*
3 Tbsp oil
½ c. minced onion
dash of Tabasco
salt & pepper to taste
¼ tsp. garlic salt
broth to moisten**
12 corn tortillas
lettuce
tomatoes
cheese

* turkey may be substituted
   for chicken
** chicken or mushroom soup
   may be substituted for broth

DIRECTIONS
Fry shredded chicken in oil, then add next six ingredients. Keep hot while you fry corn tortillas in hot fat. Fold. Fill with filling. Mix shredded lettuce, diced ripe tomatoes and grated cheese. Add to tacos as desired.

TEXAS HASH
Turtle Bayou RV Park — Wallisville, TX

This recipe is quick, easy and tastes great served with a salad and bread. You have a great meal without a lot of time and effort.

We are located halfway between Beaumont and Houston on I-10 at the 812 mile marker. We have 10½ acres. Our park is mostly wooded, and we're partially surrounded by Turtle Bayou. You'll find some of the best crappie fishing here.

INGREDIENTS
1 lb. ground meat
1 Tbsp. cooking oil
1 lg. onion, chopped
1 med. bell pepper, chopped
2 cloves garlic, chopped
1 sm. can stewed tomatoes
1 sm. can whole kernel corn
1 tsp. chili powder
1 c. cooked rice
salt & pepper to taste
grated cheese (optional)

DIRECTIONS
Brown meat in oil, stirring to break up meat. Remove meat. Add onion, bell pepper and garlic to fat. Cook until soft but not brown. Add tomatoes, tomato sauce, corn, meat, chili powder; mix well. Add rice and season to taste. Bake at 350° for 30 min. Grated cheese may be sprinkled on top for last 5 minutes.

ROAST BEEF CHIMICHANGAS
Justin's Water World and RV Park – Tucson, AZ

The Mexican influence is very strong in Tucson and is reflected in the lifestyle, the arts, and particularly the food. Justin's RV Park is situated at the base of the Tucson Mountains and adjoins the beautiful Tucson Mountain Park. The park is host to The Arizona Sonora Desert Museum, Saguaro National Monument, and Old Tucson. The atmosphere is peaceful and serene. Once a year we like to invite the Mexican Folkloric dancers out for an afternoon of entertainment. At that time, we "fiesta" on roast beef chimichangas and other traditional Mexican dishes.

INGREDIENTS
- 8 lg. tortillas
- 2 c. shredded beef (canned roast beef works great)
- melted butter
- chopped onion
- spices
- shredded lettuce
- chopped tomato
- sliced avocado
- chopped green onion
- grated cheese
- sour cream
- guacamole
- salsa

DIRECTIONS
Heat roast beef in juice or gravy. Add chopped onion and spices. Spoon about ¼ cup of the warmed shredded beef mixture in a line across center of tortilla. Fold tortilla over, roll once, fold ends in, and continue to roll all the way, making a burro. Place these burros side by side in a shallow buttered baking dish. Brush melted butter generously on tops and sides of burros. Bake in a hot oven (500°) for 5 to 10 min, until browned. Watch closely while baking and baste with more butter if necessary. Serve hot.

Garnish with a salad of shredded lettuce, chopped tomato, chopped green onion, sliced avocado, and grated cheese. Top chimichanga with sour cream, guacamole, and/or salsa.

Makes 8 chimichangas and serves 4-8 (depending on how hungry you are!)

SOUTH TEXAS ENCHILADAS
Magic Valley Trailer Park – Weslaco, TX

This is a recipe that my mother gave to me and it's one of my favorites. I have lived in Texas all my life and want to share this with you, hoping you and your family will enjoy it as much as my family does.

Magic Valley is located 6 miles from the Mexican border. We are a large and very active park, offering a heated pool, hot tub, horseshoes, 10 pool tables and one of the finest shuffleboard courts in the area.

INGREDIENTS
- 2 lbs. ground beef
- 1 Tbsp. chili powder
- 1 tsp. salt
- 1 tsp. pepper
- 1 garlic clove
- 2 c. longhorne cheese
- 1 can condensed tomato sauce
- 24 corn tortillas

DIRECTIONS
Brown the ground beef. Add chili powder, garlic, salt and pepper. Drain grease and add tomato sauce and one can of water. Simmer for 10 min. Put two heaping tablespoons of meat in each tortilla. Roll up tortillas and place in long cake pan. Top tortillas with cheese and remainder of meat. Bake at 350° for 30 min.

TORTILLA HASH (CHILAQUILES)
Pecos River RV Camp – San Jose, NM

We're located 40 miles east of Santa Fe and 25 miles west of Las Vegas, NM at exit 319 on I-25. We offer level pull-thrus, full hookups, barbeque pits and tables, laundry, store, and tile restrooms with large showers. While you're here, you can enjoy fishing, self-guided trails, Indian artifact hunting, movie & VCR rentals, Santa Fe Trail ruts, video games, rock hunting, beautiful views, National Monuments, national forests, playground and recreation hall for group activities. Come visit us and see for yourself the spectacular river view from the Old Santa Fe Trail.

INGREDIENTS
12 corn tortillas, broken in quarters
⅓ c. lard or beef fat
3 onions, diced and browned
1 c. red chile powder
1 c. water
2 cloves garlic, or ⅔ tsp. garlic powder
1 pinch oregano
1 pinch cumin
½ lb. grated longhorn cheese

DIRECTIONS
Fry the tortillas in grease until they are light brown. Mix the chile powder with water, and stir until free from lumps. Mix all ingredients together, but save back some of the cheese to sprinkle over the top. Bake in a preheated 350° oven for 20 min. or until tortillas are soft.

SOUPER MEX
Shiloh Pines – Tyler, TX

This recipe is quick and easy. It offers an authentic Mexican flavor so often found here.

Shiloh Pines offers 75 spacious acres of beautiful towering trees and gently rolling hills. We're located within the city limits of Tyler, near medical facilities, restaurants and shopping. We provide 24-hour security, equipped clubhouse, laundry facilities, two swimming pools, spacious shady lots and more. Move up to the best and pay no more! Come experience the Shiloh Pines difference.

INGREDIENTS
12 corn tortillas
1 can cream of mushroom soup
1 can cream of chicken soup
1 can cheddar cheese soup
1 can green chiles & tomatoes
1 lb. ground beef
chopped onions
grated cheddar cheese

DIRECTIONS
Brown and drain ground beef. Mix with soups and drained chiles and tomatoes. Line 9" x 13" pan with tortillas. Top with half the beef mixture. Cover with remaining tortillas and other half of mixture. Top with onions and cheese, cover with foil and bake at 350° for 45 min.

WESTERN BEEF TACO
Yogi Bear's Jellystone Park – Bandera, TX

When large groups of people gather, food is one of the main topics of discussion. Since Texas produces beef in abundance, and the area has a rich Hispanic heritage, Mexican food is a very popular food item for large groups.

Yogi Bear's Jellystone Park is located in Bandera, Texas in the heart of the hill country on the Cypress lined banks of the Medina River. The resort offers many organized activities including canoeing, cookouts, swimming, horseshoes, volleyball, card parties, guided tours of the area, as well as golf on two nearby 18 hole golf courses. Pari-mutual and quarterhorse horse racing and rodeos are also featured. There is an abundance of deer, turkey and other wild game that attracts not only the sportsman but camera buffs as well.

INGREDIENTS
- 1 lb. lean ground beef
- 1 med. onion, finely chopped
- 1½ tsp. chile powder, or to taste
- ½ tsp. oregano leaves
- ½ tsp. paprika
- ¼ tsp. rosemary leaves
- ¼ tsp. pepper
- ½ tsp. salt
- 3 Tbsp. HOT prepared taco sauce
- 2 tsp. Worcestershire sauce
- salad oil
- 10-12 corn tortillas
- 1 sm. head iceberg lettuce, shredded
- 2 tomatoes, chopped
- 1 can ripe olives, chopped
- 1 c. onion, chopped
- 1 c. shredded cheddar cheese
- bottled taco sauce

DIRECTIONS

Brown beef in frying pan until crumbly; add onion and cook. Keep stirring until limp. Drain off excess fat. Stir in chili powder, oregano, paprika, rosemary, pepper, salt, three tablespoons of taco sauce and Worcestershire. Blend well and simmer for approximately 20 min.

While the taco filling is simmering, heat ¼" of salad oil in a large frying pan over high heat. Fry tortillas, one at a time, for about 15 seconds. Fold in half and fry on each side until slightly crisp or leave flat if desired. Fill each shell with 2 to 3 tablespoons of the taco mixture. Sprinkle with chopped onion, tomato, olives and shredded cheese. Place under broiler until cheese is melted. Serve hot with shredded lettuce and additional taco sauce. Makes 10-12 tacos. This recipe can easily be increased to serve as many people as you wish.

MEXICAN PILE-ON
Amarillo KOA – Amarillo, TX

This recipe was introduced to us by an RV club spending the weekend. It is so popular and easy to prepare that we use it for winter potlucks. Every RV has one or more of the ingredients on hand.

Amarillo, the "Yellow Rose of Texas" is the economic and cultural capitol of the panhandle, where the old west still lingers on. Palo Duro Canyon, the American Quarterhorse Association Headquarters, Texas' largest cattle auction and the Helium capitol of the world are just a few of the reasons visitors come our way.

INGREDIENTS
Fritos
canned chili (no beans)
shredded jack cheese
chopped onions
chopped green olives
chopped black olives
chopped tomatoes
shredded lettuce
chopped walnuts or pecans
shredded coconut
picante sauce

DIRECTIONS
Heat chili and serve from crockpot. Set up table as for potluck. Line begins with a layer of Fritos and each person piles on whatever of the selection he desires.

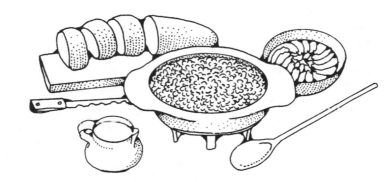

CASSEROLES

HOT SEAFOOD CASSEROLE
San Francisco RV Park – San Francisco, CA

Throughout the year our employees have potluck get-togethers. This scrumptious, easy to prepare casserole is one of their favorites.

Right in the heart of San Francisco, this is where you'll find San Francisco RV Park. We're close to all your favorite sightseeing spots and conveniently located near the freshest seafood available. Our large party room has seen some of the best crab feeds held by visiting RV clubs. This recipe is a favorite here and is very San Francisco.

INGREDIENTS
½ lb. fresh crab
½ lb. sm. fresh shrimp
1 c. celery, chopped
6 Tbsp. green pepper, chopped
3 Tbsp. onion, chopped
½ tsp. salt
½ tsp. pepper
dash of Worcestershire sauce
1 c. mayonnaise
1 can cream of celery soup
3 c. cooked rice
potato chips

DIRECTIONS
Toss all ingredients together and put in greased 9" x 13" pan. Top with crushed potato chips. Bake at 350° for 45 min.

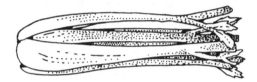

SEAFOOD CASSEROLE
Fayetteville-KOA – Wade, NC

We're a perfect halfway overnite stop between New York City and Disney World. We're open all year and we have clean restrooms, spacious, level sites and a quiet atmosphere. We offer a pool, fishing, game room, convenience store, RV supplies and LP gas.

INGREDIENTS
½ lb. steamed sm. shrimp
½ lb. bay scallops
½ lb. crabmeat, picked
½ c. chopped celery
½ chopped green pepper
¼ c. melted butter
2 Tbsp. flour
1 c. milk
1 egg yolk, beaten
2 Tbsp. lemon juice
½ tsp. salt
dash of pepper
Topping:
1 Tbsp. melted butter
¼ c. bread crumbs

DIRECTIONS
Cook celery and green pepper in melted butter until tender. Blend in flour. Add milk slowly and stir until smooth and thick. Stir a little of flour mixture into egg yolk and blend with remaining sauce, stirring constantly. Add lemon juice, seasonings and seafood. Blend well. Place in greased 1 qt. casserole dish. Combine bread crumbs and melted butter and sprinkle on top. Bake at 350° for 20-25 min. or until brown.

BACHELOR'S LIFE SAVER
Canoe Creek Campground – St. Cloud, FL

Being a single parent, I found this recipe allowed me to make a quick, wholesome dinner that my family really enjoyed. And since it freezes well, it is definitely a bachelor's (or bachelorette's) life saver!

Canoe Creek Campground is a clean, friendly, adult oriented park. Our 178 site shady campground offers paved and lighted streets, a swimming pool, group activities, a store and reasonable prices. We're also conveniently located to attractions in central Florida.

INGREDIENTS
- 8 oz. pkg. mashed potatoes
- 2 lbs. ground beef
- ½ lb. ground sausage
- 1 bell pepper
- 2-3 oz. cans chunky vegetable soup
- 1 c. rice
- ½ c. instant oats
- 1 onion
- 3 eggs

DIRECTIONS
Mix all ingredients together except mashed potatoes. Place mixture into bread pans. Top with mashed potatoes. Bake at 375° until done. You now have a meat and potatoes meal. This recipe makes enough for several meals, so freeze what you want and eat the rest later.

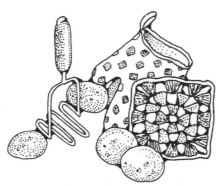

HAMBURGER HOT DISH
Northern Terrace Mobil Home & RV Park – Ely, MN

Northern Terrace is located on the edge of Ely's city limits, away from the congested city traffic. We offer RV parking with full hookup sites and we also rent trailers to our customers. We're conveniently located near the Boundary Waters Canoe Area where you'll find great fishing.

INGREDIENTS
- 1 lb. ground beef
- 1 med. onion, sliced
- 3 carrots, sliced
- 5-6 potatoes, sliced
- 1-15 oz. can tomato sauce

DIRECTIONS
In medium casserole dish, layer ½ lb. of ground beef, then half the onion, potato and carrot slices. Repeat layers. Pour tomato sauce over all and bake at 350° for 2 hrs.

MEXICAN LASAGNA
Five Forks Motel and Campground-Williamsburg, VA

This is a quick and easy Mexican dish which we love. We hope you enjoy it as much as we do.

Five Forks offers spacious, wooded sites. We have full and partial hookups as well as tent sites. Our amenities include laundry room, game room, swimming pool, playground, and much more. We welcome catered events.

INGREDIENTS
- **1 lb. ground beef**
- **1-12 oz. jar thick & chunky salsa**
- **6 tostada shells**
- **1 c. refried beans**
- **1 c. sour cream**
- **4 oz. cheddar cheese, shredded**
- **shredded lettuce for garnish**

DIRECTIONS

In skillet, brown beef. Drain. Stir in ½ c. salsa. Spread ¼ c. salsa in 10″ pie plate. Top with 3 tostadas. Top with half of each of the beans, meat mixture, sour cream and cheese. Repeat layers. Cover with foil. Bake at 350° for 30 min. Top with lettuce, remaining salsa and sour cream. Makes 6 to 8 servings.

ONE POT TUNA PASTA
Always Welcome Traveller Camp Sites-Gettysburg, PA

Our park, located on the site of the second day's battle of the Gettysburg campaign, takes its name from General Robert E. Lee's favorite horse, Traveller. While being convenient to museums and other points of interest, the park's own potluck suppers are very popular.

INGREDIENTS
- **3½ c. water**
- **4 chicken bouillon cubes**
- **⅛ tsp. pepper**
- **1 tsp. basil leaves**
- **2 c. (8 oz.) elbow or spiral pasta**
- **1 (4 oz.) jar pimientos**
- **1 (9 oz.) pkg. frozen cut green beans**
- **2 c. milk**
- **1 c. American cheese**
- **1 (7 oz.) can tuna, drained & broken into chunks**
- **¼ c. chopped parsley**

DIRECTIONS

Bring water, bouillon cubes, pepper & basil leaves to a boil in a 4-qt. pot. Gradually add uncooked pasta so that water continues to boil. Cover and simmer for 7 min., stirring occasionally.

Meanwhile, dice pimientos. Stir pimientos, beans and milk into pot. Cover and simmer 6-8 min. longer until pasta and beans are tender. Stir in cheese, tuna and parsley until cheese is melted. Serve from pot or turn into serving dish. Serve immediately.

TURKEY IN THE STRAW
Holiday Camping Resort – New Era, MI

We are located in Oceana County, MI, the asparagus capital of the world. Many of our campers attend the 3-day National Asparagus Festival held annually the 2nd weekend of June. The Asparagus Smorgasbord on Saturday evening is one of the main events. This is one of the favorite dishes served.

We are situated in a pine forest on a hill with a scenic view of the rolling hills and fields of the quiet countryside. Stony Lake, Silver Lake, and the sandy beaches and dunes along the shores of Lake Michigan are nearby.

INGREDIENTS
1 lb. fresh sliced asparagus
½ c. water
2 c. diced cooked turkey
½ c. butter
1 box (12 oz.) cornbread stuffing
chicken stock or boullion
salt & pepper to taste

DIRECTIONS
Prepare stuffing as directed on box (for liquid use chicken stock). Add raw asparagus, turkey, butter and water. Add salt and pepper as desired. Mix well. Cover and bake as directed on stuffing mix box.

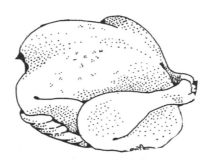

KING RANCH CHICKEN CASSEROLE
McFarland Park – Florence, OR

McFarland Park is located on the banks of the Tennessee River in a beautiful wooded area within the city limits of Florence. We're located off Highway 20, only a few blocks from the major business district. There is an 18-hole golf course in the park, picnic shelters, picnic tables, barbecue grills, playgrounds, boat launching ramps, and fishing piers.

INGREDIENTS
1 fryer chicken, boiled & cut into bite-sized pieces
1 lg. pkg. cheese flavored corn chips
1 lb. grated medium cheddar cheese
1 can tomatoes
1 can cream of mushroom soup
1 can cream of chicken soup
1 lg. onion, chopped
1 bell pepper, chopped
1½ tsp. chili powder
dash of garlic salt
2 Tbsp. bacon fat

DIRECTIONS
To make sauce, saute onion and pepper in bacon fat in large skillet. Add soups and tomatoes until well blended; then add chili powder and garlic. In 3-qt. casserole, layer chips, chicken, cheese and sauce. Layer again with all, ending with cheese. Bake at 375° for 30 minutes.

MARITIME MADNESS
Heritage Farm Campground – Mactaquac, NB

Campers enjoy participating in our Sunday evening potluck suppers held in our recreation barn. We usually have two potlucks each month and this recipe is a favorite served with whipped potatoes or potato salad. In the year 1787, Jonathan Brown, a United Empire Loyalist, settled on the banks of the Saint John River. This scenic property is what is now the campground. Our children, the 6th generation, still live here. The land was farmed until 1977 when some of it was converted into Heritage Farm Campground.

INGREDIENTS
- **1 lb. ground beef**
- **10 oz. cream of mushroom soup**
- **½ c. chopped onions**
- **1 Tbsp. parsley flakes**
- **1 tsp. salt**
- **¼ tsp. pepper**
- **½ tsp. sage**
- **3 Tbsp. ketchup**
- **1 Tbsp. barbeque sauce**
- **½ tsp. garlic powder**
- **¼ c. grated cheddar cheese**
- **½ c. chopped green pepper (optional)**
- **½ c. rolled oats**

DIRECTIONS
Combine all ingredients in large bowl. Mix together well. Pat down in 1½ quart casserole. Bake covered 50 min. at 350°. Remove cover and bake about 15 min. to brown.

OUR FAVORITE MEAT LOAF
Stillwell RV Park – Alpine, TX

We have used this recipe for many park picnics and it is a park favorite. Our park is located at the top of Big Bend National Park, the biggest tourist attraction in Texas. Beautiful mountains, many pre-historic canyons and many kinds of workable rocks can be found in this area.

INGREDIENTS
- **1½ c. soft bread crumbs**
- **1 envelope onion soup mix**
- **2 lb. ground beef**
- **2 eggs**
- **¾ c. water**
- **⅓ c. catsup**

DIRECTIONS
Preheat oven 350°. Crumble meat in bowl. Add other ingredients and mix well. Put in 4" x 9" loaf pan. Bake for 50-60 min.

SPANAKOPETA (Spinach Pie)
Houston Leisure RV Park – Highlands, TX

Houston is a melting pot for many different cultures. Houston Leisure RV Park is particularly interested in Greek dishes since our "Fearless Leader" comes directly to us from Kavala, Greece. For this reason our camp-outs frequently include Greek dishes. Our campers love to sample these delicious delicacies such as Spanakopeta, occasionally served with complimentary Greek wine.

INGREDIENTS
3 pkg. frozen chopped spinach (room temp.)
1 lb. cottage cheese (small curd)
1 lb. Feta cheese, crumbled
½ c. grated Romano cheese
1 lg. egg
1 med. onion, grated
16 filo sheets
½ lb. melted butter
¼ c. grated Romano cheese

DIRECTIONS
While preparing recipe, place filo between damp towel. Allow spinach to stand at room temperature, to defrost completely. Squeeze dry in colander. Combine first 6 ingredients and mix thoroughly in large bowl. Lightly butter bottom of 11″ x 16″ pan. Arrange 6 filo in bottom of pan, brushing each with butter. Add spinach mixture on top of filo in pan. Cover with remaining filo and brush with butter. With sharp knife cut through top layer of filo in serving size squares. Sprinkle remaining Romano cheese on top. Bake at 350° for 50 or 60 min. until golden brown on top. Serve warm and watch your campers say, OPA!!!

ITALIAN BROCCOLI CASSEROLE
Casini Ranch Family Campground-Duncan Mills, CA

This recipe is an old Casini family favorite and has been passed down through the years.

We're located ½ mile east on Moscow Rd., off Hwy. 116 in Duncan Mills. We're a full service campground with riverview sites, open or shaded. Take advantage of our clean restrooms, hot showers, general store, laundry, arcade, pull-thru full hookup sites, tent sites, trailer rally area, rec hall, and canoe and boat rentals. Hiking, horseback riding, golf, wine tasting, the seashore and redwood scenic area are all nearby.

INGREDIENTS
2-10 oz. pkg. cut broccoli
2 eggs, beaten
1 can condensed cheese soup
½ tsp. dried oregano, crushed
8 oz. stewed tomatoes
3 Tbsp. Parmesan cheese, grated

DIRECTIONS
Cook cut broccoli in unsalted water 5 to 7 min. Drain. Combine eggs, soup and oregano. Stir in stewed tomatoes and cooked broccoli. Put mixture into a 10″ x 6″ x 2″ baking dish. Sprinkle with Parmesan cheese. Bake uncovered at 350° for 30 min. or until heated through. Makes 6 to 8 servings.

HOT TACO CASSEROLE
Wilderness RV Park & Campground-Robertsdale, AL

This dish is a big hit whenever I serve it. The dish is always empty at the end of the meal.

We are located between Pensacola, FL and Mobile, AL, 1½ miles off of I-10 at exit 53. We're in a quiet, remote setting among pine trees. Deer and a variety of birds are seen daily in our park along with other wildlife. Two ponds, nature trails, pavilion for group activities and an outdoor barbeque grill for feeding large groups are also provided. We welcome tenters.

INGREDIENTS
- 2 Tbsp. oil
- 2 onions, chopped
- 3 lbs. hamburger
- 1 can mushroom soup
- 1 can cream of chicken soup
- 1 jar hot taco sauce
- 1 jar mild taco sauce
- 1 lg. bag tortilla chips, crushed
- 2 c. grated American cheese

DIRECTIONS
Brown onions and hamburger in oil. Add soups and taco sauces. Alternate layers of hamburger mixture, chips and cheese in buttered casserole dish. Bake at 350° for 30-40 min. or until bubbly.

ENCHILADA CASSEROLA
Posada del Sol – Harlingen, TX

Palm trees, cottonwoods, bougainvillea bushes and other foliage native to the Rio Grande Valley make our park green and appealing. Also native to the area is Mexican cooking and we are only 20 miles from the Mexican border. The taste of hot and spicy beef, tomato and tortilla chips makes for an easy, filling, and good meal. This casserole is a potluck special on Thursdays.

INGREDIENTS
- 1 c. chopped onion
- 1 clove garlic, minced
- 2 Tbsp. margarine or butter
- 2 lbs. ground beef
- 1 can (10½ oz) cream of mushroom soup
- 1 can tomato sauce
- 1 can (6 oz.) tomato paste
- 2 cans peeled green chiles, chopped
- 1 tsp. salt
- 1 pkg. (8 oz.) tortilla chips
- ¾ lb. Longhorn cheese, shredded
- sour cream, optional

DIRECTIONS
Saute onion and garlic in margarine. Add meat and brown. Stir in soup, tomato sauce, tomato paste, chiles and salt. Cook until mixture begins to boil. Place half of tortilla chips in bottom of 9″ x 13″ baking dish. Pour meat mixture over tortilla chips. Top with remaining tortilla chips and cheese. Bake at 375° for 20-25 minutes. Serve with sour cream if desired.

JIMMIE'S CASSEROLE FROM TEXAS
St. Charles Bay Trailer Inn – Rockport, TX

This dish is easy to prepare and is even good as leftovers!
Our park is located on Saint Charles Bay, just outside of Rockport. We have a 500 ft. lighted pier for fishing with boat docking nearby. Oysters are plentiful in the bay area. In addition to fishing we offer a clubhouse, laundry facilities and a large swimming pool.

INGREDIENTS
oleo
¾ lb. hamburger
1 onion, chopped
4 celery stalks, chopped
1 sm. can Spanish style tomato
   sauce
1 can cream of celery or cream
   of mushroom soup
macaroni or spaghetti, cooked
   according to directions
cheddar cheese, grated
salt & pepper to taste

DIRECTIONS
   Saute onion and celery in oleo. Add hamburger and brown slightly. Add cooked pasta. Stir in remaining ingredients. Place in casserole dish and cover with cheese. Bake at 350° until bubbly.

MEXICAN SPOON BREAD
Towerpoint Resort – Mesa, AZ

Towerpoint Resort is located in the middle of the desert. The area is rich in Indian heritage. We have 1123 spaces in the park and our guests are made up of winter visitors that come to Arizona to enjoy not only our great winter weather, but also the lifestyle that has become very well known throughout the U.S. The lifestyle here leans toward a more active retirement area.

INGREDIENTS
1 lb. cream style corn
1 c. cornmeal
⅓ c. margarine, melted
2 eggs, beaten
1 tsp. baking soda
4 oz. green chiles, drained &
   chopped
1½ c. shredded longhorn
   cheese

DIRECTIONS
   Combine the first 6 ingredients; mix well. Pour half the batter into a greased 9" x 9" x 2" pan. Then sprinkle with chilis and half the cheese. Pour on remaining batter. Sprinkle with remaining cheese. Bake at 400° for 45 min. Cool 10 min. before serving.

DUNGENESS CRAB CASSEROLE
Als R.V. Park – Port Angeles, WA

We are located on the upper Olympic Peninsula of Washington state in a prime area for salmon, bottomfish and shellfish. There are also many sights and activities of interest to history buffs and nature lovers, not the least of which is the Olympic National Park. We are located within minutes to either the mountains or the water. There is an abundance of recipes for preparing the "catch of the day" and we would like to share with you a favorite recipe for preparing Dungeness Crab.

INGREDIENTS
1 pt. fresh Dungeness Crab (or canned crab)
½ c. butter
½ c. flour
2⅔ c. milk
1½ c. chopped celery
½ c. chopped green pepper
2 Tbsp. minced onion
1 Tbsp. parsley
½ c. mayonnaise
½ c. slivered almonds, chopped
4 hard cooked eggs
2 tsp. salt
⅛ tsp. pepper
several dashes of Tabasco
1 c. shredded cheddar cheese
buttered bread crumbs or seasoned crumbs
paprika

DIRECTIONS
Preheat oven to 350°. Melt butter in saucepan. Add flour and mix well. Remove from heat and slowly add milk. Heat again, stirring constantly until sauce thickens. Add all other ingredients except crumbs, cheese and paprika. Pour into a 3-qt. casserole dish. Top with crumbs, cheese and paprika. Bake 30-35 min. Can be frozen. To freeze, omit cheese, paprika and crumbs until ready to bake. Serves 8. For a complete meal, serve with rice and a green salad.

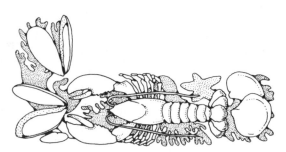

SEAFOOD CASSEROLE
Bayou Haven R.V. Park – Galveston, TX

Seafood dishes are very popular in Galveston. We prepare this recipe for Thanksgiving, Christmas and New Year's to enjoy along with the turkey.

Our park has 84 sites with full hookups. We are next to the Offats Bayou, 2 blocks off 61st and near a big shopping area.

INGREDIENTS
1 lb. cooked shrimp
1 lb. cooked crab
1½ c. chopped celery
¾ c. chopped green peppers
¼ c. chopped onions
¼ tsp. salt
1 c. mayonnaise
1 Tbsp. Worcestershire sauce
crumbled potato chips

DIRECTIONS
Combine all ingredients except chips. Place in a greased casserole pan. Top with crumbled potato chips. Bake at 400° for 20-25 min.

SCALLOPED CRAB, SHRIMP OR LOBSTER
Arvi Park – Beaumont, TX

This recipe offers a unique way to prepare shellfish. It's always a hit for holiday meals or any special occasion.

Arvi Park offers 40 full hookups, concrete streets and large concrete parking slabs. We provide picnic tables shaded by over 100 trees, laundry, propane, phones and security lights. There's even a marketplace within walking distance. Stay with us and experience Beaumont's finest.

INGREDIENTS
- 4 Tbsp. butter
- 4 Tbsp. flour
- 2 c. half & half
- ½ tsp. salt
- dash pepper
- dash cayenne
- dash paprika
- ½ tsp. Worcestershire sauce
- 2 Tbsp. parsley
- 2 c. cut crab, shrimp or lobster
- ¼ c. soft buttered bread crumbs

DIRECTIONS

Melt butter. Add flour, then half & half and seasonings. Stir until thick. Add crab. Put in casserole dish and top with crumbs. Bake at 350° for 20 min.

SEAFOOD CASSEROLE
Elm River Park – Debert, NS

Many types of seafoods are available in our area; either bought or caught by our guests. This recipe is a favorite when we are asked how to use a number of fish varieties together.

Our park is 12 acres of level pull-thru sites bordering on the Debert River. It is situated 10 miles from Truro — the Hub of Nova Scotia, and near the Bay of Fundy.

INGREDIENTS
- 3 c. celery
- 2 c. onion
- ¼ c. butter
- ¾ c. flour
- 5 c. milk
- 1 lb. Velveeta cheese
- 2 c. cooked lobster
- 1 lb. cooked scallops
- 1 c. cooked crab meat
- 2 c. shrimp

DIRECTIONS

Saute celery and onions in butter. Blend in flour and gradually blend in milk. Add Velveeta cheese and slowly cook until cheese is melted. Place sauce in large casserole dish and add fish. Bake at 350° for 30 min.

BREAKFAST CASSEROLE
Eagle River Village MH Community – Edwards, CO

The men in our family request this breakfast casserole whenever we plan a camping trip.

Our park, near the winding Eagle River, is surrounded by the beautiful Rocky Mountains. You can ski Beaver Creek or Vail and we even provide free shuttle buses to some ski areas. We're only minutes from Eagle River Village, and fishing, river rafting, golf, hunting, hiking, and more are close by.

INGREDIENTS
- **8 slices bread, cubed**
- **½ c. grated cheddar cheese**
- **4 eggs, beaten**
- **½ tsp. dry mustard, optional**
- **1 tsp. salt**
- **2 c. milk**
- **1½ lbs. bulk sausage, hot**

DIRECTIONS

In casserole dish, layer bread, sausage, and cheese, ending with cheese on top. Mix eggs, milk, salt, and mustard. Pour over layers. Let stand overnight. Bake at 350° for 1 hr. We like Territorial or Picante sauce served with the casserole.

COUNTRY BREAKFAST PIE
Bristol/Kingsport KOA – Kingsport, TN

We've found that this dish is great as a one-dish family breakfast, served at home or on the go.

We are located on 23 acres of beautiful Eastern Tennessee countryside. We are surrounded by trees for a quiet night's rest. Come stay with us and enjoy the historical sites in the area. Or relax and take advantage of the many recreational activities we offer at our campground.

INGREDIENTS
- **1 pkg. ground sausage**
- **9″ deep dish pie shell**
- **1½ c. grated cheddar cheese**
- **¼ c. chopped bell peppers**
- **¼ c. chopped red bell peppers**
- **2 Tbsp. chopped onion**
- **4 eggs, slightly beaten**
- **1 c. light cream**

DIRECTIONS

Fry sausage until done. Crumble and drain. Mix cheese and sausage together. Sprinkle into pie shell. Combine beaten eggs and remaining ingredients. Pour into shell. Bake at 375° for 40-45 min. Cool on rack 10 min. before serving.

BROCCOLI CASSEROLE
Parkway Travel Park – Harrison, AR

This is a favorite recipe from a favorite Aunt. Although it's not a dish I serve at our park, it's one our family enjoys.

We have a small campground with 25 spaces. Cleanliness and compatibility are the order of the day here at Parkway Travel Park. We have concrete patios and cabanas at each pad and our rates include full hookups with free cable TV. We also offer a children's playground and a swimming pool.

INGREDIENTS
- ⅓ c. salad oil
- 1 tsp. salt
- 1 c. grated cheese
- 1 lg. egg
- 1 c. milk
- 1 sm. onion, chopped fine
- 1 c. cooked rice
- 1-10 oz. pkg. frozen, chopped broccoli, prepared as directed and drained

DIRECTIONS
Mix all ingredients together and put in a buttered casserole dish. Bake at 350° for 1 hr.

AUNT FRANCES' ZUCCHINI CASSEROLE
Best Holiday Trav-L-Park Memphis – Marion, AR

Our favorite Aunt from Wisconsin shared this with us. It is easy to prepare and our time is limited when running a campground. It has become one of our favorites and we hope it becomes one of yours as well.

For southern hospitality at its best, try the Best Holiday tradition! Marion, Arkansas is just 15 min. from downtown Memphis, TN. Graceland, Mud Island, dog racing, and the famous Peabody Hotel are just minutes away. We are glad to be able to share this recipe. Come see us!

INGREDIENTS
- 3 c. grated zucchini
- 1 med. onion, chopped fine
- ½ c. grated cheese
- ¼ c. chopped parsley
- ½ c. oil
- ½ tsp. oregano
- ½ tsp. garlic powder or salt
- ½ tsp. salt
- ½ tsp. pepper
- 1 c. Bisquick
- 4 eggs, beaten

DIRECTIONS
Mix all the ingredients together. Bake in a casserole dish or 8" x 8" pan at 375° for 45 min.

HOME-MADE MARZETTI
Hickory Grove Lake Family Campground-Marion, OH

We are located about 10 miles west of Marion, out in the country away from the city traffic. We have a 9 acre lake and are located in a partially wooded area. We offer activities to keep the whole family busy. One of our special activities occurs over Father's Day. We ask our campers to bring Dad's favorite dish to our Father's Day Potluck. This dish happens to be my husband's favorite. We hope you and your family can stay with us this Father's Day and share your Dad's favorite recipe with us.

INGREDIENTS
- **2 lbs. ground beef**
- **1 c. celery**
- **1-16 oz. pkg. broad noodles**
- **1-10¾ oz. can cream of mushroom soup**
- **1 lg. onion**
- **1 sm. green pepper**
- **1 lb. colby longhorn cheese, chopped**
- **2-10¾ oz. cans tomato soup**

DIRECTIONS

Fry ground beef, celery, onion and green pepper together. Drain excess grease. Cook noodles in salt water, then rinse well in cold water. Line a roaster pan with aluminum foil. Layer noodles, cheese, ½ can of mushroom soup and ½ the hamburger mixture. Cover with one can tomato soup. Repeat above procedure, add other can of tomato soup. Bake at 350° for 1 hr.

ST. REGIS SOUR CREAM BAKE
Best Holiday Trav-L-Park Campground-St. Regis, MT

This delightful one-dish meal is easily prepared in any RV oven and was always one of our greatest favorites as we motor-homed across the continent. Prepare and eat this meal as you enjoy one of our shady, park-like sites. We're located at Exit #33 on Interstate 90; which just happens to be the exact halfway point between Billings, MT and Seattle, WA as well as being the scenic gateway to Glacier Park and the National Bison Range.

INGREDIENTS
- **2 c. baking mix**
- **½ c. cold water**
- **1 lb. ground beef**
- **2 med. tomatoes, thinly sliced**
- **¾ c. chopped green pepper**
- **1 c. dairy sour cream**
- **⅔ c. mayonnaise**
- **1 c. shredded Cheddar cheese**
- **2 Tbsp. chopped onion**

DIRECTIONS

Mix baking mix and water until soft dough forms. Pat in greased 9" x 13" x 2" pan with floured hands, pressing ½" up sides.

Cook and stir ground beef until brown; drain. Layer beef, tomatoes and green pepper on dough. Mix remaining ingredients, drop spoonfuls over top. Sprinkle with paprika. Bake at 375° for 25 to 30 min.

BROCCOLI AU GRATIN
Turtleback RV Park — Lake Panasoffkee, FL

We're a family-owned and operated park located on Lake Panasoffkee. We have shady, grassy sites with full and partial hookups. We offer a wide variety of winter activities including shuffleboard, mini-golf, rec halls, swimming, nature study area and naturalist trails.

INGREDIENTS
- 1½ lbs. fresh broccoli
- 1½ c. water
- 1 Tbsp. sugar
- 2 Tbsp. butter or margarine
- 2 Tbsp. all-purpose flour
- 1 c. milk
- ¾ tsp. salt
- ⅛ tsp. nutmeg
- 2 Tbsp. butter or margarine, melted
- 2 Tbsp. fine dry bread crumbs

DIRECTIONS

Wash and trim broccoli. Place in large saucepan; add water and sugar. Cover. Boil over high heat. Reduce to medium heat and cook for 5-8 min. Drain.

While broccoli is cooking, melt butter in saucepan. Add flour and stir until smooth. Add milk and bring to boil. Cook until thick, about 2 min. Add salt and nutmeg; set aside.

Arrange cooked broccoli in oven-proof dish and pour sauce over broccoli. Combine melted butter and crumbs; sprinkle over broccoli. Bake at 350° for 30 min.; or cover and store for cooking at a later date. Serves 4.

BROCCOLI CASSEROLE
Zachary Taylor Camping Resort — Okeechobee, FL

We serve this recipe frequently at covered dish dinners. However, when we share it with others, we double the recipe.

Located on Taylor Creek, we offer riverside sites, partial and full hookups. We have 1500 feet of waterfront where you can fish, boat and swim. Lake Okeechobee is only 1000 feet away from us. We offer a variety of amenities including boat rentals and guides, shuffleboard, horseshoes, a large rec hall, groceries, RV supplies, bait and tackle and lots of trees for shade. Come visit us where the fishing is good and the folks are friendly!

INGREDIENTS
- 2 pkgs. frozen chopped broccoli
- 1 c. mayonnaise
- 1 c. cream of mushroom soup
- 1 c. sharp cheese, grated
- 1 sm. onion, grated
- 2 eggs, well-beaten
- salt and pepper to taste
- 1 c. cracker crumbs

DIRECTIONS

Cook broccoli until tender, drain well. Combine other ingredients except crumbs. Add broccoli to mixture and blend well with spoon. Put in buttered casserole dish. Top with crumbs. Bake at 400° for 20 min.

WILD RICE CHICKEN CASSEROLE
Stony Point Resort – Cass Lake, MN

Wild rice is harvested on our area lakes by the local Chippewa Indian tribe making it great area food. We are located on the southeast side of Cass Lake in beautiful pine and hardwood forests. We cater to overnight campers or all types of travel units. Many retired people spend the summer in permanent mobile homes parked on our 1500 ft. boat canal. Children enjoy our safe, sandy beach, rec hall and playground. The whole family enjoys dining in the Canal House Restaurant and Lounge where they can feast on delicious Bar-B-Que Pork Ribs, Chicken, Pizza and numerous sandwiches all available for carry out as well.

The wild rice casserole has been used for our potluck camp fish fries and we have also served it to the local bridge club luncheon. Hope you enjoy it as much as we have.

INGREDIENTS
4 Tbsp. butter
5 Tbsp. flour
1 c. chicken broth
1½ c. evaporated milk
1 tsp. salt
1 c. wild rice
2 c. diced chicken
¾ c. sliced mushrooms
¼ c. diced pimiento
⅓ c. chopped green pepper
½ c. sliced almonds (optional)

DIRECTIONS
Prepare sauce by melting butter, then adding flour and blending with broth and milk. Cook until thickened. Add salt. Meanwhile, mix other ingredients and put into 6" x 10" pan. Pour sauce over all. Top with almonds and bake at 350° for 45-50 min. Serves 4-6.

JOX CAMPING NIGHT GOURMET DINNER
Lakeside KOA – Henderson, NE

Not only is this dish easy to prepare and bake in an hour, it's also very nutritious and delicious.

Located at the Henderson Exit #342 on I-80, Lakeside KOA offers a travel shop, gas station, and quiet, tree shaded, grassy sites. Enjoy our sandy beach, boat rentals, mini golf, playground, and Kamping Kabins. Our 13 acre campground is open from the beginning of March until the end of October and tenters are welcome.

INGREDIENTS
4 boneless chicken breast
  halves, fresh or frozen
½ bunch of broccoli, fresh or
  frozen
4 oz. sliced Swiss cheese
1 can cream of chicken soup
1 can cream of mushroom soup
1 can cream of celery soup
1 box chicken flavor dressing,
  prepared according to
  directions

DIRECTIONS
Blend soups together. In baking dish, layer blended soups, then chicken, then a little more soup, then cheese slices, more soup, broccoli spears, and rest of soup. Cover with dressing. Bake at 350° for 1 hr. Enjoy!

CANADIAN WILD RICE CASSEROLE
Wogenstahl's Canadian Resort – Vermilion Bay, ONT

Canadian wild rice — a grain that is rare, unique, and highly prized for its nutty flavour and soft, chewy texture, grows in the wilds of Canada. It is an organic food, free from all artificial growing aids. It is also very digestible, being low in fat content, high in protein and rich in Vitamin B. The great French explorers were probably the first white men to enjoy this delicacy.

Canadian wild rice which I prepare and serve at our parties has been a real delight to our guests. Our park is 16 acres on the lakefront with 36 pull-thru sites on Cedar Lake. We have good fishing and lots of fun.

INGREDIENTS
1 c. long grain wild rice
4 c. cold water
½ c. chopped green pepper
1 c. chopped onion
1 c. chopped celery
1 c. mushrooms
½ lb. bacon (fried crisp)
soy sauce to taste

DIRECTIONS
Add water and rice to a heavy 2-quart saucepan and bring to a hard boil. Reduce heat, cover tightly and boil gently for 30 min. Shut off heat and let stand on burner for 25-35 minutes until rice reaches the desired texture. Drain.

Melt small amount of butter in skillet and saute onion, celery and green pepper until tender. Combine with rice and remaining ingredients in a large casserole dish. Cover and bake at 325° for 30-45 min.

MACARONI & SAUSAGE CASSEROLE
Fox Den Acres – New Stanton, PA

Our park is in its 30th year of catering to the overnight traveller. Located at the foothills of the Laurel Highlands, we offer a variety of amenities and all kinds of recreation the whole family can enjoy. You may also visit our free wildlife museum and old time trading post.

INGREDIENTS
1 box macaroni
1 lb. sausage links
1 can whole or crushed
    tomatoes
1 pkg. cheddar cheese

DIRECTIONS
Boil macaroni. Boil sausage in skillet for 15 min. In casserole dish, add macaroni, tomatoes and cheese. Lay sausage on top. Bake at 350° for 40 min.

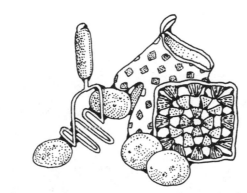

SIDE DISHES

PAT'S COLESLAW
Anvil Campground – Williamsburg, VA

This coleslaw is served as a side dish at Anvil Campground's free cookouts held every Friday from April through October. The cookouts are as fun for the owners as they are for their guests. The recipe most requested is "Pat's Coleslaw". It is delicious and different.

Anvil Campground has been headquarters for almost 35 years for thousands of guests who come to visit restored Colonial Williamsburg, Busch Gardens, Historic Jamestown and Yorktown. The free cookouts first began in 1975 and demonstrate the campground's attitude toward hospitality.

INGREDIENTS
- **2 lbs. cabbage, shredded**
- **2 lg. ripe tomatoes, diced fine**
- **1 onion, quartered and thinly sliced**
- **1 c. mayonnaise**
- **3 Tbsp. milk**
- **1 c. sugar**
- **½ c. vinegar**
- **salt & pepper to taste**

DIRECTIONS

To shred cabbage, cut into manageable wedges and slice wedges thinly. Mix all ingredients well, cover and refrigerate until served.

CREAMY COLE SLAW
Gulfstream Trailer Park – Marathon, FL

Gulfstream Trailer Park, located on the Gulf of Mexico, is family owned and operated. Swim in our pool or participate in our many activities. We start our winter months together by having a Christmas party for our guests. In February, we have a week long fishing contest and trophies are awarded. The festivities are ended by a fish fry which is very popular at our park. We are very proud of the park and its friendly, family atmosphere.

INGREDIENTS
- **¾ c. mayonnaise**
- **¼ c. sour cream**
- **2 Tbsp. grated onion**
- **2 Tbsp. chopped parsley**
- **2 tsp. Dijon mustard**
- **1½ tsp. celery seed**
- **½ tsp. salt**
- **½ tsp. fresh ground pepper**
- **8 c. shredded red cabbage**
- **8 c. shredded green cabbage**
- **4 grated carrots**

DIRECTIONS

In a large bowl, whisk mayonnaise, sour cream, onion, parsley, mustard, celery seed, salt and pepper. Add red and green cabbage and carrots. Toss until well mixed. Can be made ahead of time. Cover and refrigerate up to 24 hours. Makes 12 cups.

SWEET POTATO PIE
P & L Trailer Park – Palestine, AR

I love sweet potato pie and this is the best recipe I have found yet. We are located midway between Little Rock, Arkansas and Memphis, Tennessee. We offer a nice country setting with easy access to I-40. Come by and visit with us.

INGREDIENTS
- 2 c. sweet potatoes, baked or boiled
- 6 Tbsp. butter
- 1 c. sugar
- 3 eggs, beaten
- 1 tsp. vanilla
- 1 tsp. apple pie spice
- 1 c. milk
- ¼ tsp. salt
- 2 9″ pie crusts

DIRECTIONS
Melt butter and add to potatoes. Add sugar, beaten eggs, vanilla, salt, spice and milk. Mix well. Pour into 2 unbaked pie shells. Bake at 350° for 40 min. or until filling is firm.

VIDALIA ONION "PIE"
Moonshine Creek Campground – Balsam, NC

The campers organize potluck cookouts at the pavilion known as "RC's Meating Place" on Saturday nights and special occasions. The camper's cooking talents come from all over the country. When the recipes are unusual or outstanding we compile them into a Moonshine Creek cookbook. This recipe comes from one of our campers and is representative of food from the area.

Moonshine Creek is located in the heart of the Blue Ridge Smoky Mountains and is a quiet, cool and secluded retreat in an unspoiled scenic area. It is a great place to get away from it all, relax and unwind. Just put your feet up, listen to the ever present creek rushing by and the other sounds of nature surrounding you.

INGREDIENTS
- corn flake crumbs
- ¾ c. melted margarine
- 2 c. sliced Vidalia or sweet onion
- 2 eggs
- ¾ c. milk
- ½ tsp. salt
- grated sharp cheddar cheese

DIRECTIONS
Pour corn flake crumbs into bottom of pie plate (cover well). In sauce pan, melt margarine and saute sliced onions and pour over crust. Beat eggs and add milk and salt and pour over onions. Next add grated sharp cheddar cheese over top. Bake at 350° for 30-35 min.

EASY PA. DUTCH POTATO FILLING
Eagles Peak Campground – Robesonia, PA

This recipe (often doubled and tripled) is served at our annual Chicken BBQ. It gets rave reviews each year and everyone thinks our Pennsylvania Dutch cook has slaved hours peeling potatoes, etc. to create it. No one can taste any shortcuts and this recipe sure saves us time on a busy weekend.

Eagles Peak Campground lies in the heart of the Pennsylvania Dutch Country. Mennonites, Amish folk and vast farmlands surround us. The Dutch are famous for their delicious food and hearty meals. If you visit this area, you won't go home hungry.

INGREDIENTS
1 13½ oz. box of instant mashed potatoes
1 6 oz. box of Stove Top stuffing for chicken
2 eggs
1 qt. of milk or more if needed
¼ lb. butter or margarine

DIRECTIONS
Heat milk and butter in a large oven-proof container until steaming. Add potatoes & eggs. Stir until smooth. Add Stove Top stuffing mix and stir again. You may add more milk if needed. Bake uncovered at 350° for 30-40 min.

PENNSYLVANIA DUTCH POTATO FILLING
Schlegel's Grove & Campsites – Bechtelsville, PA

Each year at the end of our camping season, we have a free dinner for our seasonal campers. We try to have homemade Pennsylvania Dutch recipes. Our potato filling has become a favorite item among the campers.

Our campground is located in Pennsylvania Dutch country. It is a very quiet park with grass, trees, and two ponds for fishing. We also have a creek flowing through the meadow and a Pennsylvania Dutch barn for dancing and suppers.

INGREDIENTS
8 lg. potatoes
2 eggs
4 slices bread, cubed
1 med. onion, chopped
1 Tbsp. parsley flakes
milk
salt & pepper to taste
2 Tbsp. butter
1 tsp. brown sugar

DIRECTIONS
Saute chopped onion and cubed bread in frying pan. Set aside to cool. Cook and mash potatoes. Mix in eggs, parsley flakes, onion mixture, brown sugar, butter, salt & pepper to taste. Add milk to make nice consistency. Place in buttered casserole dish and bake at 350° for 45 min.

SAUGEEN COLE SLAW
Saugeen Tent & Trailer Park – Hanover, ONT

We hold a Thanksgiving B.B.Q. for the campers and this is our cabbage salad our campers like.

Our park is on the banks of the Saugeen River surrounded by cedar and maple trees. It has quiet, green, relaxing surroundings with friendly campers.

INGREDIENTS
1 head shredded cabbage
1 green pepper
1 c. chopped celery
½ onion, sliced
1 c. vinegar
¾ c. sugar
¼ tsp. dry mustard
½ c. oil
2 tsp. salt

DIRECTIONS
Mix vinegar, sugar, pepper, dry mustard, salt and oil in a frying pan and bring to a boil. Place vegetables in a large bowl and pour mixture over vegetables. Mix well. Will keep for one week.

SPANISH RICE
Joe Hominick RV Park – Robstown, TX

This dish is very good with beans or a salad. For those of us watching our cholesterol levels, this dish is a tasty way to do it.

We have a nice, quiet and clean park. We're just 15 min. from the bayfront of Corpus Christi. We offer grassy sites, laundry facilities, swimming pool and rec hall. And since we're open all year you can take advantage of all that we have to offer any time you'd like!

INGREDIENTS
1 c. long grain rice
1 14½ oz. can of tomatoes
1 clove garlic
1 sm. chopped onion
3 Tbsp. oil
1 sm. chopped green pepper
1 tsp. cumin
salt & pepper to taste
1½ can water (use tomato can)

DIRECTIONS
Brown rice in oil. Add all ingredients except water. Stir and add water. Stir again. Cover and do not stir again. Cook until done — about 30 min.

ADIRONDACK GARBAGE
Whispering Pines Campground

We are located 6 miles south of Lake Placid, near the high peaks of the Adirondacks. Sometimes black bears are a nuisance when it comes to our campers' garbage. This "garbage", however, is something our campers have come to enjoy as their side dish to hamburgers and hot dogs at our annual Campers Cookout. Come visit us and experience our shady, wooded sites, our clean, quiet atmosphere and all the activities we have to offer.

INGREDIENTS
1 16-oz. pkg. Kluski noodles
½ lb. bacon
4-5 med. red potatoes
½ head cabbage
3-4 lg. onions

DIRECTIONS
Cook noodles in salt water. Rinse well. Wash potatoes and boil. Let cool and skin. Cut potatoes as for potato salad. Cut bacon in 4 strips, fry until crisp; remove from grease with slotted spoon. Chop cabbage and onions and simmer in remaining bacon grease until tender and transparent. In a large bowl, toss all ingredients, season to taste and serve as a side dish to BBQ chicken, pork chops, hamburgers or hot dogs. Serve hot.

SQUASH DRESSING
Mom's Campground – Madisonville, TX

This recipe was given to me by an RV guest. My park is the homesite of this guest. Descendants of the first settlers along the O.S.R. (Old San Antonio Road) came back for a family reunion.

Mom's Campground faces part of the last section of the O.S.R. (Old San Antonio Road) with the original roadbanks, little varied. This is the route of the cattle drives of early Texas history.

INGREDIENTS
5 c. cooked squash
1 6-oz. bag Mexican cornbread
   mix, cooked
1 can cream of chicken soup
1 c. finely chopped celery
1 lg. finely chopped onion
1 stick butter
1 egg
salt & pepper to taste

DIRECTIONS
Crumble cornbread into cooked squash. Mix well. Add soup, egg, softened butter and vegetables. Add salt and pepper. Mix well. Pour into a slightly greased oblong baking pan. Bake 30-35 min. in a preheated oven of 400° until brown.

STUFFED ZUCCHINI
Cheerful Valley Campground – Phelps, NY

These vegetables are plentiful in our area during summer and stuffed zucchini is a great dish for potluck suppers.

Cheerful Valley Campground is located in the Finger Lakes Area of New York — famous for scenic beauty and friendliness.

INGREDIENTS
1 lg. zucchini
1 sm. zucchini
1 green pepper
1 onion
1 rib celery with leaves
1 tomato
1 carrot
½ c. grated Italian cheese
1 tsp. celery salt
½ tsp. garlic powder
black pepper to taste

DIRECTIONS
Wash large zucchini and cut in half lengthwise. Scrape out seeds. Chop remaining vegetables. Toss cheese and seasoning with chopped vegetables. Fill zucchini cavity with stuffing. Put into 9" x 13" pan with ¼ inch of water in the bottom. Cover with aluminum foil and bake at 350° for 20-30 min.

WILD RICE HOT DISH
Stardust RV Park – Las Vegas, NV

My husband and I are former residents of Minnesota where the real wild rice abounds. We always take this dish to potlucks to promote this healthy and nutritious food.

Our park is located on the famous strip in Las Vegas directly behind the Stardust Hotel and Casino. We have a beautiful and quiet park which is newly refurbished and landscaped. We host people from all over the world and United States and they love staying in our park overlooking the excitement and bright lights.

INGREDIENTS
- ½ lb. 100% pure wild rice
- ¼ c. chopped onion
- 1-4 oz. can mushrooms (optional)
- 1 can cream of mushroom soup
- 1 can cream of celery soup
- ½ lb. hamburger
- 3 c. water
- salt & pepper to taste

DIRECTIONS

Rinse wild rice well until the water is clear. Cook rice in 2 qt. saucepan in 3 c. boiling water until done, about 15 min. Stir occasionally. Pour off any excess water and rinse. Fry hamburger with onions until browned. Mix hamburger, wild rice and other ingredients together and bake at 350° for 30-45 min.

RICE PILAF
Arizona Beach – Gold Beach, OR

Arizona Beach is located on Highway 101, just 14 miles north of Gold Beach. Our unspoiled natural setting among the trees also offers ½ mile of beach front. We have RV hookups and tent sites, lots of amenities and plenty of things to do.

INGREDIENTS
- 1-10 oz. pkg. coil vermicelli
- 2 cubes margarine
- 10 cubes chicken bouillon
- 4 c. converted rice
- 8 c. boiling water

DIRECTIONS

Brown vermicelli in margarine. Dissolve bouillon cubes in boiling water. Add bouillon mixture and washed rice to vermicelli. Cook covered on low for 1 hr.

CAMPERS DELIGHT
Hunters R.V. – Lakeview, OR

This recipe is served at our yearly 4th of July festival. Our park is surrounded by a large variety of wild game, natural mineral pools, a natural geyser and forested mountains. Also, our park is a world famous museum and a sports and lodging center.

INGREDIENTS
- 6 cans red kidney beans
- 2 cans pinto beans
- 1 can lima beans
- chopped red onions to taste
- hot barbeque sauce to taste

DIRECTIONS

Pour all beans in a large pot. Add chopped red onions and hot barbeque sauce to taste. Simmer for several hours until onions are done. Serve with barbeque ribs and bread.

CAJUN STYLE WHITE BEANS
Cajun Farms RV Campground – Houma, LA

Cajun Farms RV Campground invites you to relax at a real Cajun resort in Houma, Cajun capital of the world. We're situated on a working crawfish farm, with two fishing lakes (no fishing license needed), nature trails, boat ramp, hayrides, and tent camping. We're conveniently located near Cajun restaurants and attractions.

INGREDIENTS
- **1 lb. dried white beans (Great Northern or Navy)**
- **1 lb. salt pork or ham**
- **1 lg. onion, chopped**
- **cooking oil, optional**
- **¼ c. chopped fresh parsley**
- **¼ c. chopped fresh shallots or onion tops**
- **salt to taste**

DIRECTIONS

Method 1: If time permits soak dried beans overnight; otherwise wash thoroughly. Boil salt pork until tender and discard water. Chop into bite-sized cubes. Add all ingredients to pot with enough water to cover. Boil over low fire until tender. (Some cooks add parsley and shallots about 15-20 min. before beans are done.)

Method 2: Boil and chop salt pork. Fry pork in cooking oil until it is slightly browned. Add chopped onion and saute until tender. (Don't brown the onions.) Add beans and other ingredients and boil until tender. Serves 6-8.

Note: Be careful when adding salt. Salt pork will add salt to the dish even after boiling. Method 2 will produce a dish that is creamy and sweeter than the first method due to the cooking oil and sauteed onions. Serve over rice or as a side dish.

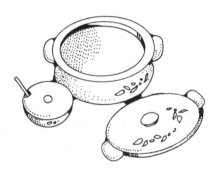

ANNETTE'S 4TH OF JULY BEANS
Nancy Lake Marina Resort – Willow, AK

We hold a 4th of July picnic and this is always a big hit. Our campground has 50 campsites on the shore of Nancy Lake. We're adjacent to a state recreation area. Located 65 miles north of Anchorage on Parks Highway, Nancy Lake Marina Resort is a rustic campground offering modern restrooms and showers. We also offer a camp store, fuel, propane, fishing and boat rentals.

INGREDIENTS
- **1 lb. bacon**
- **4 lg. onions**
- **1 c. brown sugar**
- **½ c. vinegar**
- **1 tsp. dry mustard**
- **1 lg. can pork and beans**
- **1 can kidney beans, drained**
- **1 can butter beans, drained**

DIRECTIONS

Cut up and fry bacon. Do not drain fat. Chop and add onions. In a large pot, mix all ingredients together. Simmer for at least 1 hr. Enjoy!

BBQ PIG BAKED BEANS
Diamond Point RV Park – Sequim, WA

A BBQed pig is standard fare every Memorial Day. The leftover meat makes a wonderful difference to the baked bean dish which we prepare every weekend for the rest of the summer.

We are located 10 miles east of Sequim, away from the hustle and bustle of the city. From our park it's an easy walk to 5 miles of state beaches that offer clam digging, fishing and beachcombing. We also serve all-you-can-eat low-cost breakfasts and dinners on weekends during the summer.

INGREDIENTS
2 lbs. barbequed pig meat, cut in lg. chunks
2 gal. baked beans
2 lg. onions, diced
garlic powder
salt & pepper

DIRECTIONS
In large baking dish, add pig meat, beans and onions. Stir in seasonings. Bake at 350° for 1 hr.

WESTERN BAKED BEAN DISH
Bayshore RV Park – Tokeland, WA

We are located right on Willapa Bay, known as the banana belt of the south coast. We cater dinner to our tourists as well as our camping groups and we include this dish in our western dinners.

INGREDIENTS
2 lg. cans pork & beans
3 lbs. hamburger
24 oz. bacon
½ onion
2 cans stewed tomatoes

DIRECTIONS
Brown hamburger and onion. Fry bacon. Drain grease and add pork & beans and stewed tomatoes. Cover with foil and bake in 350° oven for 45 min.

BEANEY WEANEY
Fuller Lakes Campground — Corinth, NY

This recipe is ideal for campers because it's quick and simple and it can be cooked inside your RV or over hot coals.

Fuller Lakes is a family-oriented campground with a back-to-the-basics atmosphere. Our rural, wooded sites, restroom facilities, picnic tables, swimming pool, boating and fishing facilities and other amenities help make your stay with us a relaxing one.

INGREDIENTS
1 pkg. hot dogs
1 can pork and beans
onions, diced
mustard

DIRECTIONS
Cut up hot dogs and mix with beans, onions and mustard in pot or bowl. Cook in oven or over stove, or over open campfire until bubbling.

WILDERNESS BAKED BEANS
Green Acres Tent & Trailer Park — Shequiandah, ON

This recipe has been handed down from generation to generation for over 200 years. We hope it becomes a favorite, if not a tradition, with your family.

Our park is situated on Hwy. 6, on Manitoulin Island in Ontario, Canada. We have 85 shady, grassy, serviced sites and modern conveniences. Our park overlooks Shequiandah Bay of Georgian Bay. And this area is almost biting-insect free. Our 1,000 feet of safe, sandy beaches and awesome sunrises complement the great fishing.

INGREDIENTS
- **4 c. white beans**
- **2 whole med. onions**
- **1 lb. salt pork, sliced or
  1 lb. bacon and 1 Tbsp. salt**
- **1 lb. pure lard**
- **1 c. brown sugar or molasses,
  or ½ c. each**

DIRECTIONS

Soak beans for 12 hrs. or boil for 1 hr. Place onions in bottom of pot. Add drained beans, lard, molasses and brown sugar. Place meat slices on top. Add water just covering meat. Cook in oven at 300° for 4 hrs. Or, in wilderness: Build campfire. Enjoy evening of song, dance and fishing stories. Before bedding down, dig hole in sand 18" deep. Dump all hot coals in hole. Place pot on hot coals, cover pot with aluminum foil to keep dirt out. Bury with 4" sand over pot. Grab some Z's, and wake up to a perfect authentic French Canadian wilderness breakfast.

KENTUCKY BEANS
Kamptown RV Park – Cadiz, KY

Our park is in a quiet, country area located on the Little River Bay of Lake Barkley. We specialize in relaxing and fishing. We are just a few miles from Western Kentucky's "Land Between the Lakes" recreation area.

Cadiz is known as the "Ham Capital of the Nation." Every October the pig is glorified during the Country Ham Festival. Country ham is delicious by itself, but it's especially good for seasoning.

INGREDIENTS
- **2 lbs. Country Ham ends
  and pieces**
- **10 oz. pkg. dry pinto beans**
- **10 oz. pkg. dry navy beans**
- **lg. sweet onion, chopped**
- **1 Tbsp. jalapeno pepper**
- **1 Tbsp. garlic powder**
- **pepper to taste**

DIRECTIONS

Add all the ingredients together. Fill pot with water. Best if cooked in a big cast iron pot over hickory wood, but also delicious if cooked slowly in a crockpot. Serve with any meal or as the whole meal accompanied with cornbread.

HARRY TRODLIER'S FRIJOLES
Woody Acres Park – Fulton, TX

Harry and Dorothy Trodlier run at large up at Sinton, which is just across the pasture from Corpus Christi. As far as being an international chef, Harry isn't. He is what you might call a "One-Note Johnny". He only attempts to cook one dish and that's beans, or frijoles as Texans call them. Harry doesn't use any blueprints when he builds a pot of beans. Like my Grandma made cornbread, he does it by instinct. Getting any kind of a scientific formula for his frijoles was like trying to get weather information from a lockjawed oyster. Let's get loose on a pot of Harry's frijoles. Like he does, we'll play it by ear.

Our park offers acres of beautiful shady oak trees, private fishing lakes, all kinds of recreation and deluxe facilities. Why not join Harry and me for a taste of frijoles at our annual barbeque?

INGREDIENTS
2 lb. well rinsed pinto beans
1 level tsp. black pepper
1 med. onion, diced
1 garlic clove, diced
½ tsp. celery seed
½ tsp. cominos, whole or powdered
1 whole jalapeno pepper, canned or fresh
1 Tbsp. chili powder
salt to taste

DIRECTIONS
Place all ingredients in a large pot and cover with a close fitting lid. Add water to cover beans and let simmer over low heat approximately 3 hr. 40 min. During the last stages of simmering add salt to your craving. In addition to adding flavor to the frijoles, the jalapeno tends to reduce the . . . shall we say buoyancy content. Makes 6 large servings. Tastes great with cornbread.

Note: I'm glued to the contention that beans shouldn't be boiled to a pulpy mess of potage. They should be slowly simmered until they're plump and soft but not mushy. Each bean should retain its own individuality.

OPEN FIRE SAUSAGE & BEANS
Basswood Country RV Park – Platte City, MO

Our 75 site park offers full hookup sites, laundry facilities, grocery items, RV supplies and a whole lot more. We have excellent fishing in 12 acres of stocked lakes, shuffleboard courts and hiking trails. We're only 10 miles NE of Kansas City International Airport and we welcome senior citizens and RV clubs. Hope to see you soon!

INGREDIENTS
1 smoked sausage link
2 cans pinto beans
¼ c. bar-b-que sauce
½ chopped onion

DIRECTIONS
Cut sausage into bite size slices. Put in a kettle with other ingredients. Cook over open fire for 30 min. to 1 hr. The longer it cooks the better the flavor. This is especially good served with hot cornbread.

QUICHE LORRAINE
Miami South KOA – Miami, FL

This is a favorite of our winter seasonal campers. We are a 50-acre campground located in the countryside amid avocado and mango groves. We offer spacious, grassy sites and huge, heated swimming pool and hot tub.

INGREDIENTS
- 3 eggs
- ½ c. melted butter or margarine
- ½ c. Bisquick
- 1½ c. milk
- ¼ tsp. salt
- dash of pepper
- 1 c. grated cheese
- 1 c. cut-up ham *or*
- ½ c. bacon bits

DIRECTIONS
Place all ingredients in blender except cheese and ham. Spread cheese and ham in a greased 8″ pan. Pour mixture over. Bake 45 min. at 350°.

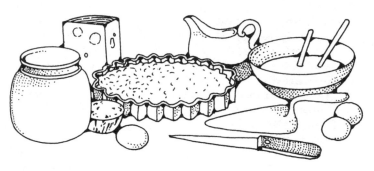

GREEN BEANS AND PEARS
Riverbend Park – Mount Vernon, WA

Riverbend Park is located along the Skagit River with great fishing. Our campground is convenient to the freeway, restaurants and shopping. An orchard of Bartlett pear trees surrounds the common area. By late August the pears are ripe and can be enjoyed by all.

INGREDIENTS
- 2 pears, peeled and diced
- ¼ lb. bacon, fried and crumbled
- 1 Tbsp. bacon drippings
- 1 Tbsp. flour
- ¼ c. white wine (optional)
- 1 c. chicken broth
- 2 lbs. green beans, blanched

DIRECTIONS
Saute pears in bacon drippings until tender. Remove pears. Stir in flour and cook 2 minutes. Add wine and broth and simmer until thickened. Add blanched beans and cook until tender. Stir in pears. Serve immediately topped with crumbled bacon. Serves 8.

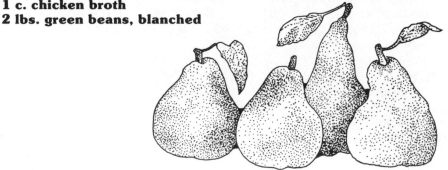

COUNTRY ROASTED CORN
Country Roads Campsites – Gilboa, NY

Our area is comprised of rich farming land. As a result, there is a vast variety of corn to choose from. While we are centrally located for lots of attractions, our park is secluded and we look for things to do that are comfortable, low key, and "country". Corn roasts give our guests the chance to enjoy one another and the local produce. Our campers love to relax on our mountain-top and enjoy nature's bounties — beautiful view, cooling forests, crisp, clear stars, fresh air, and GREAT CORN!

INGREDIENTS
fresh corn in husks
melted butter or margarine
salt and pepper

DIRECTIONS
Soak corn in water at least 15-30 min. Build a wood fire, keeping fire at a consistent cooking height. Place grill about 8" over wood. Place corn on grill, cover, and turn every few minutes so corn cooks evenly. Cook about 15 min. (covered). Husks may look charred. Peel back husks carefully — corn will be steaming — dip in butter and come back for more!

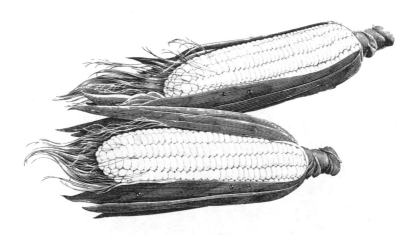

CORN PUDDING
Alligator Point KOA – Alligator Point, FL

This dish is easy to prepare and is a great side dish to pass along at potlucks.
Alligator Point KOA offers lakeside and oceanfront sites, a fully stocked grocery store, 2 swimming pools, boat ramp and dock, and fresh water and ocean fishing. We invite you to come stay with us and enjoy Florida's natural abundance of sun, surf and friendly people. Folks have enjoyed our service for over 14 years and keep coming back for more.

INGREDIENTS
1 can cream style corn
1 can evaporated milk
1 c. sugar
3 Tbsp. cornstarch
2 eggs
¼ tsp. salt

DIRECTIONS
Beat eggs slightly. Add milk and salt. Add remainder of ingredients. Mix well. Turn mixture into buttered casserole. Dot with butter. Bake at 350° for about 1 hr.

Side Dishes   153

COUNTRY POTATOES
Zilpo Recreational Area — Salt Lick, KY

Kentucky has long been known for good country cooking and southern hospitality. The Zilpo Recreational Area, located on the shores of Cave Run Lake in northeastern Kentucky, is frequently the scene of shared meal preparation when families and friends camp together. Country potatoes are equally as good when served with hamburgers grilled over a fire or freshly caught bass or crappie.

INGREDIENTS
- **10 lbs. white potatoes, washed and sliced**
- **2 medium yellow onions, chopped**
- **2 bell peppers, chopped**
- **salt & pepper to taste**
- **1 tsp. garlic powder**
- **1 tsp. seasoned salt**
- **2 oz. liquid margarine**

Variation:
- **½ lb. bacon**
- **6 drops Tabasco sauce**
- **2 c. shredded cheddar cheese**

DIRECTIONS

Line a large casserole pan with foil and grease foil with margarine. Layer sliced potatoes, onions, peppers and seasonings three times and spread liquid margarine over each layer. Cover with foil and bake at 350° for one hour (or until tender).

Variation: Add layer of bacon to bottom of pan and to top of each of the three layers. Add 2 drops of Tabasco to top of each layer. Cover with foil and bake 40 min. at 350°. Remove foil, cover top with shredded cheese. Bake uncovered for additional 20 minutes.

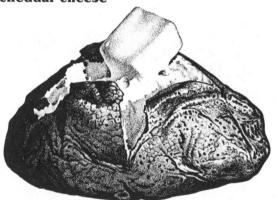

PICNIC POTATOES
Hills Family Campground – Fairview, PA

Throughout the season we do a lot of pig and turkey roasts at our pavilion for our campers, travel club groups, and various organizations who rent our pavilion. These potatoes are well liked and easy to prepare.

Our campground is located next to Erie, the third largest city in Pennsylvania. We are at Exit 5 I-90, Route 832, the direct route to Presque Isle State Park, which consists of 3,202 acres of sandy beaches jutting 7 miles into Lake Erie. There is swimming, fishing, boating, hiking, picnicking, bird watching, and much more to do.

INGREDIENTS
- **5 lbs. potatoes, washed and scrubbed**
- **2 sticks margarine**
- **2 pkgs. dry Italian dressing**

DIRECTIONS

Melt margarine sticks in 9″ x 12″ pan. Cut unpeeled potatoes into chunks. Place in pan. Sprinkle with dry Italian dressing. Cover with foil and bake 1 hour covered and 1 hour uncovered or until done. Serves about 25.

PIZZA BEANS
Bluewater Campground & Boat Dock – Dayton, TN

We often have bean dinners here at the park. The kids really enjoy this recipe — I guess it reminds them of pizza.

We are a small family campground surrounded by water on three sides. Our main activity is fishing and boating. We are situated on eleven acres, mostly wooded, with a good view of the water from all vantage points. Come visit us and camp on the beautiful Lake Chickamauga.

INGREDIENTS
- 1 lb. pinto beans
- 6 c. water
- 4 med. tomatoes, peeled & diced
- 1 onion, chopped
- ¼ c. chopped pepper
- 1 clove garlic, crushed
- 2 tsp. salt
- ½ tsp. oregano
- ¼ tsp. rosemary
- 1 c. shredded mozzarella cheese
- ¼ c. Parmesan cheese

DIRECTIONS

Soak beans in water overnight. In slow cooking pot, cook soaked beans in water on high for 2-3 hrs. or until tender but not mushy. Drain, saving liquid. In Crockpot, combine beans with remaining ingredients except cheese. Add 2 c. liquid from beans. Cover and cook on low for 8-10 hrs. Add cheeses and cook on high for 15-20 min. Let stand for a few minutes before serving. Makes 6 to 8 servings.

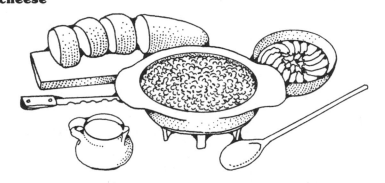

BROWN BAKED BEANS
Pioneer Camp Ground – French Creek, WV

Whenever we have a cookout or gathering, I always make sure I'm in charge of the B-B-Q. These baked beans are always a favorite.

Our campground offers a peaceful, quiet atmosphere. We have all wooded sites with full and partial hookups. We offer picnic tables, fire rings, playground, hiking trails and pond fishing.

INGREDIENTS
- cranberry beans
- salt & pepper to taste
- onion, sliced
- dark brown sugar
- catsup
- vegetable oil

DIRECTIONS

Saute beans in vegetable oil. Salt and pepper to taste. Cook until beans are almost done, but still solid. Place in baking dish. Mix catsup and sugar together. Pour over beans. Top with onion and bake until done.

BAKED BEANS
Frazier RV Center & Campground – Swannanoa, NC

This recipe is a favorite with everyone, especially at our covered dish suppers!
We are located in the Swannanoa Valley, six miles east of Asheville. Our campground has 66 full hookup sites, a pavilion, and is convenient to shopping centers, restaurants, laundry and outlet stores. We are only about 4 miles from the beautiful Blue Ridge Parkway, and approximately 7 miles from the most magnificent mansion in America, The Biltmore Estate.

INGREDIENTS
1½ lb. ground beef
10 slices bacon
½ c. onion, chopped
⅓ c. packed brown sugar
⅓ c. granulated sugar
¼ c. catsup
¼ c. barbeque sauce
2 Tbsp. pure prepared mustard
2 Tbsp. molasses
½ tsp. salt
½ tsp. chili powder
½ tsp. pepper
3 (16 oz.) cans pork and beans*

* May use 1 can kidney beans,
drained, 1 can butter beans
and 1 can pork and beans

DIRECTIONS
Brown meat and drain. Add onion and cook until tender. Add combined sugars, catsup, barbeque sauce, mustard, molasses and seasonings; mix well. Add beans. Pour into 3-quart casserole. Bake at 350° for 1 hr. Makes 10-12 servings.

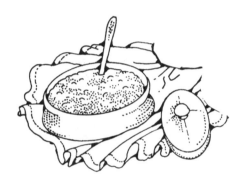

"WOODSY" BAKED BEANS
Lil Thicket Travel Park – La Marque, TX

This recipe was handed down through my family and it exemplifies the very best in "Down Home Southern Cooking". We use it whenever we barbeque out on the grills in the park.
Our park is in a small, secluded, woodsy area near but not on the busy interstate between Houston and Galveston. Our park offers a quiet, peaceful interlude after enjoying an active and busy day at the beach in Galveston or the many activities in Houston. Lil Thicket is a wonderful place to unwind after enjoying the many wonderful historical sights of our area.

INGREDIENTS
1 16 oz. can pork & beans
4 slices bacon, cut into
sm. pieces
1 sm. onion, diced
3 Tbsp. sorghum or dark
Karo syrup or honey
3 Tbsp. brown sugar

DIRECTIONS
In a large cast iron skillet, brown bacon. Add diced onions and saute until soft. Do not drain grease. Add beans and mix well. Add syrup and brown sugar. Move to the side of the grill and cook slowly for 20 min. (If cooking indoors, bake in oven for 20 min.) Stir before serving. Serves 4.

COOK SHACK BEANS
Buena Vista Family Campground – Buena Vista, CO

This dish is served in our restaurant as part of our Buffalo Burger Chuckwagon dinners.

We are located in the upper Arkansas Valley of the Colorado Rockies, an incredibly beautiful area with breathtaking scenery and a mild climate. Our campers enjoy a friendly western atmosphere, fantastic view of the Continental Divide and delicious home-cooked meals at our "Cook Shack". We hope you will enjoy this recipe we have shared with you. Come camp with us for a spectacular view of Colorado!

INGREDIENTS
1 2-lb. can pork and beans
¼ lb. Polish sausage, diced
3 Tbsp. chopped onion
2 tsp. Dijon mustard
3 Tbsp. ketchup
2 Tbsp. brown sugar
dash Tabasco sauce
salt & pepper to taste

DIRECTIONS
Mix all ingredients in a 2-qt. baking dish. Bake at 350° for 1½ hrs.

EASY BAKED BEANS
Tincup Campers' Park – Mahomet, IL

Our park is set among trees and rolling terrain. Because the park is situated high, our guests can enjoy the quiet, scenic setting. We have all types of hookups and can accommodate all sizes of groups and RVs. This recipe is great for our potlucks — an easy and tasty dish for campers and campground owners alike to prepare!

INGREDIENTS
½ lb. bacon
½ c. chopped onion
1 16 oz. can pork & beans
1 16 oz. can butter beans
1 16 oz. can kidney beans
1 c. sharp cheddar cheese
  shredded (optional)
¼ c. brown sugar
¼ c. catsup

DIRECTIONS
Saute onions and bacon until fairly crisp. Pour off drippings. Add all cans of beans (drain off small amount of liquid from each) and pour into 9″ x 13″ casserole pan. Mix in brown sugar and catsup. Add cheese on top if desired. Bake at 350° for 1½ hrs.

BEANS TEXAS STYLE
Hatch R.V. Mobile Home Park – Corpus Christi, TX

Early Cowboys & Mexicans alike ate beans cooked over the campfire around South Texas. However, it took the Texas woman with a little Mexican seasoning to add the spice. Corpus Christi hugs the Bay and the Gulf making the weather very mild for most of the year. Outside cooking and barbeques are great for get togethers. Our park has lots of shade and of course the Mesquite Tree for our barbeques. But, DON'T FORGET THE BEANS!

INGREDIENTS
2 lbs. pinto beans
ham or bacon, chopped
onion, chopped
3 tsp. salt
2 tsp. garlic powder
cilantro (tops pulled off stems)
green chili peppers; seedless,
    diced (optional)

DIRECTIONS
Wash pinto beans well. Soak beans for 2 hrs. or overnight in water with 1 tsp. salt added. Make sure the water completely covers the beans. After soaking, drain water and add fresh water that fills the pan at least 3/4 full and add 1 tsp. salt and 1 tsp. garlic powder. Simmer over low heat for about 3 hrs. Then add another tsp. salt, another tsp. garlic powder, 1/2 cup of onion, ham or bacon, 1/2 cup cilantro tops and about 2 Tbsp. diced green chili peppers — optional. Cook for 2 more hrs. or until very soupy. Serves: 12-15.

SUGGESTIONS: Beans freeze well or add to Taco Seasoned Ground Meat for GREAT Chili.

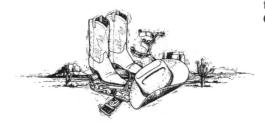

RANCH BEANS
Apache Skies – Apache Junction, AZ

This recipe is a tasty side dish that goes with any main dish.
Apache Skies is located in Apache Junction with a wonderful view of the Superstition Mountains. We offer full hookup sites, laundry facilities, rec hall, heated swimming pool, whirlpool, shuffleboard courts and more!

INGREDIENTS
1 lb. hamburger
1 pkg. onion soup mix
2 cans pork & beans
1 can kidney beans, drained
1 c. ketchup
2 Tbsp. mustard
¼ c. brown sugar
1 lb. bacon

DIRECTIONS
Brown hamburger. Add all other ingredients. Place in baking dish. Lay strips of uncooked bacon across the top. Bake at 400° for 30-40 min.

COWBOY BEANS
San Diego Metro KOA – Chula Vista, CA

This is very tasty, easy, smells good, and our campers really like it. We serve this with BBQ hamburgers and all the trimmings.

The San Diego Metro KOA is a 270-site full-service RV Park located in the suburb of Chula Vista. Many of our campers remark that we have a very rural, country "feel" even though we are right in the middle of Metropolitan San Diego. One of our hallmarks is service to our campers. Once a week, during the busy season, we serve up a hearty hamburger BBQ dinner. We always serve "Cowboy Beans" and use this recipe, created by Carol Bell. One of the unique things about the recipe is that it has no sugar and very little salt and yet has a savory, full flavor. Enjoy!

INGREDIENTS
5-7 lbs. pinto beans
water to cover
1 Tbsp. salt
1 Tbsp. dry sage
2 Tbsp. chili powder
3 Tbsp. dried, minced onions
1 tsp. garlic salt
1 tsp. pepper
½ lb. salt pork, cubed

DIRECTIONS
Soak beans overnight. Add the rest of ingredients. Cook slowly 3-4 hrs., stirring occasionally. Add more water if needed to keep juicy.

CHUCK WAGON BEANS
Camp-A-Way – Lincoln, NE

These beans are a great favorite at outdoor gatherings.

Camp-A-Way is a medium-sized campground with large shade trees and large grassy areas. We offer full and partial hookups and plenty of amenities to make your camping trip a pleasant one. It's only minutes to downtown Lincoln where you can visit fine restaurants, historical sites, museums and the zoo.

INGREDIENTS
1 15-oz. can pork & beans
¼ c. light molasses or brown
  sugar
½ c. coarsely chopped onion
½ c. catsup
3 slices bacon, fried and cut up
1 Tbsp. Worcestershire sauce
½ green pepper, cut in sm.
  slices

DIRECTIONS
Mix all ingredients in heavy cast iron kettle. Bake slowly at 325° for 2 hrs. or put over outdoor campfire, stirring often.

SANDWICHES

BRATWURST-WISCONSIN STYLE
KOA-The Kamping Place on Devils Lake-Haugen, WI

Wisconsin is bratwurst country. We are a quiet family campground located on a peninsula surrounded by the waters of upper and lower Devils Lake. Our 112 acres of woods and 2 miles of shoreline make us a super destination!

INGREDIENTS
- **8 bratwurst**
- **1 med. onion, sliced**
- **1 med. green pepper**
- **1 can flat beer**

DIRECTIONS

Brown brats on grill. Cook slowly so skin does not burn. Place pan of beer in center of grill — if you use coals on side it won't boil out as fast. Add onions, peppers, and brats. Cover and cook 30 min. Serve on buns.

SPIEDI MARINATE
Pine Valley Campground — Endicott, NY

Pine Valley is snuggled among picturesque rolling hills. We have spacious campsites in a variety of wooded and open settings. Spiedies are a local favorite and we encourage our campers to attend the Annual Spiedi Fest and Balloon Rally held in nearby Binghamton.

INGREDIENTS
- **5 lb. cut up beef***
- **⅓ c. oil**
- **½ c. vinegar**
- **2 tsp. garlic powder**
- **1 tsp. salt**
- **½ tsp. pepper**
- **1 tsp. celery salt**
- **1 tsp. garlic salt**
- **1 tsp. basil**
- **1 Tbsp. parsley**
- **1 Tbsp. rosemary**
- **1 bay leaf**

* venison or pork may be substituted for beef

DIRECTIONS

Mix all ingredients together and add meat. Marinate for 3 days, stirring occasionally. Place marinated meat on skewers and char-broil over grill until done. Serve on slices of French or Italian bread.

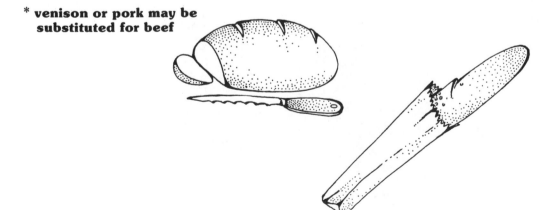

LOBSTER ROLL
Meri-Mist Acres – Bayfield, NB

During lobster season, lobsters are fished right before your eyes in the Northumberland Strait and are available to our campers.

We have a beautiful view from every campsite. Our park is located on the Northumberland Strait, Cape Tormentine, New Brunswick, Canada.

INGREDIENTS
1 lobster
1 tsp. Miracle Whip
dash of paprika
few drops of lemon juice
hot dog buns
butter
lettuce

DIRECTIONS
Cut cooked lobster meat into bite size pieces. Add Miracle Whip and lemon juice. Mix together. Butter outside of hot dog buns and fry until golden brown. Place a lettuce leaf in each bun and fill with lobster meat. Sprinkle top with paprika and ENJOY!

BAKED HAM & CHEESE SANDWICHES
Windy City Beach & Camping Resort – Mokena, IL

After a day of visiting Chicago, our guests come back to a dip in the lake and supper at our renovated turn-of-the-century barn. These sandwiches are a favorite.

Windy City is the closest campground to Chicago. We are near a commuter train for easy service to the city. Our park is full service with a springfed lake, swimming, hayrides, and other planned activities.

INGREDIENTS
½ c. butter
¼ c. chopped onion
¼ c. mustard
1 Tbsp. poppy seeds
Swiss cheese
sliced, boiled ham
12 dinner rolls

DIRECTIONS
Saute butter and onion. Add mustard and poppy seeds. Mix well. Split each dinner roll and spread with mustard mixture. Add 1 slice cheese and 1 slice ham. Wrap in foil and bake at 350° for 15 to 20 min. May be frozen.
Note: Do not overfill sandwich.

BARBECUE PORK ROAST SANDWICHES
Hickory Grove Lake Family Campground-Marion, OH

The third Saturday in August, we have a Luau/Pig Roast at the campground. If there is left over pork from this, I freeze the pork and in September I fix the Barbecue Pork Sandwiches. Hickory Grove Lake Family Campground is located about 8 miles west of Marion. Our hickory trees and nine acre lake offer a country haven away from city traffic. Although our Luau/Pig Roast takes place in summer, our campground is a pretty place to visit spring, summer, winter and fall.

INGREDIENTS
- 2 onions, chopped
- 2-3 celery stalks, chopped
- 1 tsp. paprika
- ½ tsp. pepper
- 1 Tbsp. soy sauce
- 3-4 lb. pork roast
- 1 c. brown sugar
- 2 tsp. prepared mustard
- 14 oz. catsup
- ¼ c. vinegar (mix with broth from meat to make liquid)

DIRECTIONS
Cook pork, take off bone and shred. Use two cups of broth and mix the remaining ingredients in the broth. Simmer until onion and celery are almost done. Add pork to broth mixture andd simmer for 45 min. to 1 hr. You can add more broth if needed. Beef may be substituted for pork. Serve on sandwich bread or rolls.

ROSE BAR B-Q
Rose Gardens Resort KOA – Crittenden, KY

This old Kentucky recipe has been handed down in the Rose family for over half a century. The staff at Rose Gardens Resort loves it! Rose Gardens Resort KOA, just south of Cincinnati, Ohio in the Bluegrass country of Kentucky is an ideal vacation spot. This 35 acre campground was a barren hayfield when building started nearly 20 years ago. Thousands of trees and shrubs planted by the Rose family have turned it into a beautiful arboretum and bird sanctuary. The large flower gardens are enjoyed daily by campers from the first crocus in February, through the Iris and Daylillies of the Summer to the last Rose that is killed by November's hard freezes.

INGREDIENTS
- 2 lg. onions, chopped
- 1½ lb. ground chuck or lean ground beef
- 1 Tbsp. chili powder
- ½ tsp. pepper
- 2 Tbsp. Worcestershire sauce
- ½ bottle tomato catsup
- ½ bottle chili sauce
- ½ c. water

DIRECTIONS
Saute onions in skillet. Add ground chuck and brown. Stir in other ingredients. Cover and simmer for about 1/2 hour. Serve on heated buns with pickle relish.

BARBECUE BURGERS
Pine Mountain Campgroud – Pine Mountain, GA

This recipe is served here on the 4th of July and Labor Day. It is loved by young and old alike. They often come back for seconds. It will be a hit at your next barbecue.

Our park is a beautifully shaded area, with a relaxed atmosphere and friendly people. Located 12 mi. from Warm Springs and F.D. Roosevelt's Little White House and 1½ mi. from lovely Callaway Gardens.

INGREDIENTS
4 lb. ground chuck
2½ Tbsp. Heinz 57 Sauce
2½ Tbsp. A-1 Sauce
1 med. chopped onion
3 dashes Worcestershire sauce
1½ tsp. pepper
1½ tsp. salt
3 slices moist white bread
barbecue sauce

DIRECTIONS
Mix all ingredients except barbecue sauce in a large bowl. Then make large patties and grill to your liking. When done, top with barbecue sauce and serve on seeded buns with potato chips.

BARBEQUE BEEF — DEER PARK STYLE
Deer Park Campground – Buffalo, WY

Deer Park Campground is located in the shadows of the Big Horn Mountains along the Bozeman Trail in northeastern Wyoming. This is beef country. When we opened our little restaurant at Deer Park we decided to feature our favorite beef recipe. Our restaurant has an indoor dining room and an outdoor deck with a spectacular view of our pool and spa with the snowcapped Big Horn Mountains in the background. After dinner, campers may enjoy our 1 mile private walking path in a natural setting where white tailed deer may be seen most evenings.

INGREDIENTS
4 lbs. cut up stew beef
mesquite seasoning
1 c. catsup
¼ c. brown sugar
¼ c. vinegar
4 tsp. prepared mustard
4 tsp. Worcestershire sauce
1 Tbsp. chopped parsley
¼ c. chopped onion
dash pepper

DIRECTIONS
Lightly sprinkle 4 lbs. stew meat with mesquite seasoning. Place in crockpot on low setting. Do not add water. Cook for 4 to 6 hrs. Stir remainder of ingredients, to make sauce, into meat and its natural juices. Continue to cook on low for 4 hrs. Serve with your own favorite dishes. Serves 6.

CHEESE DELIGHT
Goodwin's RV Park – San Jacinto, CA

This recipe was handed down to me from my mother. It's a quick and tasty entree I sometimes serve at potlucks.

Goodwin's is "the friendliest park in town". This is our motto and the tenants and management try very hard to live up to it. We are located 1 hr. from the desert, 1 hr. from the mountains and 1 hr. from the beaches. Our average temperature year round is 70°. We have a very nice rec hall, jacuzzi and pool. What more could you ask for?

INGREDIENTS
- 1½-2 lbs. med. sharp cheddar cheese
- 1 can black pitted olives, chopped
- 1 jar stuffed green olives, chopped
- ½ sm. onion, minced
- 1 can tomato sauce
- 1 pkg. sourdough rolls

DIRECTIONS

Grate cheese in blender. Blend olives and onions with tomato sauce. Spread tomato mixture on rolls and top with cheese. Melt in broiler. Serve hot.

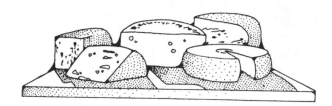

GRILLED CHEESE
Jellystone Park – Lebanon, TN

When working outside most of the morning, this sandwich is a quick, hot, high protein lunch. It keeps me going all afternoon.

Just 15 minutes east of Nashville (off of I-40), Jellystone Park sits on a scenic hill overlooking the city of Lebanon. With 100 sites, pool, country store, open air pavilion, tennis court, clean washrooms, and a fishing pond, Jellystone Park offers the camper the quiet of the country and the bright lights of the city.

INGREDIENTS
- 2 slices of bread
- your favorite cheese
- peanut butter
- butter
- bacon

DIRECTIONS

Cook bacon. Spread light coat of peanut butter on inside of both slices of bread. Cover each slice with cheese. Place bacon strips between bread slices and grill sandwich in butter.

JUST SANDWICHES
West 40 Camp Area – Shamrock, TX

Our campground offers peaceful country camping. We offer shady, flat and grassy or gravel sites with full and partial hookups. Hot showers, grocery items, laundry facilities, swimming pool and indoor rec room help make your stay with us a comfortable one.

INGREDIENTS
- ¼ c. margarine, melted
- 2 c. milk
- 2 pkgs. active dry yeast
- ¾ c. warm water
- 5½ c. flour
- 2½ tsp. salt
- ¾ c. sugar
- cooking oil
- 1 sm. pkg. salami
- 1 sm. pkg. cooked ham slices
- 1 c. shredded mozzarella cheese
- 1 c. shredded cheddar cheese

DIRECTIONS

Melt margarine in a medium saucepan. Remove from heat and add milk. In a small bowl, combine yeast and warm water. When margarine and milk are lukewarm, add to yeast mixture. In large bowl combine salt, sugar and 4 cups flour. Add liquids and mix to form dough. Place in oven or microwave with a pan of hot water until dough rises. Place dough on floured surface and knead in enough flour so that the dough will roll out easily. Roll remaining dough out to the length of the long cookie sheet. Place salami, cooked ham and shredded cheeses on top of the rolled out dough. Fold the dough over the filling and close edges by mashing the dough together. Place on oiled cookie sheet and spread oil over the top of the dough so it browns evenly. Bake at 350° until golden brown.

RANCHBURGERS FOR A CROWD
Bel Aire Mobile Home & RV Park – Austin, TX

This is easy to fix for a few or a lot!

Our cozy, shaded park in Austin offers you easy access to all local points of interest in the surrounding area. Visit Aquarena Springs, LBJ Ranch and Library, fine restaurants and golf courses. Or if you'd rather, just relax in our friendly park.

INGREDIENTS
- 4 lb. hamburger
- 6 eggs
- 16 crackers
- 2 c. milk
- 2 tsp. pepper
- 3 tsp. salt
- 4 Tbsp. mustard
- 1 8-oz. can tomato sauce
- 1 c. catsup
- 2 onions, chopped

DIRECTIONS

Mix all ingredients in large pot and cook slowly. Stir often. When cooked thoroughly dip a scoop onto a hamburger bun. Yum. Yum.

HAMBURGER STUFFED FRENCH BREAD
Town and Country RV – Roswell, NM

This recipe is quick, easy and delicious. It can even be prepared on a barbeque grill.

Town and Country RV offers clean facilities in a quiet atmosphere. Our amenities include laundry facilities, clean, private restrooms, a rec room, horseshoes and playground. We're close to town and we're only 96 miles from Carlsbad Caverns. We offer daily, weekly and monthly rates year 'round.

INGREDIENTS
- 1 loaf French bread
- 1½ lbs. hamburger
- 1 med. onion
- 1 Tbsp. parsley flakes
- 1 c. grated cheese (your choice)
- 1 egg, beaten
- salt, pepper & garlic powder to taste

DIRECTIONS

Brown meat and onion with salt, pepper and garlic powder to taste. Drain and set aside. Cut approximately 2 inches off one end of loaf. Hollow out center of loaf, leaving about ¾ inch thickness. Tear bread in pieces. In a mixing bowl, add bread, meat mixture and remaining ingredients. Mix well. Put into hollowed loaf. Put end on and secure with toothpicks. Wrap loaf in foil. Bake at 350° for 30 to 45 min.

DESSERTS

CHOCOLATE SHEET CAKE
Gordon's Camping – Wolcottville, IN

Each year we serve this cake at one of our potlucks. Of course it takes 3 or 4 of these cakes to go around, but even then these cakes don't last long! Our campground offers a variety of amenities and lots of recreation. Why not visit us and take advantage of all that we have to offer — chocolate cake and all!!

INGREDIENTS
- 2 c. flour
- 2 c. sugar
- 2 eggs
- 1 tsp. vanilla
- 1 tsp. cinnamon
- 1 tsp. baking soda
- ½ c. buttermilk
- 1 stick margarine
- ½ c. vegetable oil
- 1 c. water
- 4 Tbsp. cocoa

Icing:
- 1 stick margarine
- 6 Tbsp. milk
- 4 Tbsp. cocoa
- 1 tsp. vanilla
- 1 box powdered sugar
- 1 c. chopped pecans

DIRECTIONS
Mix together flour and sugar. Bring margarine, oil, water and cocoa to a rapid boil. Add to flour mixture and mix thoroughly. Add eggs, vanilla, cinnamon, baking soda and buttermilk to mixture. Pour onto cookie sheet and bake at 400° for 20 min.

Icing: Bring margarine, milk and cocoa to a rapid boil. Add vanilla, powdered sugar and pecans to mixture. Stir well. Spread on cake while it is still warm.

LINDA'S CHOCOLATE CAKE
Inscription RV Park – El Morro, NM

This chocolate cake is a great success at our weekend BBQs. Inscription RV Park is located ¼ mi. from El Morro National Monument. We provide RV Spaces and 2 cabins along with a store and a restaurant.

INGREDIENTS
- 3 c. flour
- 2 c. sugar
- 2 tsp. baking soda
- 1 tsp. salt
- ¼ c. cocoa
- 10 Tbsp. oil
- 2 Tbsp. vinegar
- 2 tsp. vanilla
- 2 c. hot water

DIRECTIONS
Sift together dry ingredients. Stir in remaining ingredients with a spoon — no need for a mixer. Pour into a 9″ x 13″ pan. Bake at 350° for 30 minutes.

BUSY-DAY CAKE
Estes Park – Tulsa, OK

This is a plain and simple cake that is delicious and so easy to make even after a busy day. So you can understand why it's a favorite with our family.

Estes RV Park is located in a residential neighborhood, close to shopping malls, grocery stores, and points of interest in Tulsa. We are a clean, quiet, family owned, retirees court with plenty of trees to provide shade.

INGREDIENTS
- 2½ tsp. baking powder
- 1 tsp. vanilla
- ¼ tsp. salt
- 1 egg
- 1 c. sugar
- 1⅔ c. flour
- ⅓ c. shortening
- ⅔ c. milk

DIRECTIONS

Mix all ingredients together in a mixing bowl. Beat for 2 minutes. Pour batter into a well greased and floured baking pan (1 9″ round pan or 8″ square). Bake for 25-30 min. at 350°. You can add chocolate if you like.

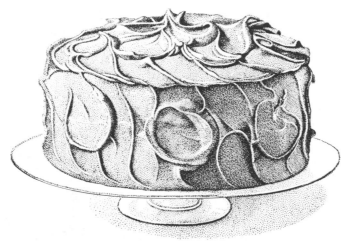

HOT MILK CAKE
La Grande Estate Camping Resort-Leonardtown, MD

My husband loves this dessert — and you'll be surprised how easy it is to make this homemade cake!

La Grande Estate is set in the midst of 33 acres of unspoiled Maryland countryside. Deer and a large variety of birdlife can be found throughout the large varieties of tall timber here. While relaxing here, you can enjoy year round fishing or boating in nearby waterways. In addition, many historical points of interest are at your fingertips. So, come take advantage of our modern facilities and let us make your visit a pleasurable experience.

INGREDIENTS
- 4 eggs
- 2 c. sugar
- 2 c. sifted flour
- 1 c. milk
- ¼ lb. butter
- 1 tsp. baking powder
- 1 tsp. vanilla

DIRECTIONS

Beat eggs and sugar at high speed until creamy. Add flour slowly. Heat milk and butter. Add to mixture. Mix slowly at low speed. Add baking powder and vanilla. Bake in tube pan at 350° until top splits. No icing is needed.

BIG MAMA'S CHOCOLATE CAKE
KOA-Nashville I-24 – Smyrna, TN

At KOA-Nashville I-24 Campground, located just south of Nashville, this special chocolate cake is served at our annual 4th of July celebration. In addition to our 4th of July celebration, our guests also enjoy the many attractions the Nashville area has to offer. We invite you and your kin to come and stay with us for a spell!

INGREDIENTS
Batter:
- 2 c. sugar
- 2 c. plain flour
- 1 stick margarine
- ½ c. vegetable oil
- 1 tsp. baking soda
- pinch of salt
- 2 Tbsp. cocoa
- 1 c. water
- 2 eggs
- ½ c. buttermilk
- 1 tsp. vanilla

Icing:
- 1 stick margarine
- 8 Tbsp. buttermilk
- 3 Tbsp. cocoa
- 1 tsp. vanilla
- 1 c. nuts
- 1 box powdered sugar

DIRECTIONS

Batter: Add baking soda to buttermilk and let stand. Bring butter, cocoa, water and oil to a boil. Pour over sugar, salt and flour. Add one egg at a time and beat after each. Add vanilla to buttermilk mixture. Bake in 9″ x 13″ x 2″ pan at 350° for 30 min.

Icing: Bring margarine, buttermilk and cocoa to a boil. Pour mixture over powdered sugar and beat. Stir in vanilla and nuts. Place icing on cake when cool.

DUMPIT CAKE
Round Top Campground – Gettysburg, PA

This is the recipe that won the baking contest a few years ago, entered by our reigning queen, Miss Round Top. It's easy for campers to prepare and requires no mixing.

Our park is mostly wooded on rolling hills and is located next to the Civil War battlefield at Gettysburg.

INGREDIENTS
- 1 can cherry pie filling
- 1 can crushed pineapple with juice
- 1 box yellow cake mix
- 1 stick butter
- 1 c. nuts or coconut (optional)

DIRECTIONS

Dump above ingredients into 9″ x 13″ pan in order given above. Make each layer as even as you can. Cut butter into pats and place over top of ingredients. Bake at 350° for 1 hr.

JB CUPCAKES
Jantzen Beach RV Park — Portland, OR

Quick, easy and yummy too! Aunt Hazel gave me this recipe, and it's always been one of my favorites.

We're a beautiful, complete hookup park. Close to downtown Portland, you can conveniently take care of medical, social and business matters. Entertainment and recreation can be found right at the park. We have the feel of the country and the convenience of the city.

INGREDIENTS
- 4 eggs
- 1¾ c. sugar
- 1 c. oil
- 1 c. flour
- 14-oz. pkg. shredded coconut
- 1 tsp. vanilla
- 1 tsp. salt

DIRECTIONS
Beat eggs in large bowl with sugar. Add oil and blend well. Gradually add flour, mixing thoroughly. Stir in coconut, add vanilla and salt. Bake at 350° for 25-30 minutes. Makes 20 cupcakes.

CHOCOLATE TORTILLA TORTE
Good Life RV Resort – Mesa, AZ

Located in the desert Southwest, much of our food has Mexican or Indian influence — as this recipe illustrates. At our park, recipes are swapped at potlucks and social gatherings. We even printed our own recipe book one year.

Good Life RV Resort is an adults only, activity oriented park. Snowbirds find that our two swimming pools, whirlpool, shuffleboard courts, group activities and local tours keep them plenty busy. Our visitors from the Snowbelt also find this area and its food exotic and unusual. We invite you to visit us and experience the Good Life.

INGREDIENTS
- 1-12 oz. pkg. semi-sweet chocolate chips
- 1-8 or 9 oz. milk chocolate bar
- 2 pt. sour cream
- 5 Tbsp. powdered sugar
- ½ tsp. cinnamon
- 8 or 9-8″ flour tortillas

DIRECTIONS
Melt chocolate chips over hot water or low heat. Add sour cream, powdered sugar and cinnamon. Blend well. Spread mixture over each tortilla, layering tortillas one on top of another. Frost top and edges. Sprinkle grated milk chocolate bar over top and edges. Cover with plastic wrap and chill overnight. Slice in thin wedges.

APPLE CAKE
Talisman Campark — Madison, GA

This is a wonderful recipe for soft apples. It is also my grandmother's favorite cake. I bake her several apple cakes every month.

Talisman Campark is open year 'round and is located in Madison, Georgia. It is a clean, comfortable campground located on 30 beautiful acres. Come stay with us and visit historic Madison.

INGREDIENTS
- 2 c. sugar
- 1½ c. vegetable oil
- 3 eggs
- 3 c. flour
- 1 tsp. baking soda
- 1 tsp. salt
- 1½ tsp. vanilla
- ¾ c. coconut
- 3 c. apples, grated
- 1 c. nuts

DIRECTIONS

Mix ingredients together. Pour into tube pan. Bake at 325° for 1½ hours. Delicious!

CHOCOLATE-CINNAMON SHEET CAKE
Brookside RV Park – Rochester, MN

We have a family night potluck each week and this cake with chocolate sauce and ice cream is always a winner.

Our park is just 12 blocks from downtown Rochester and is a home away from home for our guests. Many are here for medical treatment or temporary job assignment. Here our visitors check on each other daily and get together in the evening or morning for coffee to see how their neighbor is doing. We are not a recreation camp area, but a home since 90% of our guests are patients at the medical facility here. Their stay here can be difficult so we try to offer the support and home and caring they need.

INGREDIENTS
- ¼ c. cocoa
- 1 c. water
- ¾ c. vegetable shortening
- 2½ c. flour
- 1 tsp. baking soda
- 1 tsp. salt
- 1 tsp. cinnamon
- 2 c. sugar
- ½ c. buttermilk
- 1 tsp. vanilla
- 2 eggs

Icing:
- ½ c. butter or margarine
- ¼ c. milk
- ¼ c. cocoa
- 2 c. powdered sugar
- 1 tsp. vanilla
- ½ c. chopped nuts

DIRECTIONS

Mix cocoa and water in saucepan. Add shortening. Bring mixture to a boil then cool slightly. Sift together flour, baking soda, salt and cinnamon. Blend together (do not beat) sugar and eggs in a large mixing bowl. Blend in cocoa mixture. Add sifted dry ingredients alternately with buttermilk, stirring after each addition until well blended. Stir in vanilla. Pour into greased (15½" x 10½" x 1") jelly roll pan. Bake in a hot 400° oven for 20 min.

Icing: Melt butter or margarine in milk in small saucepan. Mix cocoa with powdered sugar and stir into milk mixture. Add vanilla. Spread on cake. Top with chopped nuts.

FUNNEL CAKE MIX
Mill Bridge Campresort – Strasburg, PA

Funnel cakes have been a favorite tradition of the Pennsylvania Dutch for generations. They originated as a mid-morning snack for the hard working Pennsylvania farm hands. The thrifty housewives of these farmers used excess pancake batter from breakfast. The batter was poured through a funnel into hot lard and fried until golden brown and then sprinkled with powdered sugar.

Our funnel cakes at Mill Bridge Campresort, which is located in the heart of Pennsylvania Dutch Country in Lancaster County, are made and served to our visitors daily. The batter is made from stone-ground yellow cornmeal from our 260 year old grist mill.

INGREDIENTS
- ½ c. sugar
- 2 c. cornmeal
- 6 c. flour
- 1 tsp. salt
- 4 tsp. baking powder
- 2 eggs
- 1 c. milk

DIRECTIONS
Mix dry ingredients together. In a separate bowl, beat eggs and add milk. Add this liquid to 2 cups of the dry mix. Stir until smooth. Pour some batter into a funnel, holding your finger under the funnel spout. Hold funnel over a fry pan filled with hot deep fat or frying oil (350°). Release finger letting batter flow and move the funnel in a slow circular motion, shaping a round cake. Fry until crisp and golden on one side; turn and fry on other side. Dust generously with powdered sugar and serve immediately.

DONNA'S HOOTENANNY STIR UP CAKE
V.I.P. Resort – Apache Junction, AZ

This recipe is a favorite BIG CAKE to serve a crowd. Our park seems to draw "country folks" who like the simple life: friendly people, country music and room to breathe.

We're located close to downtown Apache Junction, but are off the main busy street, with a beautiful view of the Superstition Mountains. We have a nice recreation room for activities, shuffleboards, horseshoes, bingo, crafts & potlucks. Reservations recommended November through March. We hope you'll "Come for a Day" or "Come to Stay".

INGREDIENTS
- 1 lg. cake pan,
  13½" x 8½" x 1½"
- 1 pkg. yellow cake mix
- 1 pkg. instant vanilla pudding
- 1 pkg. instant butterscotch pudding
- 4 eggs
- ½ c. cooking oil
- 1 c. water
- 2 tsp. vanilla
- Topping:
  - 1 c. diced walnuts
  - 1 c. brown sugar

DIRECTIONS
Beat all 7 ingredients with an electric beater for 10 min. and pour ½ of batter into the cake pan.

Topping: Sprinkle half the walnuts and brown sugar over the batter in the pan. Spread remaining batter over topping and the rest of the walnuts and brown sugar on top. Bake at 350° for 45 min. or until a toothpick inserted comes out clean. No need to frost. Best served warm to toe tappin', guitar pickin', happy singin' campin' folks.

HAPPY BIRTHDAY USA CAKE
Capitol KOA Campground — Millersville, MD

Each year one of our 4th of July activities is to serve complimentary Happy Birthday USA cake and punch. We decorate a large serving table with a red, white and blue color scheme and use fresh flowers and flags as centerpieces. A huge birthday cake adequate to serve all campers is the focal point of the table. Following cake and punch, complimentary sparklers are provided for the children. This has been a tradition on our campground for 11 years and it is greatly enjoyed by all our guests.

Capitol KOA Campground is situated on 50 acres in the middle of the Washington/Annapolis/Baltimore triangle. Full amenities include swimming pool, hiking trails, recreation room, badminton, volleyball, ping-pong, horseshoes and full activity program. Tours and shuttle transportation for Washington, D.C. are offered, as well as a daily touring program and orientation. Camping Kabins are available plus a choice of open or wooded sites. A fully stocked store, propane station, laundry, and two restroom/shower facilities are offered for the comfort of our guests.

INGREDIENTS
- **2 boxes white cake mix**
- **½ tsp. cherry flavoring or red food coloring**
- **½ tsp. blueberry flavoring or blue food coloring**
- **½ tsp. coconut flavoring**

Icing:
- **white icing**
- **1 can coconut**
- **1 can drained & chilled blueberries**
- **¼ tsp. blue food coloring**
- **3 cans drained & chilled cherries**

DIRECTIONS
Prepare cake mix and divide into thirds. Add ½ tsp. flavoring or coloring to each third (1-red, 1-blue, 1-coconut). Alternate pouring batter into two oblong cake pans in ½ inch strips. Bake according to directions. Cool. Place cakes side by side to form a long cake. Knife trim long sides of cake to look like flag waving in the breeze.

Icing: Pipe white icing around edges of the cake. Spoon blueberries into square in upper left corner. Divide remainder of cake into 5-7 wavy stripes with red and white. Spoon cherries onto red stripes. Generously pipe on the white icing between cherries. Top white icing with coconut. Pipe small white icing stars on the field of blueberries. Chill before serving.

OATMEAL CAKE
Lionshead RV Park Resort – West Yellowstone, MT

Lionshead Resort is conveniently located just 8 min. west of West Yellowstone at the base of Lionshead Mountain. The 150 full hookup RV spaces, combined with shady campsites, square dance hall, and famous Alice's Restaurant specializing in German cuisine makes Lionshead Resort an all around popular resort. Open year 'round to serve Snowmobilers in the winter, we also offer trout fishing, hunting, hiking, tours to Yellowstone Park and all-around family fun. As a matter of fact this recipe is a favorite late night snack for many of our active guests. It's especially popular with the square dancers after a busy night of "promenading".

INGREDIENTS
- 1 c. quick oatmeal
- 1½ c. boiling water
- ½ c. oleo
- 1 c. brown sugar
- 1 c. granulated sugar
- 2 eggs
- 2½ c. flour
- 1 tsp. baking soda
- 1 tsp. salt
- 1 tsp. vanilla

Topping:
- 5 tsp. butter
- ½ c. brown sugar
- ¼ c. canned milk
- ½ tsp. vanilla
- 1 c. coconut
- 1 c. nuts

DIRECTIONS
Batter: Pour boiling water over oatmeal and let stand 20 min. Cream oleo, brown sugar and granulated sugar together. Add eggs and oatmeal mixture. Mix in flour, baking soda, salt and vanilla. Bake at 350° for 40 min.

Topping: Mix all ingredients together — do not cook. When cake is finished, spread topping over cake evenly. Place cake in broiler 3 – 6 min. or until coconut is browned.

BANANA SPLIT CAKE
Indian Creek Camping – Geneva on the Lake, OH

We are located in the village of Geneva on the Lake, which has the oldest family resort in the state of Ohio. We are situated on over 110 acres with many amenities. We have lots of great get-togethers in our large pavilion. Come and see us for unlimited family fun. Here's hoping everyone has a great camping season.

INGREDIENTS
- 2 c. graham cracker crumbs
- 3 sticks margarine
- 2 eggs
- 2 c. powdered sugar
- 3-5 sliced bananas
- 2 cans crushed pineapple, drained
- Cool Whip
- maraschino cherries, optional
- nuts, optional

DIRECTIONS
Melt 1 stick margarine. Combine with graham cracker crumbs and press into 9″ x 13″ baking pan. Mix 2 sticks margarine, eggs and powdered sugar at medium speed for 15 min. Spread mixture over crumb crust. Layer bananas and pineapple. Cover with Cool Whip. Decorate with cherries and nuts. Chill and serve.

HUMMINGBIRD SHEET CAKE
Camp Toodik Family CG & Canoe Livery-Loudonville, OH

We have used this recipe for 15 years for our special events: Christmas in July, season camper parties, factory or club outings, and other catered events. This is so sweet that everyone will hover around and come back for second and third helpings.

Camp Toodik Family Campground and Canoe Livery has scenic shaded sites on rolling terrain overlooking the Mohican River Valley. We offer river edge tenting sites as well as a variety of hookup sites in the main camping area. We're located in Holmes county, home to the world's largest Amish settlement, cheese factories and succulent home cooked family style meals.

INGREDIENTS
Dry ingredients:
  12 c. flour
  2 tsp. salt
  4 tsp. baking soda
  4 tsp. cinnamon
  8 c. sugar
Moist ingredients:
  6 c. oil
  12 eggs (beaten)
  4 c. pineapple
  8 c. chopped bananas
  4 c. coconut
  6 tsp. vanilla
Icing:
  2 lb. powdered sugar
  ½ c. butter or margarine
  2 tsp. vanilla
  milk

DIRECTIONS
Sift all dry ingredients together. Combine with moist ingredients and mix well. Divide into three 12" x 17" x 1" sheet pans and bake at 325° for 45 min. to 1 hr.

Cream the margarine and add powdered sugar gradually, then add vanilla. Add milk slowly while stirring until proper consistency is reached. Spread on cooled sheet cake. Serves 80-100 people.

NO-STIR CHERRY PINEAPPLE CAKE
Wood Smoke Campground – Irmo, SC

We have cookouts on some holidays and this is an easy recipe for those of us always on the go and with lots of things to do. This recipe is one of my favorites.

Our park is shady and peaceful, yet close enough to Columbia to meet any needs. We have full hookups, dump station, propane gas and a small camp store for our campers.

INGREDIENTS
  1 can cherry pie filling
  1 20 oz. can crushed pineapple
    with juice
  1 reg. size box yellow cake mix
  1 c. coconut
  1 c. chopped walnuts
  1 c. melted butter

DIRECTIONS
Preheat oven to 350°. Grease and flour a 9" x 13" pan. Place ingredients in pan in order. Do not stir. Bake for 1 hour.

Note: Cake will not be hard set, the center will be soft.

STRAWBERRY DELIGHT CAKE
Seaway R.V. Village – San Benito, TX

Seaway R.V. Village is a small RV Park offering a whole lot of fun. We offer excellent fishing opportunities for trout and redfish from our 450 ft. seawall or from our lighted piers. We also have a rec hall, where you can play card games every night or why not take one of our tours to Mexico. This recipe is easy to prepare, yet it is so refreshing — especially after a long, hot Texas day!

INGREDIENTS
- **1 box white/yellow cake mix**
- **4 eggs**
- **½ c. oil**
- **1 sm. pkg. strawberry Jell-O dissolved in ½ c. hot water**
- **½ sm. pkg. frozen strawberries**

Icing:
- **1 stick margarine**
- **1 box powdered sugar**
- **½ box frozen strawberries**

DIRECTIONS
Mix all cake ingredients in large mixing bowl and beat on med. speed for about 4 min. Pour into sheet pan and bake for 35-40 min. at 350°. While cake is baking, mix icing ingredients in large mixing bowl. When cake is cool, spread icing on top.

BANANA SPLIT CAKE
Lonesome Pine Campground – Waynesville, NC

This is the cake that never gets left. Served at our covered dish dinners, it's a favorite of all our guests.

We have a cozy park that runs along Jonathan Creek. There's plenty of trout for you fishermen and we're just a stone's throw away from beautiful Maggie Valley. Open all year so you can visit us anytime you like!

INGREDIENTS
Bottom Layer:
- **2 c. crushed vanilla wafers**
- **1 stick butter, softened**
- **3 tsp. sugar**
- **¾ c. walnuts**

Filling:
- **2 c. powdered sugar**
- **2 sticks butter, softened**
- **2 eggs**

Top Layer:
- **12 oz. crushed pineapple**
- **5 bananas, sliced lengthwise**
- **9 oz. whipped cream**
- **cherries**
- **coconut**

DIRECTIONS
Bottom Layer: Mix vanilla wafers, butter, sugar and walnuts and press into the bottom of a 9″ x 13″ pan. Bake at 375° for 5 min. Let cool.

Filling: Beat sugar, butter and eggs on high speed until firm. Spread mixture over bottom layer.

Top Layer: Add a layer of drained pineapple, then a layer of bananas. Add a layer of whipped cream. Sprinkle top with coconut and a few red cherries and walnuts. Refrigerate 2 hrs.

CARROT CAKE
Issaquah Village RV – Issaquah, WA

This is an old family recipe that's a favorite with us. It's easy to prepare and is always a hit.

Our park is surrounded by mountains and is nestled around the "old setting" town of Issaquah. We're only minutes from Bellevue and Seattle and all their attractions. We offer full hookups, restroom and laundry facilities, picnic tables, patios, basketball, horseshoes and playground. We hope you enjoy this old family recipe. Stop by and tell us what you think of it.

INGREDIENTS
Cake:
    2 c. sugar
    1½ c. oil
    3 eggs
    2 c. grated carrots
    1 c. crushed pineapple,
       drained
    1 Tbsp. vanilla or rum
    2½ c. + 2 Tbsp. flour
    1 tsp. salt
    1 tsp. baking soda
    1 tsp. baking powder
    1 tsp. cinnamon
    ½ c. chopped nuts
Frosting:
    ½ stick margarine
    3½ c. powdered sugar
    4 oz. cream cheese
    lemon extract to taste

DIRECTIONS
    Blend sugar, oil and eggs. Add carrots, pineapple and vanilla or rum. Mix well. Add remaining ingredients and mix well. Pour into greased and floured pan. Bake at 350° for 45 min. or until done.
    Frosting: Beat all ingredients until smooth. Spread over cooled cake. Enjoy!

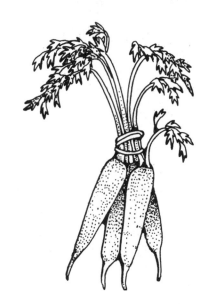

POUND CAKE
Nature's Campground – Homosassa, FL

This is a favorite family recipe. It tastes great topped with fresh strawberries or your favorite fruit.

Nature's Campground offers shaded, secluded sites on the Halls River. Enjoy fishing, swimming, boating and a full marina. Our 275 site campground offers a variety of amenities and we welcome tenters.

INGREDIENTS
    ½ c. butter or oleo
    ½ c. crisco
    2½ c. sugar
    3 c. flour, sifted
    1 tsp. baking powder
    1 tsp. vanilla or almond extract
    1 c. milk
    4 eggs

DIRECTIONS
    Combine all ingredients together in a large bowl. Beat with mixer until well blended. Place in well greased pan. Bake at 350° for 1 hr.

SUNRISE HEALTH CAKE
Sunset RV Park – Fort Worth, TX

I invite the tenants to the office for coffee and a taste of cake so everyone can get acquainted. Our park has large shade trees and friendly people. We are close to the Convention Center, museums, and shopping centers. There is also a laundromat and grocery store close by.

INGREDIENTS
- 1 ripe banana, mashed
- ½ c. low calorie margarine, softened
- ¾ c. egg beaters (or 3 eggs)
- ½ c. unsweetened crushed pineapple (undrained)
- 1 apple, peeled & chopped fine
- 1 c. unsweetened apple juice
- 1 tsp. vanilla
- 3 c. unbleached flour
- 1½ tsp. baking powder
- 1 tsp. soda
- 1 tsp. cinnamon
- ½ tsp. nutmeg
- 1⅔ c. whole dates, chopped
- ½ c. chopped walnuts or pecans*

* European chestnuts are much lower in fat if you can find them.

DIRECTIONS
Blend mashed banana and margarine together. Add other liquid ingredients and mix well. In separate bowl mix flour, baking powder, soda, cinnamon and nutmeg together. Then add dry ingredients slowly to liquid while mixing at a low speed on the electric mixer. Lastly, add dates and nuts. Bake at 350° for 30-40 min. Cake is done when a knife or toothpick inserted comes out clean.

DIRT CAKE
Sharyland Villa – Mission, TX

This is a potluck favorite dessert. Although it sounds unusual, it's surprising how good it really is!

Sharyland Villa is located in the Rio Grande Valley where produce, citrus, and beauty abound. The semi-tropical climate, south of winter, makes Sharyland a warm, popular haven. We are a small, caring community of retirees in a convenient, safe, central location.

INGREDIENTS
- 16 oz. softened cream cheese
- 1 stick oleo, softened
- 1 c. powdered sugar
- 1½ c. milk
- 2 pkgs. instant vanilla pudding
- 12 oz. whipped cream
- oreo cookies

DIRECTIONS
Mix first three ingredients together. In a separate bowl, mix remaining ingredients, except cookies. Blend the two mixtures together. In a new 6½" flower pot, layer cookies, then mixture. Continue layering, ending with cookies on top for "dirt". "Plant" a silk flower or use a drinking straw and a real flower in center of flower pot.

HOLIDAY FRUITCAKE
V.I.P. Resort – Apache Junction, AZ

This is a "fun" recipe that always gets a laugh. It seems appropriate during the Christmas holiday season.

We're located close to downtown Apache Junction, but are off the main busy street, with a beautiful view of the Superstition Mountains. We have a nice recreation room for activities, shuffleboards, horseshoes, bingo, crafts & potlucks. Reservations recommended November through March. We hope you'll "Come for a Day" or "Come to Stay".

INGREDIENTS

- 1 c. butter or margarine
- 2 c. sugar
- 2 c. mixed fruit
- 3 c. all-purpose flour
- 2 tsp. baking powder
- 1 c. chopped nuts
- 1 tsp. soda
- 1 Tbsp. lemon juice
- 2 Tbsp. brown sugar
- 1 c. high performance rum

DIRECTIONS

Follow directions carefully. Before starting, sample rum, check for quality. Good? To begin, select a large bowl, measuring cup, etc. Sample rum again. It must be just right. With an electric beater, beat 1 cup butter, 1 teaspoon sugar and beat again. Add 2 large eggs and 2 cups dried fruit. Beat until very high. (?) (If the fruit gets stuck in the beater, pry out — with a knife). Sample rum and check for consistency. (Hic!) Delicious!! Next, sift in 2 cups baking powder (?), add a pinch of the rum, 1 teaspoon soda and 1 cup of salt (or was it pepper?). Anyway, don't fret, sample the rum again — HicZowie!! Next, shift in ½ pint lemon juice, fold in chopped buttermilk and strained nuts! Shample rum again - Hic! Now, 1 tablespoon brown sugar or whatever color you have around, Hic! Mix this well. Don't forget to grease the oven and — oops, turn on the cake pan, Hic! Now, pour the whole mess in the oven and — OOPs. Oh well, you can clean the oven later. On second thought, just forget the cake — drink the rest of the rum and go to bed!!!
MERRY CHRISTMAS!!!!

COUNTRY TIME VANILLA ICE-CREAM
Sun Ray R.V. Park – Dateland, AZ

We use this recipe for our park potlucks. Our park is an oasis in the desert off I-8 out of Dateland. We have a solar heated swimming pool, gas barbeque and many other extras to offer in our family type park.

INGREDIENTS
- 4 eggs
- 1⅓ c. sugar
- 2 Tbsp. vanilla
- ¾ tsp. salt
- 1 qt. half and half
- 1 pt. whipping cream
- 2 c. milk

DIRECTIONS
Beat eggs until slightly thickened. Add sugar, gradually beating until mixture is thick. Add vanilla and salt. Mix well. Stir in creams and milk. Pour into chilled ice-cream can. Freeze in electric freezer or hand cranked freezer. Use 1 part rock salt to 10 parts ice.

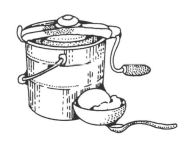

MILKY WAY ICE CREAM
Lake Hartwell KOA – Anderson, SC

This is a favorite dessert at our campground potluck suppers.
We're a quiet, friendly, family campground nestled among pine trees. We offer a rustic atmosphere and all the amenities to make your camping experience a pleasant one. There's plenty to do while you're here whether it's swimming, fishing, mini golf or hiking. We're located just one mile from I-85, midway between Atlanta, GA and Charlotte, NC.

INGREDIENTS
- 6 Milky Way candy bars
- 2 cans condensed milk
- 1 Tbsp. vanilla
- milk

DIRECTIONS
Melt candy bars in double boiler. Add condensed milk and stir well. Add vanilla. Pour into freezer container and add milk to fill line. Freeze in ice cream freezer.

SIX THREES ICE CREAM
River Oaks Park — Toledo, WA

This recipe has been a 4th of July favorite in our family for 40 years. We now serve it, along with other favorites, at our annual 4th of July celebration right here at River Oaks Park.

Our park is located along the banks of the Cowlitz River in beautiful Washington State. We offer a quiet country setting with full hookups, pull-thrus, tenting sites, restroom facilities, fire rings, barbecue grills and more. You can boat, fish and swim in the Cowlitz River. Or, if you're a landlubber, you can take advantage of the other amenities at our park.

INGREDIENTS
3 c. cream
3 c. milk
3 c. sugar
3 bananas
3 oranges, juiced
3 lemons, juiced

DIRECTIONS
Combine milk, cream and sugar. Blend bananas and fruit juices and add to cream mixture. Pour into freezer container and freeze according to manufacturer's directions.

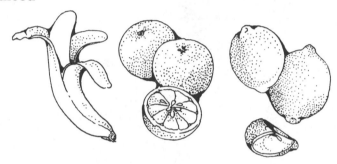

PINA COLADA ICE CREAM
Hudson Bend Camper Resort — Austin, TX

We have an "Ice Cream Crank Off" every Labor Day. Everyone brings their "secret recipe" and all freezers are numbered. Everyone gets to taste all of the entries and vote for the one they like the most. The winner gets a prize — what else? An ice cream cone windchime! We are located on Lake Travis just outside Austin. Lake Travis is a great lake for water sports, skiing, etc. with lots of sail boats. We are open year 'round.

INGREDIENTS
1-3 oz. box instant pudding mix
2 c. milk
1 can evaporated milk
½ c. white Karo syrup
1 can condensed milk
1 can pina colada mix
1 sm. can crushed pineapple
half & half

DIRECTIONS
Mix pudding mix with milk. Mix in other ingredients. Stir in pineapple with juice. Pour in freezer and fill with half & half. This recipe is correct — no eggs.

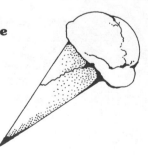

HOT FUDGE
Oil Creek Camp-Resort – Titusville, PA

The oil industry was born in Pennsylvania and among the sites of early oil boom towns in that state is Oil Creek Camp-Resort in Titusville. South of the campground is the Drake Well Park and Museum which marks the site where Colonel Drake struck oil in 1859. The museum contains a detailed history of those early days of oil. Despite the reminders of this "black gold" everywhere, Oil Creek campers' favorite topic is ice cream. The park is noted for its Ice Cream Party; an annual scooping and saucing event. Nona Koller decided to share one of her famous ice cream topping recipes with us.

INGREDIENTS
- **1½ c. granulated sugar**
- **½ c. brown sugar, packed**
- **¾ c. cocoa**
- **¼ c. flour**
- **½ tsp. salt**
- **12 oz. can evaporated milk**
- **1 c. water**
- **2 Tbsp. butter**
- **2 tsp. vanilla**

DIRECTIONS
Combine all ingredients except the vanilla and cook them over medium heat, stirring constantly until boiling. Boil five minutes. Cool and stir in the vanilla. For serving, use coffee server with candle or some other means of keeping the sauce warm.

STRAWBERRY ICE CREAM TOPPING
KOA-Idaho Falls – Idaho Falls, ID

Idaho Falls gets its name from the falls created by the Snake River which flows right through the heart of town. These lovely falls add a good country feel with all the conveniences of a city. What nicer place to relax after the almost exhausting beauty and grandeur of the Teton Mountains and Yellowstone Park. Our new swimming pool helps our guests relax. Or course, we are already planning to have weekly ice cream socials. Our favorite topping is strawberry, and with this recipe, you can freeze the topping and enjoy it throughout the year.

INGREDIENTS
- **1 qt. fresh strawberries**
- **4 c. sugar**
- **¾ c. water**
- **1 pkg. sure gel**
- **1 pkg. wild strawberry Jell-O**

DIRECTIONS
Wash and cap berries. Mash well. Mix in sugar and dry Jell-O mix. Set aside for 10 min. Mix water and sure gel. Bring to a boil, stirring constantly and boil for 1 min. Pour over berries and stir for 2 min. Cover and leave at room temperature until set (up to 24 hours). Will keep for 2 weeks in refrigerator or may be frozen for later use. If using raspberries, stir an additional minute. Good Eating!

WILD BLUEBERRY GLACE PIE
Acres of Wildlife – Steep Falls, ME

Wild blueberries are picked here on the land, and we make the pie in our bakery on the premises.

Acres of Wildlife Campground is a 300 acre camper's paradise located in the Sebago Lake area of southern Maine. Over 20 miles of hiking trails provide breathtaking scenery and great blueberry picking in July and August. Fresh baked goods such as this pie, are available daily from our bakery.

INGREDIENTS
- **3 c. wild blueberries**
- **¾ c. water**
- **1 Tbsp. butter**
- **1 c. sugar**
- **3 Tbsp. cornstarch**
- **dash of salt**
- **1 tsp. lemon juice**

DIRECTIONS
Bring 1 c. wild blueberries and water to a boil. Cook gently for 4 min. Add butter, then add sugar, cornstarch and salt to hot blueberry mixture, stirring constantly. Cook slowly until thick and clear. Remove from heat, and add 1 tsp. lemon juice. Pour over two cups raw blueberries, mix gently. Turn into 9-inch baked pie shell. Refrigerate or leave at room temperature. Serve with sweetened whipped cream.

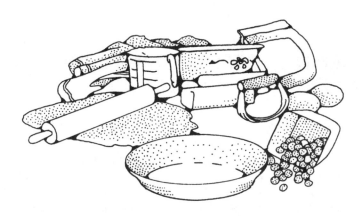

IMPOSSIBLE PIE
Belton, Temple, Killeen KOA – Belton, TX

For a great coconut custard pie that makes its own crust, try the Impossible Pie. This is a popular dessert served at some of our many trailer club rallies. We have a very nice rally building at our KOA Kampground in central Texas and we can handle groups of 15 to 20 units. We also welcome families and winter Texans to stay with us. Our swimming pool is great and we are right next door to the Bell Company Expo Center. Stop by for a visit and let us know what you think of our Impossible Pie.

INGREDIENTS
- **4 eggs**
- **1 stick butter or margarine**
- **½ c. flour**
- **¾ c. sugar**
- **2 c. milk**
- **1 tsp. vanilla**
- **1 tsp. nutmeg**
- **1 c. coconut**

DIRECTIONS
Blend all ingredients together. Pour into a well-greased, floured pie tin. Bake at 350° for 30 to 40 min. or until a sharp knife comes out clean. Pie forms its own crust.

QUICK KEY LIME PIE
Venture Out at Cudjoe Cay – Cudjoe Key, FL

Our premier, luxury RV resort is located on the ocean. We offer full hookups, tennis courts, heated pool, marina, secured grounds and planned activities. Since we're located in the lower and middle keys, it's only natural that Key Lime Pie is a favorite here!

INGREDIENTS
- 1 9" pie crust
- 1 can sweetened condensed milk
- ½ c. key lime juice
- whipped cream

DIRECTIONS
Blend milk and lime juice. Blend in whipped cream. Place in pie crust and refrigerate.

KEY LIME PIE
Safari Campground – Williamsport, MD

One of our regular campers from Florida makes this pie and was kind enough to share this tasty recipe. It's easy and delicious!

Safari campground is located about five miles from Hagerstown, Maryland. Since we're two miles from the nearest town, we offer a very peaceful country atmosphere. We are in the middle of the Civil War historical area. The Battle of Antietam, the bloodiest battle of the War, was fought nearby and troops actually camped on our grounds during the War. Whether you're a history buff or not, you'll enjoy all the amenities and activities Safari Campground has to offer.

INGREDIENTS
- 1 can condensed milk
- 4 eggs, separated
- ½ c. lime juice
- ½ tsp. cream of tartar
- 6 Tbsp. sugar
- 1 baked pie shell

DIRECTIONS
Combine milk, egg yolks, and lime juice. Beat 1 egg white until stiff and fold into mixture. Pour into baked pie shell. Beat 3 egg whites until stiff and gradually add the sugar and cream of tartar. Spoon on top of lime mixture. Bake until egg whites are brown.

HO BO PIE
Old Corundum Millsite Campground – Franklin, NC

When we first opened 20 years ago, this was introduced to us by some campers and it has been a hit ever since. We are located in the center of western North Carolina on the beautiful Cullasaja River. We have a pavilion where a campfire burns nightly. Activities and attractions nearby include a log cabin store, tubing down the river, gem mining and trout fishing.

INGREDIENTS
- 2 slices bread
- butter or margarine
- ready-to-eat pie filling (any flavor)
- HoBo Pie Maker (this can be purchased in a camp or hardware store)

DIRECTIONS
Butter both sides of bread and add 2-3 Tbsp. pie filling in center of bread. Put in pie maker and cook over open fire about 5 min. Turn and brown on both sides. Slide out on plate and sprinkle with powdered sugar on both sides.

NO-CRUST PUMPKIN PIE
Memphis East KOA — Lakeland, TN

This quick, simple and no-mess, no-stress recipe is a tastefully different change.

Memphis East KOA is located ½ mile off I-40, and only 8 miles from Memphis. We have a lovely fishing lake and 13 log kabins, as well as tent and RV sites. We have a grocery store, laundry, game room, pool, propane and more. We offer friendly service and look forward to your visit.

INGREDIENTS
- **3 eggs**
- **⅔ c. brown sugar, packed firmly**
- **3 Tbsp. butter**
- **1 c. milk**
- **1 c. canned pumpkin filling**
- **⅓ c. biscuit mix**
- **¾ tsp. cinnamon**
- **¾ c. granola**

DIRECTIONS
Preheat oven to 350°. Combine all ingredients except for granola in blender; cover, blend at low speed for 3 min. Pour into well-greased 9" pie pan and let stand for 5 min. Bake at 350° for 20 min. Take out and sprinkle with granola and continue baking for 20 more min.

DANG GOOD PIE
Ozark Vue RV Park – Omaha, AR

This is a delicious pie and it's so easy to make. At our potlucks it's always a special treat!

We are located on Highway 65, just 12 miles north of Harrison, Arkansas and 20 miles from Branson, Missouri. Plan to stay with us as you vacation in the Ozarks and enjoy the beautiful view and quiet and restful atmosphere. We offer full hookups, pull-thrus, and picnic tables. All campers are welcome!

INGREDIENTS
- **1 sm. can crushed pineapple**
- **1 can coconut**
- **1 stick of butter, melted**
- **1½ c. sugar**
- **2 Tbsp. flour**
- **3 eggs**
- **1 tsp. vanilla**
- **1 9" pie shell**

DIRECTIONS
Mix flour, sugar, butter and other ingredients and pour in unbaked pie shell. Bake at 350° for 45 min.

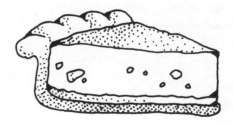

GRAPEFRUIT PIE
Fiesta Grove RV Resort – Palmetto, FL

Fiesta Grove RV Resort is a lovely 205 site park set amidst an orange grove. Enjoy our rec hall, pool and many activities. Or take advantage of the many things to see and do in the area.

INGREDIENTS
- 1 box lemon Jell-O
- 1 c. sugar
- 1¾ c. boiling water
- 3 Tbsp. cornstarch
- ¼ c. cold water
- pie shell
- 4 oz. cream cheese, softened
- 3-4 grapefruits
- whipped cream

DIRECTIONS

Dissolve Jell-O and sugar in boiling water. Add cornstarch dissolved in cold water to Jell-O mixture. Cook until clear. Cool. Peel and section grapefruit and cut into small pieces. Line pie shell with cream cheese. Add Jell-O filling and top with whipped cream.

Optional: Reserve 4 sections of grapefruit to garnish top in pinwheel fashion with a cherry in center.

GRAPEFRUIT PIE
Golden Grove R.V. Park – Mission, TX

Golden Grove gets its name from the grapefruit trees in the park. We are one of the many winter Texan parks in the Rio Grande Valley. How lucky the people are, that our valley citrus comes ripe when they are here, getting away from the cold and snow of the northern states. Golden Grove has spaces 30' x 90' between ruby red grapefruit trees. When ripe, the fruit is golden, sweet & juicy. One of the best parts of our potlucks is the grapefruit in many forms!

INGREDIENTS
- 1 9″ baked pie shell
- 32 marshmallows, cut in quarters
- ½ c. grapefruit juice
- 2½ c. ruby red grapefruit in sections
- 1 c. whipped cream
- ¼ c. shredded coconut

DIRECTIONS

Melt marshmallows in ¼ c. juice. Cool to room temperature. Add rest of juice to fruit sections. Fold fruit, marshmallows, whipped cream and coconut together. Pour into pie shell. Refrigerate at least 3 hours.

PUMPKIN PIE
Lake Mason Campground – Briggsville, WI

We often have potluck dinners here at our campground. Our campers always ask me to bring my pumpkin pie.

Lake Mason Campground is located 10 miles from Portage and 10 miles from Wisconsin Dells at Briggsville. Our campground is on beautiful Lake Mason which offers 910 acres of good fishing, boating and swimming. We have a playground, sports field, and volleyball to keep you busy. Hope you can come and see us sometime soon.

INGREDIENTS
- 1 qt. pumpkin filling
- 1½ c. sugar
- 1½ Tbsp. flour
- ½ tsp. cloves
- ½ tsp. nutmeg
- ½ tsp. ginger
- ½ tsp. allspice
- 1 tsp. cinnamon
- ¼ tsp. salt
- 5 eggs
- 3 c. milk
- 2 9″ pie shells

DIRECTIONS

Mix all ingredients together with electric beater until well blended. Pour into two 9″ pie shells and bake at 425° for 45-55 min., or until knife comes out clean.

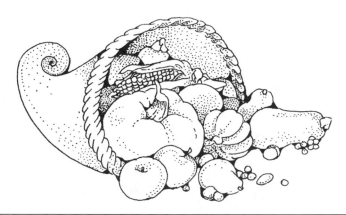

PUMPKIN PIE
Flory's Cottages & Campground – Ronks, PA

Flory's Cottages & Campground is located in the heart of Pennsylvania Dutch Country. We have spacious, shaded, level sites for RVs and tents. We're convenient to all Dutch Country Attractions. We like this recipe as pumpkins are grown in abundance here, and this pie is a delicious way to show off our area's heritage. Come visit us where the Amish are our neighbors.

INGREDIENTS
- 1 9-inch pie crust
- 2 eggs
- ¼ c. evaporated milk
- 1 c. milk
- 1 c. sieved, cooked or canned pumpkin
- ½ Tbsp. cornstarch
- ⅓ c. brown sugar, packed
- 2 Tbsp. granulated sugar
- ½ tsp. powdered cinnamon
- ⅛ tsp. powdered allspice
- ⅛ tsp. powdered ginger
- ¼ tsp. salt
- powdered nutmeg

DIRECTIONS

Prepare unbaked 9-inch pie shell. Preheat oven to 350°. Combine eggs, evaporated milk, milk, and pumpkin in glass container or bowl. Blend with electric mixer at low speed until smoothly mixed. Sift dry ingredients, except nutmeg, together into pumpkin mixture. Blend at high speed until smooth. Pour into prepared unbaked pie shell. Sprinkle lightly with nutmeg. Bake 30 min. or until crust is lightly browned and filling is set. Let cool at room temperature in pan. Makes 6-8 servings.

PEAR CRUMBLE PIE
Pine Village KOA – Leavenworth, WA

Pine Village KOA is located in the heart of Washington State's pear country. This recipe is just one of the many ways we use pears.

Green meadows, tall pines, and resort relaxation describe Pine Village KOA. We're nestled at the foot of the Cascade Mountains in central Washington's "Bavarian Village" of Leavenworth. Located on the crystal clear Wenatchee River, we offer a score of water oriented activities to keep you busy. We also offer a variety of other amenities to make your stay with us a pleasant one.

INGREDIENTS
- 6 pears, pared and cored
- 3 Tbsp. lemon juice
- ½ c. sugar
- 2 Tbsp. flour
- 1 tsp. grated lemon peel
- 1 unbaked 9-inch pastry shell

Topping:
- ½ c. flour
- ½ c. sugar
- ½ tsp. ginger
- ½ tsp. cinnamon
- ¼ tsp. mace, optional
- 4 Tbsp. butter or margarine

DIRECTIONS

Slice pears and sprinkle with lemon juice. Combine sugar, flour and lemon peel. Mix with pear slices and spoon into pastry shell. Sprinkle with topping. Bake at 450° for 45 min.

Topping: Mix flour, sugar, ginger, cinnamon, and mace together. Cut in butter or margarine until crumbly.

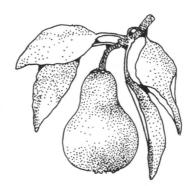

MILLION DOLLAR PIE
Holiday Trav-L Park – Ocala, FL

We have two potluck dinners a month, plus celebrations at all holidays. This pie is a favorite on the dessert counter. Holiday Trav-L Park has many talented cooks and bakers among its returning guests each year. So many of the recipes are requested again and again by our guests that two years ago we collected and published our own cookbook of the favorites. This recipe is just one among many. We are located in north/central Florida among rolling hills and surrounded by beautiful horse farms.

INGREDIENTS
- ¼ c. milk
- 8 oz. cream cheese, room temperature
- #2 can crushed pineapple, drained
- 1 lg. vanilla pudding mix
- 1 c. chopped nuts
- 2 c. coconut
- 2 c. whipped cream
- 1-9″ graham cracker pie shell

DIRECTIONS

Beat first 3 items together, then fold in balance of ingredients. Place in a graham cracker pie shell and refrigerate for several hours.

MINNIE'S CHOCOLATE CHIP PIE
KOA Anaheim – Anaheim, CA

Anaheim KOA is near all the major attractions the Anaheim area has to offer. The park is located just across the street from Disneyland. And like Disneyland, this recipe is a favorite of children of all ages. Other attractions nearby include Knott's Berry Farm, Universal Studios, the Queen Mary and Spruce Goose. The campground offers a large heated swimming pool, hot tubs and full facilities. Come stay with us, whether it be for an extended period of time or just a mini vacation.

INGREDIENTS
- **15 marshmallows**
- **½ c. milk**
- **1 c. whipped cream**
- **1 sq. grated chocolate**
- **14 graham crackers**
- **3 Tbsp. melted butter**

DIRECTIONS
Crush crackers and mix with melted butter. Press this mixture into pie pan and chill. Cut up marshmallows and add to the heated milk. Stir until dissolved and cool slightly. Add whipped cream, folding in until well blended. Add chocolate. Put into graham cracker crust and chill overnight. May garnish with a little grated chocolate.

SHOO-FLY PIE & PIE CRUST
Birchview Farm Campground – Coatesville, PA

Our park is located between Philadelphia and Lancaster, near Amish Country. This recipe is a favorite of the area and is considered an Amish pie. Our park is located in the country and offers quiet, relaxed camping as well as planned camping activities, swimming pool and playground. The choice is yours.

INGREDIENTS
Pie crust:
- **¾ c. oil**
- **¼ c. cold water**
- **2 c. flour**

Shoo-fly pie:
- **½ c. flour**
- **¼ c. shortening**
- **½ c. brown sugar**
- **½ tsp. baking soda**
- **½ c. boiling water**
- **¾ c. dark Karo syrup**

DIRECTIONS
Pie Crust: Mix oil and cold water together and beat until white. Pour over the flour and mix well.
Shoo-fly pie: Combine flour, shortening and brown sugar until it forms a crumb mix. Dissolve baking soda in boiling water. Add Karo syrup and ½ of crumb mix. Pour into unbaked pie shell and top with other half of crumbs. Bake at 375° for 35 min.

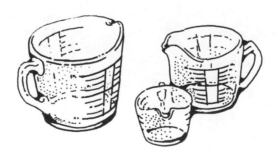

GOLDEN DELICIOUS APPLE PIE
Trailer Inns – Spokane, WA

Washington is world famous for Delicious and Golden Delicious apples and our area has many large orchards close by. We are comprised of 158 full hookup sites on black top; pull-thrus have a grassy area. Located midway between the valley and downtown area, we are surrounded by lakes for fishing and boating along with mountains for skiing. For the campers enjoyment we have a heated pool, sauna, hot tubs, tanning booth, B-B-Q Room, TV lounge and video arcade.

INGREDIENTS
- **8 c. apples, pared & sliced**
- **⅓ c. sugar**
- **1 tsp. cinnamon**
- **3 Tbsp. butter**
- **2-9″ pie crusts**

DIRECTIONS
Prepare your favorite crust. Toss apples with sugar and cinnamon. Place into 9″ lined pie pan. Top with butter and top crust. Bake at 375° for 45 min.

CRANBERRY-APPLE PIE
Pinewood Lodge Trailer Park – Plymouth, MA

We are in the heart of cranberry country. We are a medium sized park situated in the pines overlooking Pinewood Lake. The lake feeds cranberry bogs that nearly surround us. The cranberries give a new color and taste to apple pie, which is a tradition in historic Plymouth.

INGREDIENTS
- **Crust for 9″ 2 crust pie**
- **3 c. cooking apples, sliced**
- **2 c. whole fresh or thawed cranberries**
- **1¾ c. sugar**
- **¼ c. flour**
- **1½ Tbsp. butter**

DIRECTIONS
Heat oven to 425°. Mix apples and cranberries lightly in a mixture of flour and sugar. Pour into pastry lined pan. Dot with butter. Cover with top crust. Seal and flute edges. Make slits in top crust. Bake 40 to 50 minutes, until brown and juice begins to bubble through.

GRANDMOTHER'S PECAN PIE
Cedar Ridge RV Park — Glen Rose, TX

LaVoyce makes these pies and sells them. It's one of the favorites here. LaVoyce is our 75-year-old mother and she is president and partner of our park.

Located 4½ miles south of Glen Rose, Cedar Ridge sits on 5 acres in the cedar hills of Glen Rose. We have a store, laundry room, showers and hospitality room where the women gather and work puzzles. Come enjoy and relax at our very scenic park.

INGREDIENTS
- 2 c. Karo syrup (white)
- 1½ c. sugar
- 1½ c. pecans
- ½ tsp. salt
- 2 Tbsp. flour
- 6 eggs
- 1 tsp. vanilla

DIRECTIONS

Mix all ingredients together. Divide filling into two large pie pans and bake at 400° for 10 min. Reduce heat to 350° and bake until firm in center when shaken or when knife inserted in center comes out clean.

DALLAS PECAN PIE
Dallas West MH/RV Park — Dallas, TX

Our park is right in the city of Dallas, less than 1 mile from the downtown business district with all its gourmet restaurants. We have many 40 year old pecan trees on our 8 acres. In the fall, it is a contest between the squirrels and our guests to see who can get to the fallen nuts first!

INGREDIENTS
- 1 9″ prepared pie crust
- 6 oz. semi-sweet chocolate chips
- 1 stick butter or margarine
- 1 c. sugar
- 2 eggs, beaten
- ½ c. flour
- ½ c. chopped pecans
- 1 tsp. vanilla

DIRECTIONS

Melt butter. Cool. Add two beaten eggs and vanilla to butter. Mix flour, sugar and nuts together. Add butter/egg mixture and stir all together. Spread chocolate chips on bottom of prepared pie crust. Pour mixture on top. Bake at 350° for 40-45 min. Cool to at least room temperature before cutting.

LEMON CAKE TOP PIE
River Bend Resort – Brownsville, TX

This recipe was submitted by one of our residents. It's a favorite here at River Bend Resort.

The delta of the Brownsville, South Padre Island area is at the southernmost end of the Rio Grande. In this delta we produce two crops a year of all kinds of citrus. Nearly everyone has citrus trees in their yards. This is an old family favorite that is pie and cake all in one and Texas lemons make it even better!

INGREDIENTS
- 1 c. sugar
- 2 Tbsp. flour
- 1 Tbsp. butter, softened
- 2 egg yolks
- juice & grated rind of 1 lemon
- 1 c. whole milk
- 2 egg whites, beaten stiff

DIRECTIONS

Mix first 5 ingredients, add milk and mix well. Then fold in beaten egg whites. Pour into your favorite uncooked pie crust and bake until top is medium brown.

PERSIMMON PUDDING
KOA-Leavenworth/Louisville West-Leavenworth, IN

There is a persimmon grove on the back edge of the campground. Ripe fruit is offered to our campers at no charge in the fall. We are located in southern Indiana near 3 sets of caves open to the public. We offer a family-oriented atmosphere with activities on holiday/weekends and special events throughout the year.

INGREDIENTS
- 1 pt. persimmon pulp
- 1 c. sugar
- ¼ c. melted butter
- 2 eggs
- ⅓ c. sour milk
- ½ tsp. baking soda
- 1½ c. flour
- 1 tsp. vanilla
- pinch of salt

DIRECTIONS

Beat eggs and add to pulp. Mix sugar, baking soda and flour. Add to pulp. Add vanilla and melted butter. Chill and serve.

Note: Sour your milk by adding ½ tsp. of vinegar.

RICE PUDDING
Palm Harbor Marina – Rockport, TX

Rice pudding is a favorite dessert. Yet oftentimes it's difficult to find a recipe for rice pudding in cookbooks. Hope you enjoy ours!

Our park is located 4 miles south of Rockport on the Intracoastal Waterway. We catch 28-inch redfish, sea trout, flounder and sheepshead on the famous Estes Flats of the Coastal Bend. We're a family oriented, friendly park with plenty to do or not to do — depending on your mood.

INGREDIENTS
- 1 c. rice, uncooked
- 3 c. milk
- ½ stick butter
- 1 c. sugar
- 1 tsp. vanilla
- 4 eggs

DIRECTIONS

Scald milk and butter. Beat eggs. Slowly add sugar, vanilla and scalded milk. Stir in rice. Cook at 450° until inserted knife comes out clean.

DESERT SHORES BREAD PUDDING
Desert Shores – Tucson, AZ

This recipe is delicious and is one of our favorites. Although conveniently located near central Tucson and its suburban shopping centers, our tree-shaded park maintains a country-style air. Desert Shores has all modern conveniences and friendly people. It's a lovely place with a tree-lined pond. Come see for yourself.

INGREDIENTS
- 2 c. bread cubes
- 2 c. milk
- 3 Tbsp. margarine
- ¼ c. sugar
- 2 eggs
- dash of salt
- ½ tsp. almond extract

DIRECTIONS

Using day-old bread with crusts, cut into small cubes in a buttered 1 qt. baking dish. Scald the milk with the sugar and butter. Can be done in microwave oven. Beat eggs slightly, add salt, then stir in the warm milk and almond extract. Pour over the bread cubes. Set the baking dish in a pan of warm water up to the level of the pudding and bake in moderate oven (350°) for an hour or until a knife inserted in the center comes out clean. Makes 5 servings. Serve hot with plain cream.

PERSIMMON PUDDING
Free Spirit Campground – Bedford, IN

Persimmon pudding is a specialty of our area. A persimmon festival is held every year in September when this fruit is ripe. Our park is set in the woods among the maple trees where an old sugar camp is located. We want to share our neck of the woods with you, hence our recipe using a fruit grown in abundance in our area.

INGREDIENTS
- 1 c. persimmon pulp
- 1 c. milk
- ½ c. sugar
- 2 Tbsp. melted butter
- 1 egg, beaten
- 1 tsp. baking powder
- ½ tsp. baking soda
- 1½ c. flour
- 1 tsp. allspice

DIRECTIONS

Stir in soda to persimmon pulp. Add sugar, beaten egg and melted butter. Sift dry ingredients. Add dry ingredients and milk to persimmon mixture. Pour into greased 9" x 9" pan. Bake at 300° for 45 min.

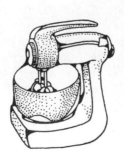

JOYCE'S BLUEBERRY SURPRISE
Crystal Lake Campground – Scottville, MI

Crystal Lake Campground is located near a 30 acre blueberry patch. Our campers often go there to pick blueberries and this recipe is one of their favorite ways to prepare this fruit.

We are a 160 site campground located on a beautiful lake. We offer clean washrooms and sites nestled in the forest.

INGREDIENTS
- 1 lg. pkg. cherry Jell-O
- ¾ c. boiling water
- 1 lg. can crushed pineapple
- 1 can blueberry pie filling
- 8 oz. sour cream
- 1 8-oz. pkg. cream cheese
- ½ c. sugar
- ½ tsp. vanilla
- ½ c. chopped pecans

DIRECTIONS

Dissolve Jell-O in boiling water. Add drained pineapple and blueberry filling. Refrigerate for about 3 hrs. and then add topping.

Topping: Mix sour cream and cream cheese together. Add sugar and vanilla. Spread on Jell-O and sprinkle top with pecans.

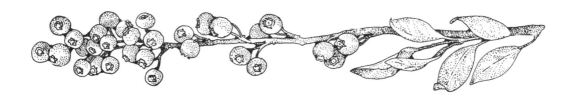

POTLUCK DESSERT FAVORITE
Sherwood Forest Family Campground – Olivet, MI

Sherwood Forest really is a "forest" with sites cut into the forest! We have all hookups, hot showers, hayrides, puppet shows, heated pool, mini-golf, petting farm and much more. Our specials include weekends with hot air balloon launches, Christmas in July and a monthly potluck dinner. At these dinners our campers supply a main dish to share. We supply the dessert and coffee. And it seems to us that this dessert is a definite favorite.

INGREDIENTS
- sliced apples
- cinnamon
- nutmeg
- cloves
- pie crust

DIRECTIONS

Spread a large cookie sheet with your favorite pie crust. Spoon on your favorite apple pie filling (we make our own pie crust and filling). Add cinnamon, nutmeg and cloves to taste. Cover with second thin layer of pie crust which has been slit to allow steam to escape. Sprinkle crust with water or milk and sugar. Bake until crust is golden brown.

STRAWBERRY DELIGHT
Bird Creek Mobile Home Park – Temple, TX

This tasty treat is a favorite and it keeps fresh in the freezer.

Bird Creek is located on I-35 at exit 302, with easy-on, easy-off access. We offer spacious sites and full hookups for all sizes of RVs. We have a swimming pool and we're convenient to all medical facilities.

INGREDIENTS
- 1 11-oz. boxes vanilla wafers, crushed
- 1 can condensed milk
- 1 box powdered sugar
- 4 eggs
- 1 tsp. vanilla
- 1 c. pecans
- ½ pt. whipped cream
- 2 10-oz. pkgs. frozen strawberries

DIRECTIONS
Mix milk, sugar and eggs. Cook over low heat until thickened. Add vanilla and let cool. Line pan with half of crushed wafers. Add milk mixture. Then add a layer of pecans, a layer of whipped cream, and a layer of frozen strawberries. Add remainder of whipped cream and top with remaining wafers. Cover with foil and freeze.

CAMPER'S CHERRY-PRETZEL DELIGHT
Brush Creek Campground — Breezewood, PA

This recipe is quick and easy. There's no cooking involved; all you need is a refrigerator. It goes well with coffee or a tall glass of ice cold milk. You're on vacation — what better time to live it up than with an easy, refreshing dessert "delight." Use it as a friendly "hello" to get to know your camping neighbors, or make little delights for kids in cereal bowls or individual pie containers. Serve with lots of love and a smile.

Get back to nature in the Blue Ridge Mountains. Our campground is situated along a state-stocked stream available for fishing. We are located 3½ miles from Breezewood with grassy and some shaded campsites. You can go hiking in the mountains or just relax by the creek with our Cherry-Pretzel Delight.

INGREDIENTS
- 1 c. pretzel crumbs
- ½ c. sugar
- ¼ c. soft butter
- 1 pkg. Dream Whip, prepared
- 1 3-oz. pkg. cream cheese
- ¼ c. powdered sugar
- 1 can No. 303 cherry pie filling or thickened blueberries

DIRECTIONS
Put pretzels in plastic bag and let the kids pound them with a "pet rock." Mix pretzel crumbs, sugar and butter. Put into 9" square dish. Whip Dream Whip according to package directions. Add the cream cheese and sugar. Whip until well blended. Spread in pan on top of pretzel mixture. Spread cherry pie filling on top of Dream Whip. Refrigerate overnight. Serve with large spoon. Serves 9.

HILLBILLY PEACH COBBLER
KOA-Nashville Opryland – Nashville, TN

All rally dinners and package dinners end with the Hillbilly Peach Cobbler as dessert. Our park is located 1½ miles north of Opryland, USA. Our KOA has a beautiful natural setting. It is a large 37 acre resort-type park with 460 sites for all types of campers — from recreational vehicles to primitive style tent campers. We feature landscaped sites with paved driveways, picnic tables and hookups for water, electric and sewer to simple grassy sites for tent camping. A large swimming pool, kiddie pool and live nightly entertainment from April thru October featuring stars of Opryland and the Grand Ole Opry all make our park a fun place to stay.

INGREDIENTS
Cobbler:
  2 1-lb. cans peaches
  2 c. sugar
  1 Tbsp. cinnamon
  ½ c. cornstarch
  1 Tbsp. vanilla
Topping:
  cinnamon
  water
  3 c. self-rising flour
  ½ c. sugar
  ⅓ c. butter

DIRECTIONS
Cobbler: Mix all ingredients together and place in pan. Set aside.

Topping: Mix flour, sugar and butter together with enough water to form mixture of "pancake batter" consistency. Spread over fruit mixture and sprinkle with ½ c. sugar. Sprinkle lightly with cinnamon. Bake at 350° for 30 min. or until browned.

E-Z PEACH COBBLER
Athens I-75 KOA – Athens, TN

We have Blue Grass festivals here at the campground on Memorial Day and Labor Day weekends. My peach cobbler is a favorite of the festival goers.

We are located just off of I-75 at exit 49 in Southeast Tennessee. It's a short drive to the Smoky Mountains, Cherokee National Forest, river rafting and many other Tennessee attractions. Campers can enjoy great Blue Grass music twice a year and explore our lovely area all year long. Our campground has extra clean restrooms, long pull-thru sites and a completely shaded tent area. Families and large groups are welcome.

INGREDIENTS
  1 c. sugar
  1 c. self-rising flour
  1 egg
  4 c. peaches
  2 tsp. tapioca, optional
  1 stick butter, finely chopped
  1 c. water

DIRECTIONS
Mix sugar and flour. Add well-beaten egg. Don't be discouraged, it will mix to rough crumbs. Place peaches in 9″ x 13″ x 2″ casserole dish. Add sugar to taste and then add water. Tapioca will thicken juice, but this is optional. Sprinkle flour mixture on top of peaches and top with butter. Bake at 350° for 1 hr. until brown.

APPLE COBBLER
Appalachian Campsites – Shartlesville, PA

Since the apple is a special part of our Appalachian Campsites' logo, apples have become almost a trademark for our campground. In fact each of the roads in our campground is named after a variety of apple. The local orchards abound with an ample supply throughout the fall so it is natural to serve an apple dessert with our chicken barbecue, steak, or ham dinners.

INGREDIENTS
Part I:
- ¾ c. sugar
- 2 Tbsp. flour
- ½ tsp. cinnamon
- ¼ tsp. salt
- 5 c. sliced apples
- ¼ c. water
- 1 Tbsp. butter or margarine

Part II:
- 1 c. flour
- 1½ tsp. baking powder
- 1 Tbsp. sugar
- ½ tsp. salt
- 3 Tbsp. shortening
- ½ c. milk

DIRECTIONS

Mix sugar, flour, cinnamon, and salt with apples. Place in oblong pan and sprinkle with water. Dot with butter, cover and bake at 375° for 15 min. Sift together flour, baking powder, sugar, and salt. Cut in shortening and stir in milk. Drop by spoonfuls on hot apples. Bake uncovered 25 to 35 min. Especially good served warm with a bit of vanilla ice cream. Makes 6 servings.

APPLE CRISP
Alpine Woods RV Resort – Hendersonville, NC

Henderson County is the 6th largest apple producing county in the United States. Surrounded by the beautiful Blue Ridge Mountains it also is a destination area for tourists wanting to explore the area's many attractions. Hendersonville is the city of seasons and claims to have the best weather in the United States because of its mild seasons. Hence, it is rapidly becoming one of the top retirement areas in the country. In October, after the harvest, Alpine Woods RV Resort provides campers with apples at no charge. Many of our guests enjoy using these apples in a variety of dishes, including this Southern dessert.

INGREDIENTS
- 5-6 apples
- 1 c. sugar
- 1 c. flour
- ¾ tsp. salt
- ⅓ c. oleo or butter
- cinnamon to taste
- 1 tsp. baking powder
- 1 unbeaten egg

DIRECTIONS

Peel apples and slice thin. Place in dish as you would for a pie. Pile high. Mix sugar, flour, salt and baking powder together. Stir in unbeaten egg to dry mixture. Put mixture on top of apples. Sprinkle with cinnamon. Pour melted oleo over the top. Bake at 350° for 30-40 min. Crust will be hard if left in too long.

DARLENE'S APPLE DUMPLINGS
Sleepy Hollow Campground – Oxford, IA

Sleepy Hollow is located 10 miles west of Iowa City on I-80. We are minutes away from the famous Amana Colonies, the Amish community of Kalona, Herbert Hoover Presidential Museum and Library, and the Old Capitol on the campus of the University of Iowa. We offer a quiet and clean family environment with planned activities. For your convenience we offer a full service restaurant, Phillips '66 gasoline, propane, lounge and mini store. Welcome to Iowa where you'll find beautiful land and lakes between two rivers.

INGREDIENTS
    golden delicious apples,
      halved
    2 c. flour
    ½ tsp. salt
    1½ tsp. baking powder
    ½ c. shortening
    ⅔ c. milk
    sugar & cinnamon in
      equal amounts
    butter
Topping:
    2 c. sugar
    2 c. water
    ½ c. butter

DIRECTIONS
    Mix flour, salt, baking soda, shortening and milk together to form dough. Roll out dough thicker than pie crust. Cut into circles or squares. Place half an apple on each square. Add 1 tsp. sugar and cinnamon and a small pat of butter on each apple. Fold dough over apple and place in buttered baking dish.
    Topping: Mix sugar and water. Add butter and bring to boil. Pour topping over dumplings. Bake at 350° for 1 hr.
    Note: Use a pan big enough that it will not boil over in oven.

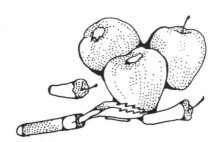

WHISPERING HILLS APPLE DUMPLINGS
Whispering Hills Recreation – Shreve, OH

Holmes County, Ohio, the location of the largest Amish settlement in the world, is famous for its down home cooking. Our specialty here at Whispering Hills Campground is home-made apple dumplings. We have two large festivals each year. The first weekend in August is the Plain and Fancy fair and the Apple Dumpling festival is the first weekend in October. Many campers come to tour the Amish country and eat apple dumplings. We also make many more Amish foods in our wood-fired outdoor oven.

INGREDIENTS
    2 c. flour
    4 Tbsp. baking powder
    ½ tsp. salt
    ½ c. shortening
    ¾ c. milk
    6 apples, peeled, cored &
      quartered
    ⅓ c. sugar
    2 tsp. cinnamon

DIRECTIONS
    Mix dry ingredients and add milk quickly. Toss on floured board. Roll dough ¼" thick, cut into 6" squares. Place an apple, 1 tablespoon sugar and a dash of cinnamon on each square. Bring up corners of dough to cover apples and place in baking pan. Mix ¾ c. sugar, 1 c. water and 1 tsp. cinnamon. Boil for 5 min. and pour over dumplings. Bake at 400° for 45 min.

OZARK CHOCOLATE DIPPED STRAWBERRIES
Tall Pines Campground – Branson, MO

Tall Pines is truly the "Pride of the Ozarks". Located between The Shepherd of the Hills Homestead and Silver Dollar City, it is quiet, peaceful and shady. We are close to the 22 different Country/Western shows performed nightly. We are family owned and operated since 1976. This delicacy is popular at our weekly "all you can eat" ice cream socials.

INGREDIENTS
fresh strawberries
1 lb. molding chocolate* (for each dozen strawberries)

* available at most candy stores in ribbon, kiss or wafer shapes

DIRECTIONS
Clean strawberries, leaving stems on. Dry thoroughly and refrigerate to cool. Melt chocolate in microwave or double boiler. Hold strawberry by the stem and immerse in chocolate. Place on waxed paper to cool. Serve at room temperature.

CIRCUS DELIGHT
Crescent City Campground — Crescent City, FL

This recipe is easy to make and is a great hit at cookouts or potlucks.
Crescent City Campground is situated on the outskirts of a quiet little town. Our park is studded with trees, and a sleepy little creek winds through our grounds. We're a very friendly park that's almost like a family. We invite you to come stay with us and enjoy Florida's sun and friendly people.

INGREDIENTS
2 pkgs. orange Jell-O
1 can crushed pineapple, drained
28 orange marshmallow circus peanuts, cut in chunks
2 c. Cool Whip

DIRECTIONS
Make Jell-O according to directions, using pineapple juice in place of water. Add circus peanuts; chill until partially set. Add crushed pineapple and fold in Cool Whip. Chill. Serve and enjoy as a salad or dessert.

JELL-O DELIGHT
Lubbock KOA – Lubbock, TX

This recipe is easy to prepare and is delightfully cool and refreshing. Not only is it pleasing to the taste buds, it also travels well so you can enjoy this treat wherever you go.
We are a convenient drive-thru campground. Most campers usually just stay with us for one night and find our pull-thru sites very easy to manage — no matter what size RV. We also offer an enclosed pool and hot tub for year 'round use.

INGREDIENTS
1 sm. box Jell-O
1 pt. ice cream

DIRECTIONS
Cook Jell-O as directed, but instead of using cold water, add ice cream and refrigerate.

CHOWNING'S TAVERN BROWNIES
Williamsburg KOA Kampground – Williamsburg, VA

We are conveniently located near all of Williamsburg's attractions. Our full service campground staff is ready to help make your stay an enjoyable one. This brownie recipe comes from Josiah Chowning's Tavern, built in 1766. It is one of the many sights in Colonial Williamsburg. We hope you will enjoy these brownies as our forefathers did. Happy Kamping!

INGREDIENTS
- 1 c. butter
- 8 oz. unsweetened chocolate
- 7 eggs
- 3 c. sugar
- ½ tsp. vanilla
- 2 c. sifted all-purpose flour
- 1 Tbsp. baking powder
- 2 c. pecans, chopped

DIRECTIONS

Preheat oven to 350°. Grease a 10½" x 15½" x 1" pan. Melt the butter and chocolate in a double boiler over hot water. Beat the eggs, sugar, and vanilla until frothy. Add the melted butter and chocolate. Add the sifted dry ingredients. Stir in the pecans. Pour into the prepared pan and bake at 350° for 30 min. Cool and cut into 3 x 3-inch squares. Yields 20 brownies.

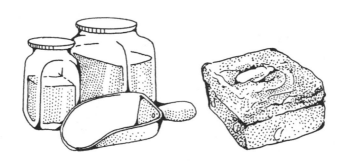

BLONDE BROWNIES
Covered Bridge Campsite – Livingston Manor, NY

This recipe is a great hit after cookouts and around the campfire — winter or summer. Covered Bridge Campsite is a rustic campground in the Catskills on the Willowemoc, a famous trout fishing creek. Great fishing and hunting are available here in the Catskills.

INGREDIENTS
- ⅔ c. shortening
- 2 c. brown sugar
- 2 lg. eggs
- 2 c. flour
- 1 tsp. baking powder
- ½ tsp. salt
- ¼ tsp. baking soda
- 1 tsp. vanilla
- chocolate chips

DIRECTIONS

Combine first 3 ingredients and mix slightly by hand. Add dry ingredients and vanilla and mix well. Spread mixture in a greased 9" x 13" pan. Sprinkle chocolate chips on top. Bake at 350° for 20 min. or until they start to fall. Do not wait for them to be firm or they will be too hard.

BROWNIES-RICH AND FAMOUS
Lake George R.V. Park – Lake George, NY

Our park was developed on the premise of combining convenience with atmosphere. In our snack bar, adjacent to the heated indoor pool and adult lounge, you will find some exotic ice cream creations. Our all time favorite is called the "Pop Up". This is made from our Rich and Famous Brownie *topped with a premium quality scoop of vanilla ice cream, hot fudge, nuts, whipped cream and a cherry on top.*

Lake George R.V. Park is located at the base of historic French Mountain located at the foothills of the Adirondacks. The Adirondacks is a name that means the great outdoors in New York State. Lake George, also known as "Queen of the American Lakes" offers 32 miles of crystal clear water and an opportunity to enjoy history from the earliest days of colonial settlement. The valley is guarded by forts in Ticonderoga and Lake George. The forests and wildlife have provided a rich source of lumber and furs. The lakeshores provided perfect settings for the "great camps" of the rich and famous.

INGREDIENTS
- ½ lb. butter
- 4 squares unsweetened chocolate
- 3-4 tsp. vanilla
- 4 lg. egg whites
- 2 c. white granulated sugar
- 2 c. walnuts (not crushed)
- 1 c. sifted flour

DIRECTIONS

Preheat oven to 300°. Butter a 9″ x 13″ pan. In double boiler melt butter and bakers chocolate. Set aside to cool. When cooled, add vanilla. In a large bowl separate 4 large eggs. Set aside whites until last step. Add white sugar, blend well. Add cooled chocolate and mix well. Add walnuts and sifted flour. Beat egg whites and add. Mix well. Spread batter evenly in pan and bake for 1 hour. Cut into 2″ squares.

MINIATURE CHEESECAKES
Eastern Long Island Kampgrounds – Greenport, NY

This is a favorite of many campers who have come to one of our great potluck suppers.

Eastern Long Island Kampground is located at the tip of Long Island. We are in a rural area noted for its seaport, Greenport, and for its farms and vineyards. The area is New England on Long Island, an hour and a half from New York City.

INGREDIENTS
- Nabisco Nilla vanilla wafers
- 2 8-oz. pkg. cream cheese
- ¾ c. sugar
- 2 eggs
- 1 tsp. vanilla
- 1 can fruit pie filling

DIRECTIONS

Line muffin tin with double paper liners. Place one Nabisco Nilla vanilla wafer in bottom of each liner. Beat cream cheese, sugar, eggs, and vanilla until smooth. Fill liners ¾ full. Bake 10-15 min. at 375°. Top should lose the shiny appearance, but not crack. While warm, spoon prepared pie filling on top. Refrigerate until serving time.

GEORGE WASHINGTON CHEESE CAKE
Hidden Valley Camping Resort – Mifflinburg, PA

Each year we open with a dessert social and this recipe is the hit of the evening. Hidden Valley Resort has over 400 sites on 115 acres. We are truly hidden in one of the many beautiful valleys of the Susquehanna. This valley was once part of the frontier of the American colonies. After the Revolution, a large number of settlers moved into the area, taking advantage of the region's rich farmland and abundant hardwoods. Many of these farms are still in operation today. The region's forests are still home to the producer of some of the nation's best furniture. The heritage of the nineteenth century can be experienced in the fascinating living museums of Susquehanna Valley towns. The Susquehanna Valley has been beckoning Americans for over 200 years. Today, its attractions are as appealing as ever.

INGREDIENTS
- 1 8″ graham cracker pie crust
- 8 oz. cream cheese
- 1 can condensed milk
- 1 tsp. vanilla
- ⅓ c. bottled lemon juice

DIRECTIONS

Beat cream cheese and condensed milk until light and fluffy. Add vanilla and lemon juice. Pour mixture into pie crust and chill at least 2 hours.

MINI CHEESE CAKES
Bud's Campground – Gearhart, OR

This recipe is very simple and easy to make. We hope to serve this treat at our campground after we open our deli.

If there's anything you want to do "Bud's Campground" will do. There's beaching, fishing, hunting, shopping, scenic sights and golfer's delight. Visit the oldest city west of the Mississippi, and numerous historical sites. Come see Mrs. Pleasant and Mr. Ouch. Come to Bud's and make lifetime friendships.

INGREDIENTS
- 24 vanilla wafers
- ⅔ c. sugar
- 3 eggs
- 3 8-oz. pkgs. cream cheese
- 1 Tbsp. vanilla

DIRECTIONS

Line a muffin pan with cupcake liners. Place a wafer in the bottom of each liner. Mix all ingredients for 5 min. or until very smooth. Pour batter on top of wafers. Bake at 325° for 15 min. Serve cold with any kind of topping.

ROSE MARINA
Chippewa Valley Campgrounds – Seville, OH

This is a light dessert and is a large crowd-pleaser. We serve it at our annual clambake and pig roast at the campground. It's always a big hit.

We offer a clean campground with a friendly atmosphere. Our large pavilion is great for family reunions or company picnics. While you're here you can swim, boat, fish or just enjoy a quiet, relaxing stay with your family and friends.

INGREDIENTS
- 1-16 oz. pkg. Rose Marina (macaroni)
- 2-10 oz. cans crushed pineapple
- 1-10 oz. can maraschino cherries
- 2 cans mandarin oranges
- ½ c. sugar
- 1 egg, beaten
- 16 oz. Cool Whip
- 2 Tbsp. flour

DIRECTIONS
Cook rose marina according to package. Drain pineapple and cherries, reserving juice. Cook juice over low heat, adding sugar, flour and egg. Cook until thick. Pour over cooked, drained rose marina. Mix in cut up cherries, drained oranges and pineapple. Cover and refrigerate overnight. When ready to serve, mix in Cool Whip.

PEAR STREUSEL
Overnite Trailer Park – Metairie, LA

We have a variety of pear trees at our park and this tasty recipe is just one way to use pears.

Our park is located 5 miles west of New Orleans. We have full hookup spaces and accept self-contained units only. Mardi Gras, the biggest free show on earth, is one of our favorite festivals. Come stay with us and enjoy all that our area has to offer.

INGREDIENTS
Batter:
- 6 c. pears, sliced
- 1¼ tsp. ground cinnamon
- ¼ tsp. ground nutmeg
- 1 c. sugar
- ¾ c. milk
- ½ c. Bisquick
- 2 eggs
- 2 Tbsp. margarine or butter

Streusel:
- 1 c. Bisquick
- ½ c. nuts, chopped
- ⅓ c. brown sugar, packed
- 3 Tbsp. margarine or butter

DIRECTIONS
Batter: Mix pears and spices; turn into pie plate. Beat remaining ingredients together until smooth — 15 sec. in blender or 1 min. on high with electric mixer. Pour over pear mixture.

Streusel: Mix all ingredients together until crumbly.

Preheat oven to 325°. Sprinkle streusel over batter. Bake for 55-60 min. or until knife inserted in center comes out clean.

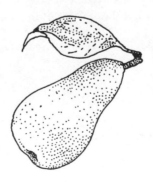

S'MORES
Holiday Trav-L-Park – Virginia Beach, VA

INGREDIENTS
graham crackers
marshmallows
chocolate bars
campfire
sticks — preferably
  "homemade"

DIRECTIONS
First of all, you spend the whole day outside. Build a sandcastle, collect seashells, swim in the ocean and then rinse off in the pools, go on the hayride, watch cartoons with the kids and then dance poolside to the nightly band. THEN, when you are good and hungry, sit around the campfire with your family and assorted neighbors. Put one or two marshmallows on your stick and, sort of lazily, start to turn it round 'n round near the flames. TAKE YOUR TIME!!! This is a process to be enjoyed and savored. When you're good and ready, make a sandwich with the graham crackers and squares of chocolate. After everyone has had one, it will then be time to make S'MORE!!!

PUPPY CHOW
Timber Trails Campground – Decatur, MI

This recipe is so easy to make and it gives everyone more time to have FUN.

Our park is located on Lake of the Woods. It is over 300 acres and is great for fishing, swimming and boating. All of our sites are grassy and shaded. We have a number of permanents, but still have room for vacationers and weekenders. We take pride in running a neat clean campground. Our play area is a favorite with the children along with the candy store. Come see us.

P.S. This recipe is for people — not pets!

INGREDIENTS
1½ c. chocolate chips
½ stick butter
½ c. peanut butter
1 box bran chex
1 c. powdered sugar

DIRECTIONS
Melt chocolate chips and butter. Stir in peanut butter. Mix in 1 box of bran chex. When hardened, sprinkle with powdered sugar.

PEANUT BUTTER EGGS
Indian Rock Campgrounds — York, PA

This smooth, delicious candy is an old time favorite!

We're a quiet relaxing park in the heart of Pennsylvania Dutch Country. Nestled in the rolling green hills of York, we're only 3 miles from many historic sites such as the First Capital, Gates House and Plough Tavern.

INGREDIENTS
1 18-oz. jar smooth peanut
  butter
1 stick margarine
1 1-lb. box powdered sugar
1 bag milk chocolate chips

DIRECTIONS
Soften margarine and blend with peanut butter until smooth. Mix in sugar and blend together. Form into egg-shaped balls. Melt chocolate. Dip peanut butter eggs with plastic fork — 1 middle prong broken out — into chocolate. Place on wax paper to set. Store in a cool place.

SAND TARTS
Panama City Beach-KOA – Panama City Beach, FL

These light colored tarts are reminiscent of the beautiful sugar white sand beaches found near our park. As a matter of fact, we're only 300 yards from the Gulf where our guests enjoy swimming and fishing. Our park is close to all major attractions in the area. There's plenty for the whole family to see and do!

INGREDIENTS
1 c. butter
2 c. self-rising flour
2 Tbsp. vanilla
1 c. chopped pecans
powdered sugar

DIRECTIONS
Mix butter and vanilla together, gradually adding flour. When well mixed, stir in pecans. Mixture will be slightly crumbly. Shape into small balls and bake in 375° oven for 10-12 min. Roll in powdered sugar and store in airtight container.

CAROLINA DELIGHTS
Holiday Trav-L-Park – Emerald Isle, NC

This recipe is a simple and delicious treat. Prepare them ahead of time and bring them along; or make them at your site.
We offer 350 spaces, most with full hookups. Enjoy our oceanfront sites, swimming pool, playground, picnic tables, recreation hall and hot showers. Located on North Carolina's spectacular crystal coast, Holiday Trav-L-Park is a beautiful place to be.

INGREDIENTS
2 c. sugar
1 stick margarine
½ c. milk
½ tsp. vanilla
½ c. peanut butter
¼ c. cocoa
2½ c. instant oats

DIRECTIONS
Combine sugar and cocoa. Add milk and margarine and bring to a boil in a saucepan. Continue boiling for 1½ min. Remove from heat. Add peanut butter and mix. Add vanilla and quick oats. Stir until well mixed. Drop from teaspoon onto waxed paper and allow to set.

MICROWAVE PEANUT BRITTLE
Davis Lakes & Campground – Suffolk, VA

This recipe takes advantage of the abundance of peanuts in our area. After all, Suffolk is known as the Peanut Capital of the world. Davis Lakes & Campground is a family oriented campground with lots to see and do. We offer great fishing and swimming and mini golf. We're only an hour's drive from Virginia Beach, Norfolk, Williamsburg and Busch Gardens. Come see what you're missing!

INGREDIENTS
- 1 c. raw peanuts
- ½ c. light corn syrup
- 1 c. granulated sugar
- ⅛ tsp. salt
- 1 tsp. butter
- 1 tsp. vanilla
- 1 tsp. baking soda

DIRECTIONS

Mix peanuts, sugar, syrup, and salt in large casserole dish. Cook on high for 4 min. Stir well. Cook 3 to 4 min. on high. Remove from oven and add vanilla and butter. Cook 1½ min. until nuts are brown. Remove from oven and quickly fold in baking soda. Pour on greased cookie sheet. Leave uncovered for 1 hour. Break into pieces. Store in tightly covered container or plastic bags. Yields approximately 1 pound.

COCONUT ICE BOX COOKIES
Clarks Skagit River Cabins & Eatery-Rockport, WA

This is a favorite as my mother served them at the suppers at the Bullerville Dance Hall in the 1930s. They taste even better as the cookies age.

We are located 6 miles east of Rockport on Hwy. 20, at the entrance to North Cascade National Park. We have 125 wooded acres and a mile of Skagit River frontage. The nearby Eatery Drive-In provides the best Cascade Burger and fresh fruit shakes. We offer full hookups, laundry and restroom facilities, a little Wildwood Chapel and many rabbits that eat from your hand. A most restful atmosphere is found here.

INGREDIENTS
- ½ c. shortening
- ½ c. brown sugar
- 1 lg. egg
- 1 tsp. vanilla
- ½ c. coconut and/or nuts
- 2 tsp. baking powder
- 1 c. flour
- ½ tsp. salt
- ¾ c. sugar

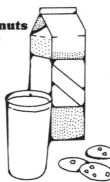

DIRECTIONS

Cream shortening and sugars together. Stir in egg and vanilla. Add dry ingredients. Mix well. Stir in coconut and nuts. Press dough into pan so it is 1" thick. Allow to refrigerate overnight. Turn dough upside down on a board and slice into ¼" strips. Lay strips on greased pan. Bake at 425° for 10 min. They should be light golden brown.

QUICK CHOCOLATE CHIP COOKIES
Bismarck Campground – Bismarck, ND

One of our friendly campers shared this recipe with us and our guests. Because it's so quick and easy, it allows our guests to take advantage of all the recreation we offer. We encourage our guests to explore Bismarck and visit all the sights. Our campground also offers a quiet and peaceful haven for those wishing to take a break from the hustle and bustle of their everyday lives.

INGREDIENTS
- 1 c. Bisquick
- 1 pkg. instant vanilla pudding
- ¼ c. oil
- 1 egg, beaten
- ½ c. chocolate chips
- 3 Tbsp. milk

DIRECTIONS

Mix all ingredients together and drop on greased cookie sheet. Dates, nuts or raisins may be substituted for chocolate chips. Bake at 350° for 8-10 min.

PERSIMMON COOKIES
Raintree Lake Campground – Scottsburg, IN

We have some "prized" persimmon trees on our grounds and we put them to good use. Raintree Lake Campground has 75 sites on 30 acres with a 9 acre fishing lake, beautiful swimming pool, laundry room, sparkling showers and restrooms as well as a variety of hookups and other amenities. Our campground is so named because of the "raintrees" on our property. Sometimes I wonder if it should have been named "Persimmon Tree Park"!

INGREDIENTS
- 1 c. chopped walnuts or pecans
- 1 c. raisins
- 2 c. flour
- pinch of salt
- ½ tsp. cinnamon
- ½ tsp. cloves
- ½ tsp. nutmeg
- 1 tsp. baking soda
- 1 c. persimmon pulp
- ½ c. butter
- 1 c. sugar
- 1 egg, beaten

DIRECTIONS

Grind nuts and raisins coarsely and mix with flour, salt and spices. Dissolve baking soda in persimmon pulp. Cream butter and sugar. Beat in eggs, then persimmon pulp. Stir in flour mixture. Drop by teaspoonfuls on greased cookie sheet. Bake at 350° for 15 min.

MICRO RECIPE — DATE SQUARES
Heritage Farm Campground – Mactaquac, NB

This delicious recipe is great for those RVers who have microwaves. It's quick and easy to prepare so you and your family have more time for fun. Our family-oriented campground offers all types of facilities as well as a variety of recreation such as swimming, group activities and a fully equipped rec hall. So throw down your aprons and come have some fun!

INGREDIENTS
- 1 lb. dates, chopped
- ¼ c. white sugar
- ½ tsp. vanilla extract
- ½ c. water (mixed with pineapple juice)
- ½ c. crushed pineapple
- 2 c. rolled oats
- 1½ c. flour
- ¾ c. brown sugar
- 1-1¼ c. soft butter or margarine (start with 1 cup and add as needed)
- dash of salt

DIRECTIONS

Place cut up dates, sugar, vanilla and water in a medium sized microwave bowl and cook 3 min. on high. Add pineapple and stir well. Cook 3 more min. on high. Let stand to cool, or place in refrigerator to speed cooling. In a large bowl, combine remaining dry ingredients and blend well. Add softened butter, not melted, and blend into mixture until it resembles coarse bread crumbs. Place half of crumb mixture into an 8" square pan. Spread date mixture evenly over all. Cover with other half of the crumb mixture and pat down. Cook 4 min. on high. Pat down. Cook 2-4 more min. on high. Cool. Cut into bars.

COWBOY COOKIES
Isla Gold Mobile Home & RV Park – Naranja, FL

Each year Isla Gold receives guests from all over the United States & Canada. Many of these guests pass along tasty recipes such as this one. We invite you to come stay in our clean, modern and friendly park and enjoy Florida camping at its finest.

INGREDIENTS
- 1 c. sugar
- 1 c. brown sugar
- 1 c. shortening
- 2 eggs
- 2 c. flour
- ½ tsp. baking powder
- ½ tsp. baking soda
- dash of salt
- 2 c. raw oatmeal
- ½ c. milk
- chocolate chips
- raisins
- nuts

DIRECTIONS

Cream first 3 ingredients together. Add eggs, flour, baking powder and soda, salt, oatmeal and milk. Mix together. Stir in chocolate chips, raisins and nuts. Place spoonfuls of batter on ungreased cookie sheet. Bake at 350° for 15 min.

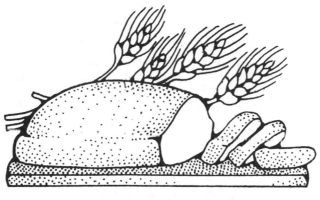

BREADS

ORANGE BISCUITS
Southern Palms R.V. Resort – Eustis, FL

We are in the heart of the southern orange groves and are located in Lake County close to good fishing, shopping and a country setting. We are a large park with 1300 full hookup sites and many accessories and activities to pamper our guests.

INGREDIENTS
Biscuits:
- 2 c. packaged biscuit mix
- 2 Tbsp. granulated sugar
- ½ c. milk
- ½ c. butter or margarine, melted

Filling:
- ½ c. orange marmalade
- ¼ c. finely chopped pecans
- 2 Tbsp. firmly packed light brown sugar
- 2 Tbsp. butter or margarine, melted

DIRECTIONS

Preheat oven to 425°. Lightly grease 8" x 8" x 2" baking pan. Make biscuits: combine ingredients, stir quickly with fork just until well mixed. Turn out dough on lightly floured surface and knead gently 8 to 10 times. Make filling: combine ingredients, except melted butter and mix well. Roll dough into a 12" x 9" rectangle; brush with 1 Tbsp. melted butter. Spread with filling mixture to within ½-inch of edge. From short side, roll up jelly-roll fashion. Cut crosswise into 9 1-inch slices. Arrange slices, cut side down, in prepared pan; brush with rest of melted butter. Bake 20 minutes or until golden-brown. Makes 9 servings.

ANGEL FLAKE BISCUITS
North Shore Park-A-Home — Channelview, TX

Our campers like to fish on weekends in either the salt water park or the fresh water Lake Sandy that's located two blocks from the park. A substantial breakfast is a must for such an outing!

North Shore Park-A-Home is a lovely, heavily shaded park close to shopping and fresh or salt water fishing. We also have a pool on site. We're only 10 miles from downtown Houston off I-10 at Exit 782 or 783 West. Amenities include two children's playgrounds, paved streets, and security lighting.

INGREDIENTS
- 5 c. enriched all-purpose flour
- 1 tsp. salt
- 1 tsp. baking soda
- 3 Tbsp. (correct) baking powder
- 3 Tbsp. sugar
- 1 c. solid all-vegetable shortening
- 1 cake yeast
- 2 Tbsp. warm water (85°)
- 2 cups buttermilk

DIRECTIONS

Sift dry ingredients together. Cut in shortening. Dissolve yeast in warm water. Add yeast and buttermilk to dry ingredients and stir with a fork until a soft dough is formed. Turn out on lightly floured board and knead briefly. Store in tightly closed plastic bag in the refrigerator. Use as needed. Pat dough out and cut with biscuit cutter. Do not let rise at any time. Bake on greased cookie sheet in preheated 450° oven 10 minutes. This dough lasts a week and yields a dozen biscuits per day.

IRISH BROWN BREAD (WHOLE WHEAT)
Lubbock RV Park – Lubbock, TX

Being from Ireland, I always have a loaf at hand. I sometimes treat my most welcome guests to a piece of my famous Irish bread.

We're a privately owned, peaceful and friendly park. We offer 30 spaces, secure premises, storm shelter, pay phone, and laundry. We're conveniently located on I-27 at exit 9.

INGREDIENTS
- **2 c. white flour**
- **2 c. whole wheat flour**
- **1 Tbsp. baking powder**
- **1 tsp. baking soda**
- **1 tsp. salt**
- **1 tsp. sugar**
- **2 c. buttermilk**

DIRECTIONS

Mix dry ingredients together. Add buttermilk. Knead dough until firm. Place dough in iron skillet. Slit top of dough. Bake at 400° for 45 min.

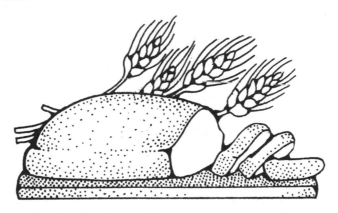

WHITE YEAST BREAD
McCarty's RV Park – Palestine, TX

Our park is located in beautiful East Texas. We're surrounded by mature oak and pine trees. Along the banks of our stream are native dogwood trees. And each March and April, Dogwood Festival activities abound. We're also convenient to attractions in the area such as a state railroad and NASA's balloon base. We welcome you all to our park.

INGREDIENTS
- **1 c. milk, scalded**
- **2 Tbsp. butter**
- **2 Tbsp. sugar**
- **1 pkg. yeast**
- **1 tsp. salt**
- **1 egg**
- **3 c. white flour**

DIRECTIONS

Combine milk, sugar and butter in a saucepan. Cook until scalded. Butter does not have to melt. Set off and cool. Put yeast in warm water and dissolve. Combine all ingredients with egg. Add flour and knead. Let rise until double in size. Knead again and let rise. Bake at 350° for 30 min.

DATE NUT BREAD
Hidden Acres Campground—Cape May Court House, NJ

Although our park is open officially 6 months, our favorite campers enjoy stopping in during the holidays and throughout the winter. The recipe is so easy to double and triple, pour into small, gift size loaf pans. It freezes well, so in addition to giving a small something to our favorite customers, I always have something to pop into the microwave and serve with a cup of coffee. We are in our 25th season, located along the Southernmost tip of New Jersey, the "Jersey Cape" area.

INGREDIENTS
- ¾ c. chopped nuts
- 1 c. chopped dates
- 1½ tsp. baking soda
- ½ tsp. salt
- 3 Tbsp. shortening
- 1 c. hot applesauce
- 2 eggs
- 1 tsp. vanilla
- 1 c. sugar
- 1½ c. sifted flour

DIRECTIONS

With a fork mix nuts, dates, soda, and salt. Add shortening and applesauce. Let stand 20 minutes. Preheat oven to 350°. Grease 5" x 9" loaf pan. Beat eggs with a fork. Add vanilla, sugar, and flour. Mix in date mixture just enough to blend. Bake 65 min. or until tester comes out clean. Cool 10 min. in pan.

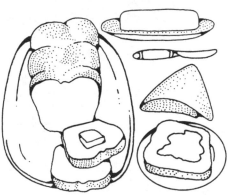

JOHNNY CAKE (from *The V. Bentley Cookbook*)
Pine Valley Resort Campground – Quechee, VT

Originally called Journey Cake, it is a traditional New England recipe and goes well with dinner and/or breakfast. This recipe is a family favorite we share with campers at breakfast coffee time.

We are a family-oriented campground conveniently located near main roads yet in the middle of scenic areas.

INGREDIENTS
- 1 c. yellow cornmeal
- ½ c. unbleached flour
- 2 tsp. baking powder
- ½ tsp. salt
- ½ c. milk
- ½ c. maple syrup*
- 1 egg
- 2 Tbsp. corn oil

* white or brown sugar may be substituted for maple syrup

DIRECTIONS

Measure dry ingredients into small bowl and set aside. Measure the remaining ingredients into a blender and blend well. Then add cornmeal mixture. Blend only until mixed, not a second more. Pour into buttered 8" square pan or muffin tins. Bake at 450° for 20 min.

MAPLE SYRUP MUFFINS
Green Acre Park – Waterloo, ONT

In the heart of Ontario, Canada, you will find the district of Festival Country. Here, fall maple trees yield a sweet sap; when refined it becomes maple syrup. At Green Acre Park, the campers enjoy this topping on the annual pancakes and sausage breakfast, not to mention all of the other various foods the syrup finds itself on.

Green Acre Park is located one hour east of Toronto and ten minutes away from the historic Mennonite Community of St. Jacobs. The quiet and conservative pace of life in the surrounding community is a reflection of what you'll find at Green Acre Park.

INGREDIENTS
- ¼ c. margarine
- ½ c. white sugar
- 1 tsp. salt
- 1¼ c. all-purpose flour
- 2 tsp. baking powder
- ¾ c. rolled oats
- ½ c. milk
- ½ c. maple syrup

Glaze
- 1 Tbsp. butter
- ½ c. icing sugar
- 1 Tbsp. maple syrup

DIRECTIONS
In a large bowl, soften margarine, blend in sugar and salt. Add dry ingredients and blend with pastry cutter until crumbly. Mix in oats. Blend milk and syrup together in measuring cup and pour over dry ingredients stirring only to moisten. Bake at 350° for 20 min. Spread glaze over when slightly cooled.

BUTTERMILK MUFFINS
Bancroft Tent and Trailer Camp – Bancroft, ONT

We are a family camp. What represents "family" more than home baking! Each day in our store I make something homemade to sell. Each day is popular; but Monday's "muffin day" is the favorite. This recipe is a large one but can be saved (sealed) up to 3 weeks.

INGREDIENTS
- 1 qt. buttermilk
- 1 tsp. salt
- 5 tsp. baking soda
- 2 c. Kellogs All Bran
- 3 c. bran flakes
- 1½ c. cooking oil
- 4 eggs
- 5½ c. flour
- 2 tsp. baking powder
- 2½ c. white sugar
- 1½ c. dates or raisins

DIRECTIONS
Combine baking soda and salt in buttermilk. Make sure all the baking soda is dissolved. Add remainder of ingredients in order given. Makes a large quantity. Keep sealed in refrigerator. Will keep for three weeks. Bake in muffin tins at 325°F. for 25 minutes.

GLAZED CRANBERRY ORANGE NUT BREAD
Pine-Aire Resort and Campground — Eagle River, WI

Pine-Aire, just north of Eagle River, is located in the midst of lakes, pines and "Cranberry Country." Annually, the first weekend of October, our native berry is celebrated during Eagle River Cranberry Fest. Thousands are attracted to bog tours, craft and quilt shows, lots of food, a fitness walk, visits by the "Cranberry People" and entertainment. A real highlight of our Fest is the Cranberry Bake-Off, where this bread recipe originated as a 1st place winner! Try it and I'm sure you'll agree this is Cranberry Cookin' at its Northwoods best!

INGREDIENTS
- 1 c. sugar
- 2 c. plus 2 Tbsp. flour
- 1 tsp. salt
- 2 tsp. baking powder
- ½ tsp. soda
- 1 c. orange juice
- grated peel from 1 orange
- ¼ c. melted shortening
- 1 c. chopped cranberries
- ½ c. chopped nuts
- 1 beaten egg

Glaze:
- ¼ c. sugar
- 2 Tbsp. coarsely chopped cranberries
- 2 Tbsp. orange juice

DIRECTIONS

Sift dry ingredients together. Combine the remaining ingredients. Lightly mix all the ingredients together. Bake in a lightly greased loaf pan at 375° for 40-50 min. Toothpick should come out clean when done.

Glaze: Mix sugar, cranberries and orange juice together. Cook slowly until a thick syrup forms. Pour over top of loaf while both are still hot.

ORANGE MARMALADE BREAD
Shady Grove Mobile & RV Park – Mesa, AZ

Shady Grove MH & RV Park is noted for its shade. All of the shade at our park is from grapefruit and orange trees. This recipe is a favorite here and we often use oranges from our trees to prepare it.

We are an adult-oriented park with an ideal in-town location. We have complete facilities including a laundry room, restrooms, patios, planned activities, rec room, shuffleboard court and more. Come stay with us in downtown Mesa where everything is just footsteps away.

INGREDIENTS
- ¾ c. orange marmalade
- 2 Tbsp. shortening, melted
- 1 egg
- 3 c. flour
- 6 tsp. baking powder
- 1 c. milk

DIRECTIONS

Put marmalade in a bowl. Add melted shortening and egg. Beat once. Add milk and dry ingredients. Mix well. Bake at 350° for 1 hr.

HOME-MADE BUTTERMILK BISCUITS
Jim Oliver's Smoke House Campground-Monteagle, TN

This recipe was handed down from my grandmother, Irene Oliver. She used to work at the Smoke House baking these biscuits every day. They are the best biscuits around.

Smoke House Campground is located 45 miles NW of Chattanooga and 80 miles SE of Nashville at Exit 134, off of I-24. The campground includes 50 sites, 20 of which have sewer, the remaining all have water and electrical hookups. 20 acres of recreation include tennis, swimming pool, volleyball, horseshoes, walking trails, children's playground, and many other things to do. Also located at this facility, is the famous Jim Oliver's Smoke House Restaurant which serves a full menu daily from 6 a.m. until 10 p.m. Also located here are honeymoon cabins, which feature hot tubs, fireplaces, kitchens, front porches, and much more. Another feature of the property is the 88 room motel which is furnished with country rockers. Also located at the Smoke House Restaurant is the Trading Post Gift Shop which features antiques, novelties, souvenirs, and many different Tennessee handcrafts.

INGREDIENTS
- 2 c. all-purpose flour
- 1 tsp. salt
- 2 tsp. baking powder
- ⅓ c. shortening
- 1 Tbsp. butter
- ¾ c. buttermilk

DIRECTIONS
Sift flour and measure. Resift with salt and baking powder. Add shortening and butter and cut in until the mixture is coarse. Stir in the buttermilk until the dough is well formed, then place on a lightly floured board. Knead lightly. Roll out dough and cut. Bake in lightly buttered sheet pan at 450° for 12-15 min. or until brown.

DONUT HOLES
South Arm Campground – Andover, ME

These donut holes are made at our park every morning and sold along with hot coffee.

South Arm Campground is located in an unspoiled wilderness area on the Richardson Lakes in the western mountains of Maine. We have 65 sites in the main camping area with full amenities plus 29 remote sites on the 17-mile lake with water access only.

INGREDIENTS
- **2 c. flour**
- **¼ c. sugar**
- **3 tsp. baking powder**
- **1 tsp. salt**
- **1 tsp. nutmeg or mace**
- **¼ c. salad oil**
- **¾ c. milk**
- **1 egg**
- **½ c. sugar**
- **1 tsp. cinnamon**

DIRECTIONS

Heat fat or oil (3 to 4 inches) to 375° in deep fat fryer or kettle. Measure flour, sugar, baking powder, salt and nutmeg into bowl. Add oil, milk, and egg; beat until smooth. Drop batter by teaspoonfuls into hot fat. Fry about 3 min. or until golden brown on both sides. Drain. Stir together ½ c. sugar and the cinnamon. Roll puffs in this mixture.

SPEEDY DOUGHNUTS
Endless Mountains Campground – Wyalusing, PA

Hi campers! If you want to just kick off your shoes, relax and enjoy a quiet countryside and clean air (2,000 ft. above sea level), then come and see us at the Endless Mountains Campground in Bradford County where you'll always meet friendly people. We have plenty of full hookups and a new pool.

INGREDIENTS
- **1 qt. oil**
- **country biscuit dough**
- **sugar**
- **cinnamon**

DIRECTIONS

Heat oil in a saucepan or deep fryer. Separate country biscuit dough. Cut hole in the center of biscuits. Fry biscuits and holes in oil for about 2 min. on each side. If desired, roll in sugar or cinnamon and enjoy!

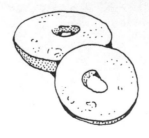

CORN BREAD
Normandy Farms Family Campground-Foxboro, MA

We print a monthly newsletter and feature recipes. This one was very popular and was listed in our July 1980 newsletter.

Normandy Farms Campground is a 400 site park located 30 miles south of Boston. We have a full-time year round activity program featuring a number of food functions as well as the regular activities. Many of our food functions feature homemade breads and desserts made by the family to accompany the group meals. This makes the events very popular with our campers. Our Boston baked beans, franks and homemade cornbread have long been a tradition of the area.

INGREDIENTS
- 1 c. white flour
- 1 c. yellow cornmeal
- 1 tsp. salt
- 4 tsp. baking powder
- ½ c. sugar or to taste
- ¼ c. powdered milk
- 1 egg
- 1 c. milk
- ½ c. cooking oil
- ½ tsp. butter-vanilla flavoring

DIRECTIONS

Sift dry ingredients in triple sifter. Add egg, milk, cooking oil and butter-vanilla flavoring to dry mixture. Bake in greased 8″ x 8″ pan at 400° for 30 min. Use toothpick test. May be used for cornbread pancakes, waffles or shortcake.

RAISIN MOLASSES COFFEE CAKE
Mt. Nebo Trailer Park — Roseburg, OR

This is an old family recipe that has been passed down throughout the years. It's one of my family's favorites and we hope your family enjoys it too.

Mt. Nebo is a trailer park with 18 RV spaces. We're located off of I-5 and are near Crater Lake and Wildlife Safari. Our amenitities include full hookups, pull-thrus, hot showers, laundry facilities and a rec room.

INGREDIENTS
- 2 eggs, slightly beaten
- ½ c. sugar
- ½ c. molasses
- ½ c. melted butter or oil
- ½ c. strong coffee
- 1 c. raisins
- 1 tsp. baking soda
- 1 c. wheat flour
- ¾ c. all-purpose flour
- ½ tsp. cloves

DIRECTIONS

Combine all ingredients in a bowl; mix well. Pour into a 9″ x 13″ greased pan. Bake at 350° for 25-30 min. Grated apple can be added to keep cake moist longer.

CORNBREAD GRIDDLE CAKES
War Eagle Mill — Rogers, AR

Simple, good tasting cornbread recipes are our specialty and a southern tradition. War Eagle Mill is a working, water-powered grist mill grinding 5 different whole grains on the War Eagle River. Our "Bean Palace" restaurant in the mill serves meals made from the grains ground on the 1st floor including War Eagle Cornbread and Buckwheat Waffles. We aren't just milling around here at War Eagle!

INGREDIENTS
- 1½ c. cornmeal
- ½ c. unbleached flour
- 2 tsp. baking powder
- 1 tsp. salt
- 1 c. milk
- 1 egg
- 1 Tbsp. honey
- oil or bacon fat

DIRECTIONS

Combine dry ingredients; add to liquid. Grease a fry pan or griddle. Over moderate heat, drop mixture by tablespoonfuls onto griddle and fry until brown, turning once. Split and serve with butter. Great cooked over an open fire.

CHEW BREAD
Two Rivers Campground — Nashville, TN

A short distance from Opryland USA, we are convenient to many attractions in the Nashville area. All of our sites include a concrete patio, picnic table and grassy area. We have a grocery store, souvenir shop and game room, also a playground and pool. We are privately owned and very proud of our knowledgeable and FRIENDLY staff. We hope you enjoy this yummy treat.

INGREDIENTS
- 3 whole eggs
- 1 box light brown sugar
- 2 c. self-rising flour
- 1 stick margarine
- 1 c. coconut
- 1 c. chopped pecans
- 1 tsp. vanilla

DIRECTIONS

Place all ingredients except coconut and pecans in mixing bowl. Beat at med. speed until well blended. Do not overbeat (batter will be stiff). Add nuts and coconut. Bake in greased 13" x 9" pan at 350° for 35 or 40 min. Cool and cut into squares.

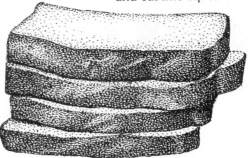

HOME-MADE FLOUR TORTILLAS
I-10 RV Park — Fort Stockton, TX

This recipe is a must when making burritos, which are very tasty and can be served with a variety of entrees. West Texas is famous for its burritos and these tortillas let you enjoy them in authentic Texas style.

We have a 20 site park with full hookups, pull-thrus and level spaces. We also provide picnic tables, barbeque pits and attractive rates. We're a family owned and operated park and you'll find that our campers are always number one with us.

INGREDIENTS
- 4 c. flour
- 1½ tsp. baking powder
- 2 tsp. salt
- ¼ c. shortening
- 1½ c. water

DIRECTIONS

Mix all ingredients together. Knead the dough until firm. Mold into 15 small balls. Roll out with a rolling pin. Cook in a flat grill until done. Makes 15 round 8" flat tortillas.

BEVERAGES

FRESH LEMON TONIC
Everett's RV Park – Cisco, TX

This drink is cool and refreshing. It quenches any thirst on a hot summer day. And best of all, you can prepare it in five minutes.

We're located in Cisco, nestled between Fort Worth and Abilene. Conrad Hilton's original hotel was built in Cisco during the oil boom days. We feature shaded, full hookup sites, pull-thrus, a pavilion and horseshoes. We invite you to come and stay with us a spell.

INGREDIENTS
- ½ c. fresh lemon juice
- lemon slices
- ¼ c. sugar
- 6 cloves
- 1½ c. chilled tonic water
- mint leaves

DIRECTIONS

Stir lemon juice and sugar together until sugar is dissolved. Add whole cloves. Pour in chilled tonic water. Serve over ice cubes. Garnish with a lemon slice and mint leaf. Preparation time: 5 min.

ORANGE JULEP
Orangeland Recreation Vehicle Park, Orange, CA

Orangeland is built on what used to be an orange grove so there are orange trees throughout the park. Our guests are encouraged to pick the oranges. This recipe is cool and soothing and is a favorite at our park.

Our park is in the heart of Orange County in southern California just a short distance from Disneyland, Anaheim Convention Center, Knott's Berry Farm, Anaheim Stadium (home of the Angels and Rams), the beaches, and several other attractions. In the Orangeland Community itself our guests can enjoy a large swimming pool, jacuzzi, video games, billiards, shuffleboard, laundry facilities, and a fully stocked store.

INGREDIENTS
- 1 c. sugar
- 1 c. water
- unstrained juice of 4 oranges
- strained juice of 2 lemons
- 1 (8¼ oz) can crushed
  pineapple
- 4 med. bananas
- chilled ginger ale

DIRECTIONS

Bring sugar and water to boil. Boil 5 min. Cool. Add orange and lemon juices and undrained crushed pineapple. Mash bananas and add to mixture. Freeze in loaf container. About 10 min. before serving remove from freezer to thaw slightly. Place 3 scoops of mixture in glass. Fill with ginger ale.

HOT CHOCOLATE MIX
Otter Creek Recreation Area — Airville, PA

We are off the beaten path, in a remote, heavily wooded area of southern York County, at the confluence of Otter Creek and the Susquehanna River (Lake Aldred). Hiking trails, wildflowers. . .nature at its best. We are surrounded on three sides by water. . .the river in front of us with fishing, boating and water skiing; and trout streams on either side of us.

After a busy day of fun, sit around the campfire and enjoy a cup of hot chocolate.

INGREDIENTS
- **25.6 oz. instant nonfat dry milk**
- **6 oz. jar powdered non-dairy creamer**
- **2 c. powdered sugar**
- **1 16-oz. can instant chocolate drink mix**

DIRECTIONS

Combine all ingredients in a large bowl. Mix well. Put in a large airtight container. Label. Store in a cool dry place. Use within 6 months. Makes about 17 cups of hot chocolate.

To make one cup of hot chocolate, add 3 tablespoons mix to one cup of hot water. Stir to dissolve. Add marshmallows if desired.

HOT SPICED RUSSIAN TEA
Roadrunner Camp Ground – Red River, NM

On long, cold, winter mornings, the smell of Hot Russian Tea warms you all over. And it is a delightful way to wake up in the winter mountains.

We have 96 sites high atop a mountain overlooking a valley. This rich setting offers many pastimes to our campers including downhill skiing & snowmobiling.

INGREDIENTS
- **2 c. Tang**
- **1 c. instant tea**
- **1 pkg. dry lemonade**
- **1½ c. sugar**
- **½ tsp. cloves**
- **1 tsp. cinnamon**

DIRECTIONS

Mix all ingredients together and store in a jar. Use 2 rounded teaspoons per cup of hot water.

MOONSHINE LIQUOR
K.O.A. Newport – Newport, TN

Cooke County was the moonshine capital of the world in 1960. We are the only campground with a real "still". Because we have our own moonshine still, this is "the" talked about recipe at our campground. Our park is 23 acres, set in the foothills of the Great Smoky Mountains. We have lots of trees, 30 pull-thru sites, and we welcome all types of RVs. Also featured at our park is a 2½ acre fishing lake that our campers use at no charge.

INGREDIENTS
- **75 lb. plain white cornmeal**
- **300 lb. sugar**
- **1 lb. yeast**
- **15 lb. bran (optional)**
- **300 gal. water**

DIRECTIONS

Mix ingredients in 6 or 7 wooden barrels for three days until the mash ferments. Then place it in a still and cook off the run. Collect steam and cool to get moonshine. Mix first run with last run to get a higher proof alcohol. This recipe yields approximately 48 gallons.

SAUCES & DRESSINGS

HOT TEXAS WEINER SAUCE
Keen Lake Campground – Waymart, PA

Our hot weiner sauce may be used in a snack bar. People love it. Reduce spices for a milder version.

We are located in the central Poconos on a beautiful 96 acre lake. The 1st steam locomotive and gravity railroad ran through the park in the early 1800's. A replica of the 1st steam locomotive can be seen in the village of Honesdale.

INGREDIENTS
- 1 lb. hamburger, browned
- 1 lg. onion, chopped
- 2 tsp. cumin
- 1 tsp. oregano
- 2 tsp. chili powder
- 2 tsp. paprika
- 2 tsp. cayenne pepper
- ¼ tsp. salt
- 1 can tomato soup
- 1 can water
- 1 sm. can tomato paste

DIRECTIONS

Mix all ingredients together. Simmer ½ hour. Spoon over hot dogs.

SHAY'S CHEROKEE HOT DOG SAUCE
Tri-State Canoe Campground – Matamoras, PA

Our riverside campground and boating livery is located on the Delaware River in Matamoras, PA, in the heart of the Pocono Mountains. Directly in front of the campground is the "Tri-State Rock" where the three states (New York, New Jersey and Pennsylvania) meet. Activities include canoeing, rafting, tubing and fishing. The Riverview Inn Restaurant constructed from an old barn of a bygone era is located on the grounds with a party room for special get-togethers, open charcoal grill, loft seating in the main dining and lounge areas, and live entertainment. We cordially invite you to stop by and we know you will enjoy this special recipe created and prepared here at our campground.

INGREDIENTS
- 1 lb. ground beef
- 2 qts. cold water
- ½ tsp. cayenne red pepper
- ½ tsp. black pepper
- 1 tsp. garlic salt
- 2 tsp. onion salt
- 1 tsp. chili powder
- 1 tsp. paprika
- 6 Tbsp. barbecue sauce
- 5 heaping Tbsp. cornstarch

DIRECTIONS

In a 4-qt. pot, brown ground beef and drain excess fat. Add 2 qts. cold water along with seasonings. Add barbecue sauce. Bring to boil and cook, stirring constantly for five minutes. Combine cornstarch with 8 oz. of lukewarm water. Add cornstarch mixture to ground beef, a little bit at a time, until sauce has gravy-like consistency. On your favorite hot dog and bun, place mustard, finely chopped sweet onions and top with Cherokee Sauce. Enjoy!

ZESTY MEXICAN SALAD DRESSING
Paradise R.V. Resort – Sun City, AZ

Resort RV guests and recreation dept. are producing a book of favorite recipes of the RVers. This recipe is one of the many contributions.

We are a 950 site destination RV resort for winter visitors. Many stay as long as six months, and become very involved in the activities within the resort, which include lawn bowling, tennis, arts and crafts, dancing, to name a few. Two attractions winter RV visitors to Arizona enjoy are the abundance of Mexican food available everywhere, and the opportunity to take side trips during the winter season into Mexico. Also, our park's potlucks invariably include some Mexican recipes.

INGREDIENTS
- 1 c. mayonnaise
- 1 c. buttermilk
- 1-2 Tbsp. chili powder (start with one)
- 1 tsp. ground mustard
- 1 Tbsp. dried parsley
- 1 tsp. celery seed
- ¼ tsp. oregano

DIRECTIONS
Combine all ingredients and mix thoroughly. Refrigerate 1-2 hours before using.

MEXICAN DRESSING
Roamer's Retreat Campground – Kinzer, PA

Several times throughout the year we host a Chicken Bar-B-Q at our campground. In addition to the chicken, we also serve a tossed salad, topped with this dressing. The campers look forward to sampling this dressing as much as the chicken.

We are a rural campground located east of Lancaster in the heart of Pennsylvania Dutch Country. As a matter of fact, our campground overlooks Amish farmlands and most of our neighbors are Amish. Our goal is to provide a clean, well-maintained campground with a quiet, friendly atmosphere.

INGREDIENTS
- 1 med. onion
- ⅓ c. vinegar
- ⅔ c. sugar
- 1 tsp. salt
- ½ tsp. pepper
- 1 tsp. celery seed
- 3 tsp. mustard
- 1 c. oil

DIRECTIONS
Mix ingredients in blender until slightly thickened.

BARBECUE CHICKEN SAUCE
Cottonwood Grove Campground — Hesston, KS

We are located just off I-135 in the heart of America, or our nation's "Bread Basket." Experience a touch of country living under the shade of a cottonwood tree. Enjoy the small clean town of Hesston that offers golf, tennis, swimming, restaurants and good friendly people. Our recipe has been a family favorite for years. We hope you enjoy it as much as we do.

INGREDIENTS
- ¾ c. salad oil
- ¾ c. vinegar
- ¾ c. water
- ½ tsp. Worcestershire sauce
- 3 Tbsp. salt
- ½ tsp. garlic salt
- 1 Tbsp. minced onion

DIRECTIONS

Mix all ingredients together. Marinate chicken in sauce for several hours; use remaining sauce to baste chicken while barbecueing. This makes enough for preparing 3 chickens.

SWEET AND SOUR BARBECUE SAUCE
Tratel Recreational Vehicle Park—Garden Grove, CA

Barbecue sauce always shows up at our Snowbirds potluck dinners in some form or other. Our guests are always on the go with so many tourist attractions surrounding us. They can use the sauce for a quick snack or a leisurely dinner, depending on the time available.

Our park is a spacious, shady oasis just minutes from Disneyland, Knott's Berry Farm, Crystal Cathedral, Anaheim Convention Center and Stadium and Queen Mary-Spruce Goose.

INGREDIENTS
- 1 c. grape jelly
- 1 c. chili sauce

DIRECTIONS

Heat until jelly melts, either on stove or in microwave. Use as a dip for meatball hors d'oeuvres; barbecue sauce for baked chicken (drain off all fat); baste ribs on grill; or cut up weiners for the kids.

BBQ SAUCE
Trailer Rancho — Encinitas, CA

My husband LOVES this recipe. It goes well with any meat you like to barbecue.

We are in an ideal location for vacationing in San Diego. We're located in North County; away from the large city, but close to all its attractions such as Wild Animal Park, the Zoo, Sea World, La Costa golfing, tennis and Del Mar racetrack. For you sun worshippers, we're only 2 blocks from the beach.

INGREDIENTS
1 c. strong coffee
1 c. Worcestershire sauce
1 c. catsup
½ c. cider vinegar
½ c. brown sugar
3 Tbsp. chili powder
2 tsp. salt
2 c. chopped onion
¼ c. minced hot chili peppers
6 cloves minced garlic

DIRECTIONS
Combine all ingredients and simmer for 25 minutes. Run through a blender. Makes 5 cups.

TEXAS HILL COUNTRY B-B-QUE SAUCE
Cascade Caverns – Boerne, TX

Texas hill country is famous for its Texas style B-B-Que dinners. This delicious B-B-Que is served to hundreds of campers each year at Cascade Caverns Park.

Located in scenic, rustic, hill country on 105 acres, we are a full service RV park with large pavilions, dance hall to accommodate large groups. Daily cave tours of Texas' only show cave with 100 foot waterfall are offered. This attraction received the 1988 Natural Attraction award. It is a designated historical site.

INGREDIENTS
2 onions, chopped
1½ c. catsup
½ c. water
4 Tbsp. vinegar
2 Tbsp. mustard
½ c. brown sugar
4 Tbsp. Worcestershire sauce
4 Tbsp. lemon juice
2 tsp. chili powder
1 tsp. salt
1 tsp. paprika
½ tsp. Tabasco

DIRECTIONS
Heat all ingredients at a slow simmer for 30 minutes, then remove from heat and let cool slowly. Can be used immediately, basting brisket every 30-45 minutes. Cook slowly over pit 4-5 hours.

SPAGHETTI SAUCE FOR A CROWD
Yokum's Vacationland – Seneca Rocks, WV

We also own a restaurant, and spaghetti, using this recipe, is on the menu. Campers frequently order this dish and it's always a hit.

Yokum's Vacationland is located on a 1,000 acre farm where sheep, cattle and horses are raised. The north fork of the Potomac River flows through our campground and offers excellent year-round trout and bass fishing. We also have a heated indoor pool, hot tub, showers, laundromat, basketball court and video games. We also offer good hunting grounds for hunters right on our farm. While you're staying with us you can climb the 960 ft. high Seneca Rock, tour the Smoke Hole and Seneca Caverns or spend a day at the Cass Scenic Railroad. Come visit us and experience our vacationland.

INGREDIENTS
6 lbs. lean hamburger
2 lg. onions, diced
¼ c. sweet pepper, diced
5 sm. hot peppers, diced
5 garlic cloves
¼ c. oregano
2 Tbsp. Italian spice
1 Tbsp. basil
salt & pepper to taste
2 qts. water
½ c. sugar
1 gal. tomato paste
½ gal. water
Parmesan cheese

DIRECTIONS
In large pot, brown hamburger, onions, peppers and spices. Add 2 qts. water and cook slowly for 1 hr. Add sugar, tomato paste and ½ gal. water. Cook slowly for 1 hr. Serve over spaghetti and top with Parmesan cheese. (Makes 2 gallons.)

THOUSAND ISLAND DRESSING
Merry Knoll Campground – Clayton, NY

"1000 Island Dressing" was made on the yacht of George Boldt by his chef Oscar of the Waldorf Astoria Hotel in New York City. Mr. Boldt was at that time building his now famous castle for his wife Louise.

Merry Knoll is on the St. Lawrence River at the heart of the Thousand Islands. From our rental boats and off our long fishing pier, fish are caught and served at our camp suppers but never without our famous 1000 Island dressing. We know you will love the dressing. Come see us to enjoy one of our fresh fish dinners.

INGREDIENTS
1 c. olive oil
1 Tbsp. vinegar
1 tsp. salt
1 tsp. sugar
⅛ tsp. pepper
⅛ tsp. paprika
¼ c. chopped green pepper
2 Tbsp. chopped stuffed olives
1 Tbsp. chopped parsley
2 Tbsp. chopped onions

DIRECTIONS
Mix all ingredients together. Beat, shake or blend until thoroughly blended. Serve over salad of choice.

PORK BBQ SAUCE
Camelot R/V Park & Campground – Malabar, FL

Weight watchers beware the 3rd weekend of February here in Malabar and Grant, Florida. This is the weekend of the Grant Seafood Festival. 40,000 people come to this area to sample the delicacies offered up by our coastal waters. At Camelot R/V Park, we are just a few miles north of the festival and we take the opportunity to double team our guests that weekend by also throwing the biggest of our BBQs. The beverages flow, two to three hundred pounds of pork loins hit the grill with our special BBQ sauce. We and our willing guests BBQ through the night. The next day when the pork is cooked, our guests bring the side dishes and no one goes hungry. After eating seafood one day and BBQ the next, you had better check the tire pressures in the camper before going home.

INGREDIENTS
1 pt. vinegar
2 Tbsp. paprika
½ c. Worcestershire sauce
1 tsp. salt
½ tsp. pepper
2 Tbsp. Louisiana hot sauce (or
  to taste)
¼ c. prepared mustard

DIRECTIONS
Mix all ingredients until all lumps dissolve. The beauty of this sauce is that it is versatile and will not burn while cooking. Marinate pork in the sauce for 2-3 hrs., then baste frequently while cooking. For a fine table sauce, catch the drippings in the BBQ sauce container while basting. Then boil the remaining sauce for 10 min. before serving.

FAMOUS SALMON BBQ BASTING SAUCE
Woodside RV Park and Campground — Ft. Bragg, CA

Many local people and tourists attend the annual Ft. Bragg "World's Largest Salmon Barbecue." We all enjoy the festivities and best of all we enjoy the salmon.

Woodside RV Park and Campground is located on the beautiful Mendocino coast just south of Fort Bragg. Our town boasts of the world's largest salmon barbecue. Every afternoon guests are welcomed at the liars' table to share good times, great trips, fish stories and recipes. One of the best is the Famous Salmon Barbecue Basting Sauce. Try it, and you can boast too!

INGREDIENTS
1 c. butter
⅓ c. lemon juice
1½ tsp. soy sauce
1½ tsp. Worcestershire sauce
1 tsp. sweet basil
1 tsp. oregano
2 Tbsp. fresh parsley
½ tsp. garlic powder
salt & pepper to taste

DIRECTIONS
Melt butter and add remaining ingredients. Baste on salmon while cooking.

WILD BLACKBERRY SAUCE
Stafford RV Park – Scotia, CA

Beautiful blackberry bushes surround our park. Campers love to pick and eat them.

Stafford R.V. Park — 15 acres of redwoods. Campsites are under the big redwoods. Pull-thrus, full hookups, electric, water and tent and group camps circle a pavilion. We are part of the Avenue of the Giants which is located near Eureka, California off Highway 101, Northern California.

INGREDIENTS
- **fresh picked blackberries**
- **1-2 c. sugar (depending on amt. of berries picked)**
- **1/8 tsp. cinnamon**
- **dash of salt**

DIRECTIONS

Mash berries, add sugar, cinnamon, and salt. Heat and stir until it becomes saucy and thickened — 10 min. or so. If you want it very smooth, cook it as long as needed to make it. Pour over hot cakes or ice cream. A square dance group, Silver Leaf Squares from Idaho, served this over pancakes one morning. We all enjoyed eating around the open fire.

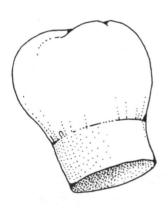

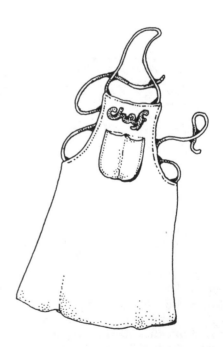

Conversion Chart

dash = less than 1/8 teaspoon

3 teaspoons = 1 Tablespoon

2 Tablespoons = 1 fluid ounce

4 Tablespoons = 1/4 cup

8 Tablespoons = 1/2 cup

16 Tablespoons = 1 cup or 8 fluid ounces

2 cups = 1 pint or 16 fluid ounces

2 pints = 1 quart

4 cups = 1 quart or 16 fluid ounces

4 quarts = 1 gallon

4 ounces = 1/4 pound

16 ounces = 1 pound

1 pound butter = 2 cups

1 stick butter = 1/2 cup

12 ounce can weighs 12 ounces

No. 300 can weighs 14 to 16 ounces or
    1 3/4 cups

No. 303 can weighs 16 to 17 ounces or 2 cups

No. 2 can weighs 1 pound, 4 ounces or
    1 pint, 2 fluid ounces or 2 1/2 cups

No. 2 1/2 can weighs 1 pound, 13 ounces or
    3 1/2 cups

No. 3 Cylinder = 3 pounds, 3 ounces or
    1 quart, 14 fluid ounces

No. 10 can weighs 6 1/2 to 7 pounds, 5
    ounces or 12 to 13 cups

One-Pound Equivalents:
2 cups butter
4 cups all-purpose flour
2 cups granulated sugar
3 1/2 cups sifted powdered sugar
2 cups milk
9 medium eggs
2 2/3 cups oatmeal or brown sugar
1 7/8 cups rice
2 1/3 cups dry beans
2 cups ground, packed meat

Abbreviations:
tsp. = teaspoon
Tbsp. = tablespoon
c. = cup
oz. = ounce
lb. = pound
pt. = pint
qt. = quart
gal. = gallon
sm. = small
med. = medium
lg. = large

Helpful hints when measuring ingredients:

Flour and powdered sugar should be spooned into the measuring cup and leveled off with a knife.

Brown sugar, butter or shortening should always be packed down into the cup and then leveled off with a knife.

MY FAVORITE RECIPES

MY FAVORITE RECIPES

MY FAVORITE RECIPES